# British Horror Cinema

Horror is one of the most popular and talked-about film genres and yet British horror films, aside from those made by Hammer, have received little critical attention. *British Horror Cinema* investigates a wide range of horror film-making in Britain, from early chillers like *The Ghoul* and *Dark Eyes of London* to modern classics such as *Witchfinder General* and *The Wicker Man*.

Contributors explore the contexts in which British horror films have been censored and classified, judged by critics and consumed by fans. Uncovering neglected gems like *Death Line*, and addressing issues such as the representation of women and the family, they consider the Britishness of British horror and examine sub-genres such as the psycho-thriller and witchcraft movies, the work of the Amicus studio, and key film-makers including Pete Walker. *British Horror Cinema* also features a comprehensive filmography and contributions from contemporary horror directors Clive Barker and Richard Stanley.

Contributors: Brigid Cherry, Steve Chibnall, Ian Conrich, Leon Hunt, Peter Hutchings, Mark Kermode, Kim Newman, Marcelle Perks, Julian Petley, Steven Jay Schneider, L.S. Smith, Richard Stanley, John C. Tibbetts, Paul Wells.

Editors: **Steve Chibnall** is Principal Lecturer in Film Studies at De Montfort University, Leicester. He is the co-editor of *British Crime Cinema* (Routledge, 1999). **Julian Petley** is Senior Lecturer in Communication and Information Studies at Brunel University. He is co-editor of *Ill Effects: The Media Violence Debate, Second Edition* (Routledge, 2001).

## British Popular Cinema
Series Editors: Steve Chibnall and I.Q. Hunter

*De Montfort University, Leicester*

At a time when there is a growing popular and scholarly interest in British film, with new sources of funding and notable successes in world markets, this series explores the largely submerged history of the UK's cinema of entertainment.

The series rediscovers and evaluates not only individual films but whole genres, such as science fiction and the crime film, that have been ignored by a past generation of critics. Dismissed for decades as aberrations in the national cinema and anaemic imitations of American originals, these films are now being celebrated in some quarters as important contributions to our cinematic heritage.

The emergence of cult genre movies from the apparently respectable lineage of British film emphasizes the gap between traditional academic criticism and a new alliance between revisionist film theorists and extra-mural (but well-informed) cinema enthusiasts who wish to take the study of British film in unexpected directions. This series offers the opportunity for both established cineastes and new writers to examine long-neglected areas of British film production or to develop new approaches to more familiar territory. The books will enhance our understanding of how ideas and representations in films relate to changing gender and class relations in postwar Britain, and their accessible writing style will make these insights available to a much wider readership.

### Books in the series:

### British Crime Cinema
*Edited by Steve Chibnall and Robert Murphy*

### British Science Fiction Cinema
*Edited by I.Q. Hunter*

### Forthcoming:

### British Historical Cinema
*Edited by Claire Monk and Amy Sargeant*

# British Horror Cinema

Edited by
**Steve Chibnall and
Julian Petley**

London and New York

First published 2002
by Routledge
11 New Fetter Lane, London EC4P 4EE

Simultaneously published in the USA and Canada
by Routledge
29 West 35th Street, New York, NY 10001

*Routledge is an imprint of the Taylor & Francis Group*

Typeset in Perpetua by
Keystroke, Jacaranda Lodge, Wolverhampton
Printed and bound in Great Britain by
Biddles Ltd, Guildford and King's Lynn

*British Library Cataloguing in Publication Data*
A catalogue record for this book is available from the British Library

*Library of Congress Cataloging in Publication Data*
A catalog record for this book has been requested

ISBN 0–415–23003–9 (hbk)
ISBN 0–415–23004–7 (pbk)

# Contents

# Illustrations

*All illustrations are courtesy of the British Cinema and Television Research Group's Archive at De Montfort University, Leicester, except figures 28 and 29 which are courtesy of Richard Stanley.*

# Notes on Contributors

**Brigid Cherry** is a lecturer in Media Arts at St Mary's College, a college of the University of Surrey, where she teaches film and television studies. She has previously published papers on the horror film audience and on vampire cinema. She is currently completing a study of female *Star Wars* fandom.

**Steve Chibnall** is Subject Leader for Film Studies and Co-ordinator of the British Cinema and Television Research Group at De Montfort University, Leicester. He is also a member of the editorial board for the *Journal of Popular British Cinema*, and a Series Editor for the books in Routledge's British Popular Cinema series. His first book, *Law-and-Order News*, was published in 1977 and he has written widely for journals, edited collections and popular magazines. His most recent books are *Making Mischief: The Cult Films of Pete Walker* (FAB Press, 1998), *British Crime Cinema* (Routledge, 1999) and *J. Lee Thompson* (Manchester University Press, 2000). He is currently writing a book on *Get Carter*.

**Ian Conrich** is Senior Lecturer in Film Studies at the University of Surrey Roehampton. He has contributed to *Sight and Sound*, and he is an editor of the *Journal of Popular British Cinema*. He is co-editor of *New Zealand: A Pastoral Paradise?* (2000), *New Zealand Fictions: Literature and Film* (2001), *The Technique of Terror: The Films of John Carpenter* (2002), *Musical Moments: Film and the Performance of Song and Dance* (2002), *Contemporary New Zealand Cinema* and *New Zealand Filmmakers* (both forthcoming).

**Leon Hunt** is Lecturer in Film and TV Studies at Brunel University. He is the author of *British Low Culture: From Safari Suits to Sexploitation* (Routledge, 1998) and has contributed chapters to *Me Tarzan: Masculinity, Movies and Men*, *British Crime Cinema*, *Unruly Pleasures: The Cult Film and its Critics*, and *Shocking Cinema of the Seventies*. He is currently writing a book about martial arts films.

**Peter Hutchings** is Senior Lecturer in Film Studies at the University of Northumbria. He is the author of *Hammer and Beyond* (1993) and *Terence Fisher* (2001) and co-editor of *The Film Studies Reader* (2000). He has also published widely on horror, science fiction, genre theory and criticism, and the films of Alfred Hitchcock.

**Mark Kermode** is a freelance film journalist and broadcaster. He has written and presented numerous television documentaries including *The Fear of God: 25 Years of The Exorcist* and *Poughkeepsie Shuffle: Tracing the French Connection* for BBC2 and *On the Edge of Blade Runner* for Channel 4. He introduces the 'Extreme Cinema' series on the Film Four Channel and Channel 4, and his radio work includes writing and presenting *Celluloid Jukebox* for BBC Radio 2. He is the author of *The Exorcist* in the BFI Modern Classics series.

**Kim Newman** is the author of novels including *The Night Mayor*, *Anno Dracula*, *The Quorum*, *Life's Lottery* and *An English Ghost Story*. His non-fiction books include *Nightmare Movies*, *Wild West Movies*, *Millennium Movies*, *Cat People* (in the BFI Classics series) and *The BFI Companion to Horror*. He is a contributing editor to *Sight and Sound* and *Empire*, and a frequent broadcaster on radio and television.

**Marcelle Perks** is an MA graduate from the Institute of Education, London. A budding horror film extra, she has written extensively about horror films in *Fangoria*, *Dark Side*, *Shivers*, *Diabolik*, *Flesh and Blood*, *Eyeball*, *Redeemer* and *Videoworld* magazine. She has also contributed to *The BFI Companion to Horror*, *Feminists Against Censorship* and *Sex Macabre*. Previously she has worked for the British Film Institute, Leicester Phoenix Arts and *Shivers* horror magazine. She currently works for a dotcom company and spends all her vacation time on film sets or at film festivals.

**Julian Petley** teaches at Brunel University and is the co-editor (with Martin Barker) of *Ill Effects* (Routledge, 2001, second edition) and (with Ian Conrich) of the third volume of the *Journal of Popular British Cinema*, which is devoted to the theme of forbidden British cinema. He is currently writing a book for Routledge on media censorship in Britain, and is the Chair of the Campaign for Press and Broadcasting Freedom.

**Steven Jay Schneider** is a doctoral student in Philosophy at Harvard University and in Cinema Studies at New York University. He is editor of *Fear Without Frontiers: Horror Cinema Across the Globe* (FAB Press, 2002) and co-editor of *Underground USA: Filmmaking Beyond the Hollywood Canon* (Wallflower Press, 2002). He has contributed to such journals as *CineAction*, *Post Script*, *Film & Philosophy*, *Journal of Popular Film & Television* and *Central Europe Review* and to the following edited collections, all forthcoming: *Horror Film Reader* (Limelight Editions), *Kathryn Bigelow: Hollywood Transgressor* (Wallflower Press), *Drive-In Horrors* (McFarland), *Shocking Cinema of the Seventies* (Noir Press) and *Weird On Top: The Cinema and Television of David Lynch* (Flicks Books).

**L.S. Smith** is a postgraduate student in the Department of Media and Cultural Production at De Montfort University, and head of an academic support service. He is currently researching Italian *orrore* and *giallo* cinema.

**Richard Stanley** is a trained anthropologist and part-time journalist. As a writer and photographer, he has documented events in South Africa, Rwanda and Afghanistan where, in 1989, he saw action as a mujahedin. As a film-maker, his work includes the features *Hardware* (1990) and *Dust Devil* (1992) as well as documentaries and music videos. He is currently completing a six-year documentary project on the Fourth Reich.

**John C. Tibbetts** is an Associate Professor of Film at the University of Kansas. He has worked as a radio producer, television presenter and as a reporter/commentator for CBS and CNN. From 1976 to 1985 he edited the bi-monthly magazine of the National Film Society, *American Classic Screen*, and he is currently a senior editor for the annual *Movie/Video Guides* published by Ballantine Books. He has been a senior consultant and contributor to several major reference works including *The New Film Index*, *The Encyclopedia of the 20th Century*, *The Oxford Companion to Mystery and Crime Writing* and *American Cultural Biography*. As well as over 200 articles, he has written six books, including *Dvorak in America* (Amadeus Press, 1993), *The Encyclopedia of Novels into Film* (Facts on File, 1998) and *The Cinema of Tony Richardson* (SUNY Press, 1999).

**Paul Wells** is Co-ordinator of the Media Portfolio at the University of Teesside. He has published *Art and Animation* (Academy Group/John Wiley, 1997), *Understanding Animation* (Routledge, 1998) and *The Horror Genre: From Beelzebub to Blair Witch* (Wallflower Press, 2000), the latter based on his Sony Award-winning radio series, *Spinechillers*.

# Acknowledgements

The gestation period for collections of original articles is usually longer than initially forecast by their editors. This collection is no exception to that rule, but although our optimism about how quickly it could be completed may have been unfounded, our optimism about the quality of contributions was not. We would like to thank all those who have contributed articles, especially those who delivered their work at an early date and have waited patiently to see the results of their labours in print. We also appreciate that a number of you have written for rates lower than your professional services usually command because you always believed that this was a long overdue project in academic publishing. Additional thanks must also go to Leon Smith, who tackled the job of compiling the lengthy filmography with considerable skill and enthusiasm at very short notice.

Steve Chibnall would also like to acknowledge the role played by the Faculty of Humanities and members of the British Cinema and Television Research Group at De Montfort University in creating a stimulating environment which encouraged the production of this book; and to thank Kara McKechnie for her unselfish support during the long hours of word processing.

Julian Petley would like to thank Brunel University for granting him sabbatical leave in order to complete this project and others; Richard Allport, Paul Douglas, David Hull, Neil Newland, Malcolm Overton of the Department of Human Sciences at Brunel not only for their technical support in producing this book but also for being such cheerful and efficient office-movers at the same time; and Mary Burt for all her love and support.

# 1 The return of the repressed? British horror's heritage and future

*Steve Chibnall and Julian Petley*

It is now nearly thirty years since David Pirie published his seminal *A Heritage of Horror*, and far too many since it was last in print. In the intervening period there has been an explosion of interest in the Gothic in general, and in horror cinema, Gothic or otherwise, in particular. Whereas the unfortunate Pirie had little more to draw on for critical sustenance than works such as Mario Praz's *The Romantic Agony* (1933), Devendra P. Varma's *The Gothic Flame* (1957) and the journal *Midi-Minuit Fantastique* – all of them admittedly formidable in their different ways – the modern enthusiast for horror in all its forms has a truly remarkable number of texts to consult, as our contributors' bulging references amply testify.

However, in the case of texts on British horror cinema, too many fail to progress beyond considering what has become a pretty limited canon. In this respect, Jonathan Rigby's recent *English Gothic: A Century of Horror Cinema* deserves particular welcome for bringing such a wide range of films within its ambit, as does the ten-part survey of British horror in the 1970s and 1980s carried out by the magazine *Flesh and Blood*. Indeed, the appearance in recent years of genre magazines written by enthusiasts for enthusiasts has been one of the most welcome developments on the horror scene, helping to create a valuable sense of community among horror fans in hostile times, allowing new writers on horror to emerge and develop, and drawing attention to neglected films and directors. Magazines such as *Little Shoppe of Horrors*, *Dark Terrors* and *Hammer Horror* have also performed an invaluable service in minutely excavating the archaeology of Britain's most prolific supplier of fantasy films, Hammer studios. In fact the diligent burrowings of the researchers associated with these Hammer fanzines, together with academic work on the studio and its leading director by Peter Hutchings (1993 and 2001) and Wheeler Winston Dixon (1991), have cleared a space for this book to explore more neglected areas of Britain's horror film heritage. In doing so, we hope to embed the fanzines' empirical findings on production histories more securely in the generic and reception contexts of the films.

In bringing together the various contributors to this book we were certainly motivated by the desire to draw attention to films and figures outside the canon,

*Figure 1*  Hammer and sickle: Peter Cushing does some vampire hunting in *Twins of Evil*
(1971), one of the Hammer studio's classic Gothic tales.

movies and people who have still not significantly benefited from the recent upsurge
of interest in British horror cinema. To extend a metaphor first used by one of us a
decade-and-a-half ago, now that the 'Lost Continent' of British fantasy cinema has
been rediscovered, we want to continue its cartography beyond the landing zone.
Hence, for example, Peter Hutchings's chapter on Amicus (dealt with fairly briefly
by Pirie, but recently celebrated by Alan Bryce's *Amicus: The Studio That Dripped
Blood* (2000), a book emanating from another fanzine, *The Dark Side*), which also
very usefully suggests that, as well as locating their films within British culture at
the time of their production, we also need to look at the American influences
at work on them. Similarly, Ian Conrich delves further into the past than Pirie to
resurrect such largely forgotten early British horrors as *Castle Sinister* (1932), *The
Ghoul* (1933) and *The Face at the Window* (1939), while Marcelle Perks contributes
the most substantial study to date of the woefully neglected *Death Line* (1972) and
Steve Chibnall explores the work of a post-Hammer 'auteur', Pete Walker, who,
for a moment in the mid-1970s, suggested new possibilities for Gothic cinema in
Britain. By taking a thematic approach, as opposed to one centred on a particular
auteur or company, Leon Hunt, Kim Newman and Steven Jay Schneider are able to
tackle an extremely wide range of films, many of which have barely received serious
consideration before, and to isolate recurring motifs and patterns which suggest the

deep cultural strains and tensions into which these films were tapping. Many of the films they discuss are original screenplays, but we are also mindful that one of the distinctive features of the horror films produced in Britain is their strong links to a tradition of fantasy literature, and these connections are foregrounded in John C. Tibbetts's close examination of the adaptation for the cinema of Henry James's novella, *The Turn of the Screw*.

This book, however, is about not simply British horror films but British horror cinema. In other words, it is concerned not simply with films as texts but with the institutions and discourses within which those texts are produced, circulated, regulated and consumed, and the book begins with three contextualizing chapters. Almost inevitably, given the amount of cutting and banning with which horror films have always had to contend in Britain, the first chapter is on censorship. Mark Kermode examines how the British Board of Film Censors/Classification has dealt with British horror films by placing this in the wider context of the Board's treatment of horror films in general. Especially valuable are his close textual readings of passages from former censor John Trevelyan's book *What the Censor Saw*, which expose many of the unspoken assumptions and attitudes underlying the censorship of the moving image in Britain. That these are extremely deep-rooted within the

*Figure 2* Literary heritage: Jon Pertwee catches up on some bedtime reading in Amicus's *The House that Dripped Blood* (1970).

British cultural establishment, of which the mainstream critics make up a key cadre, is demonstrated in Julian Petley's chapter on critical attitudes towards horror, which also suggests that, in certain respects, these attitudes have significantly hampered the development of horror cinema in Britain in recent times. The paranoia which censorship and critical denigration of the genre have fostered in many horror fans is amply illustrated by some of the remarks cited by Brigid Cherry in her study of female horror film enthusiasts. However, Cherry's main focus is the role played by horror cinema (particularly vampire films) in the lifestyle of a range of women. Her work represents an important corrective to the easy gendering of the genre's audience (and, by extension, the genre itself) as male, and offers valuable insights into the way female enthusiasts *actually* relate to the films they watch – as well as to other fans.

The last two chapters of this book attempt to bring up to date the story of the horror film in Britain. Paul Wells looks at the work of one of Britain's recent undoubted horror auteurs, Clive Barker, and, in his interview, Barker's highly articulate discussion of the genre and of his own work within it makes for a remarkable – not to say welcome and refreshing – contrast with the journeyman attitude of many of its past practitioners.[1] The same is true of the account of recent horror by Richard Stanley, who was responsible for *Hardware* (1990) and *Dust Devil* (1993), two of the last decade's most striking British entrants in the horror, or horror-related, stakes. Stanley's chapter mentions numerous British horror movies of the 1990s, but does so in a distinctly valedictory spirit, and this prompts us to conclude this introduction by reviewing the various reasons put forward for the decline of the British horror film, and by enquiring if this decline is in fact more apparent than real.

In 1973, David Pirie, in his chapter 'Towards a new horror mythology', admitted that 'the Hammer horror movie at its most traditional has inevitably suffered from an increasing public sophistication. . . . It is no longer possible to make naive straightforward English horror films that are as simple in narrative but as rich in connotation and suggestion as Hammer's early efforts' (165, 167). He also complained, with the 'Karnstein' films *The Vampire Lovers* (1970), *Lust for a Vampire* (1971) and *Twins of Evil* (1971) clearly in mind, that:

> The dark, over-laden allusiveness [of traditional Hammer] is being replaced more and more by banal sexual antics, the charged hermetic atmosphere by heavy-handed humour, the solid narrative structure by half-understood experimentation. At times the new English films even begin to look like bad imitations of the European horror films, for many of the younger British film-makers have begun to ape the overtly Freudian and surrealist intellectual quality of the French approach to horror, without understanding the essential historical value of their own tradition.
>
> (ibid.: 165)

Pirie rightly perceived the just-deceased Michael Reeves, as

> the kind of film-maker which the British cinema needed (and still needs) so desperately badly: someone who could merge the popular tradition of horror film with more avant-garde concerns without rearing the curious bastard which so often results from such experiments.

Furthermore, he contended that Reeves' *Witchfinder General* (1968)

> contains the seeds of something which could yet develop into an important cinematic idiom in this country, and one which is as intrinsically *native* to England as the western is to America. The literary romantic tradition into which it shades has as much affinity with Malory as with the Gothic and is virtually untapped by current popular English forms.
>
> (155)

Unfortunately this remains as true today as when it was written. The films based on Walpole, Radcliffe, Maturin, Lewis and other Gothic writers, which Pirie hoped to see, are still unmade, and when Pirie himself became a script writer, it was to television that he had to turn to commission his adaptations of Wilkie Collins's *The Woman in White* (1996) and Sheridan Le Fanu's *The Wyvern Mystery* (1999), as well as his Gothic-tinged original scripts *Rainy Day Women* (1984) and *Murder Rooms* (1999). In this respect it is extremely significant that Jonathan Rigby (2000) quotes Stephen Volk, the screenwriter of Ken Russell's *Gothic* (1986) to the effect that:

> In this country, the film establishment is so intellectually pompous that they wouldn't admit to *watching* Gothic horror, let alone commissioning it. It's one of the very few cultural exclusives that we could really exploit . . . but it's so hard to get anybody interested.
>
> (244)

Only very briefly, in a trio of films by Pete Walker, was Pirie's hope realized that British horror cinema might be able to follow the American example of George Romero's *Night of the Living Dead* (1968) and 'combine the best and most traditional elements of the old approach with more complex ideas and emphases' (ibid.: 167).[2] Various authors have suggested that it was precisely the British horror film's inability to keep up with modern developments in the genre which led to its alleged demise. Thus, for example, Kim Newman (1988) argues that: 'The British horror film perished because of its inability to adapt to a 1970s world beyond Home Counties Transylvania' (25), while David Sanjek (1994) similarly contends that audiences faced with the rapid and often disquieting transformations which British society was undergoing in the late 1960s and early 1970s no longer responded to the 'artificial horrors' of the Hammer school. Instead, he argued, 'to remain worthy of attention, the British horror film would have to embrace the monstrous in [the] audience', adding that, 'few horror films produced in England between 1968 and 1975 achieved this goal' (197).

Elsewhere, Ian Conrich has argued that: 'The British horror film in its generic form has become fragmented since the early 80s. The absence of any British film studios or recognised producers of horror – a Hammer, Tigon, Tyburn – has created a weakened generic image' (1998: 27). In order to illustrate his thesis, he takes the example of Palace, which, between 1984 and 1992, produced five horror-related titles: *The Company of Wolves* (1984), *Dream Demon* (1988), *High Spirits* (1988), *Hardware* (1990) and *Dust Devil* (1993), and concentrates on how these were marketed. What Conrich's article shows is that *The Company of Wolves* was successful at least in part because it was well marketed, both to a horror audience but also, more importantly, as an 'art house' product via the Angela Carter connection. It was also a critical success. *Dream Demon*, however, pleased neither the critics nor the 'arty' types, and horror fans found it merely derivative of the *Nightmare on Elm Street* films. Finally, in what seems like an act of desperation, it was sold on the attractions of Timothy Spall and Jimmy Nail! Then, when *Hardware* came along, it was sold, at first at least, purely as if it were an American film, 'the *Terminator* for the Nineties' as *The Face* put it. Conrich quotes Daniel Battsek of Palace as stating that 'there is no point from a marketing point of view in selling a horror film as British, at least not in the beginning' (ibid.: 30). This is a bitterly ironic state of affairs for films in one of the only genres Britain can claim as its own. The difficulties which home-grown horror has faced in the market place from the 1970s onwards (not least from the consequences of intense American competition) are clearly evident in Richard Stanley's chapter in the present book. As Stanley makes all too plain, Palace's valuable if limited contribution to the horror genre was finally terminated by the collapse of the entire company. In such circumstances it may not be entirely surprising that, as Jonathan Rigby argues, '1990s British horror films seemed content merely to replicate other people's horror films, and their models tended to be American ones' (op. cit.: 244).

Palace's problems and ultimate collapse suggest that we cannot look at the state of the horror film in Britain from the 1970s onwards in isolation from the condition of British cinema as a whole during this period. The fact of the matter is that, for much of this time, the indigenous production sector has been in a state of crisis that at times has seemed almost terminal. Thus, for example, in 1971 a mere 67 films of any kind were made in Britain, and in 1982 the figure had dropped to 46. It is true that, in the early 1970s, by offering a haven for low-budget film-making, the horror genre suffered less than others from the withdrawal of American capital from British film production.[3] By the end of the decade, however, even the most modest of productions were finding it impossible to recoup their costs in their home market, as more cinemas closed and audiences dwindled. During the 1980s the general plight

*Figure 3* The attractions of Timothy Spall (right) and Jimmy Nail: Palace's *Dream Demon* (1988).

of British film production improved somewhat thanks to the financial input of bodies like Channel 4 and British Screen, but their money was not directed at popular genre cinema. This has had to await National Lottery funding, but so far the main result of this largesse has been a revival of the crime, not the horror, film.

The reason for this may be quite simply that the horror genre has not yet produced its equivalent of *Lock, Stock and Two Smoking Barrels* (1998) which (without Lottery funding) did so much to re-establish the crime film in Britain. One can only speculate as to why this has not happened, but it would surely be uncontroversial to suggest that the stridently censorious campaigns against horror videos since the early 1980s, and especially in the wake of the James Bulger case, would have discouraged many producers from contemplating a foray into the genre. It is, of course, true that controversy can be good for business, but only masochists would have wanted to lay themselves open to the tirade of abuse, not to mention possible censorship, which would undoubtedly have greeted anybody foolhardy enough to contemplate a British gore film in the wake of the first 'video nasty' panic. Mark Kermode's and Richard Stanley's accounts in this book of the trials and tribulations faced by Palace in their efforts to distribute *The Evil Dead* (1983) on both film and video suggest that no one in their right mind would have attempted at that time to produce a British equivalent. And just *imagine* what would happen were a film company even to suggest making a film about, say, Fred and Rosemary West in the manner of *Deranged* (1974) (which was based on the real-life US serial killer Ed Gein) or the Bulger murder even in the mild and restrained format of *The Good Son* (1993). Indeed, even to float the idea of such projects is to risk courting controversy and to realize why Sanjek's prescription for British horror films which would confront us with the very real horrors of our own society is so problematic.[4] In a culture as jumpy and censorious as that indicated by both Kermode and Petley in this book, the idea is quite literally unthinkable. And yet, as every first-year film student knows, popular genre films can be a very effective means of exploring difficult and disturbing subjects. Not, however, the horror genre in Britain today.

This, of course, brings us back to critical attitudes towards the horror film in Britain, and leads us to the final point in our discussion about the alleged decline of the genre in this country, namely that this may be more apparent than real. In *Hammer and Beyond* (1993), Peter Hutchings notes that in the critical histories of British cinema which appeared in the 1960s and 1970s from Roy Armes, Ernest Betts, Charles Oakey, George Perry and Alexander Walker:

> Horror, one of the most commercially successful areas of British film production, is usually conspicuous by its absence or its marginality. The formulaic nature of much British horror, the way in which it seems to define itself entirely in relation to the demands of the market place, ensures that the films involved are accorded a lesser status than those films which are seen to have been made by 'artists' who in some way have transcended commercial constraints.
>
> (9–10)

Could it be that this process is still continuing? As our filmography clearly shows, a large number of British horror or horror-related titles were in fact produced during the 1980s and 1990s, but one will look in vain for any sustained discussion of them in John Hill's *British Cinema in the 1980s* (1999) and Robert Murphy's *British Cinema of the 90s* (2000), even in the chapter in the latter devoted to 'Unseen British cinema'. Contemporary British horror films have remained largely invisible to academic critics for more than twenty years, but then so had crime films before *Lock, Stock. . . .*

As we write this in early 2001, there are some signs that we might yet see the return of a repressed genre. What Pirie called 'the only staple cinematic myth which Britain can properly claim as its own' (op. cit.: 9) might be reinstated as a vital element in the national cinema. The genre in Britain may never again benefit from another Hammer studio (or even another Amicus), and it may never in the future enjoy the prominence in film production which it had in the early 1970s, but, as Guy Ritchie has demonstrated, it takes only one successful film to launch a cycle.

# Notes

1 See, for example, writer and director Jimmy Sangster's account of his work for Hammer in his autobiography (1997).
2 The Walker films were *House of Whipcord* (1974), *Frightmare* (1974) and *House of Mortal Sin* (1975). Ironically, one of the few films to be made in England which *did* follow Romero was an Italian/Spanish co-production: Jorge Grau's *The Living Dead at the Manchester Morgue* (1974).
3 Our filmography demonstrates that the peak period for the exhibition in Britain of indigenous horror films was 1970–74 when some 95 new productions were screened, 25 in 1971 alone.
4 There have been a few notable attempts to film the stories of notorious British murderers. Richard Fleischer's harrowing *Ten Rillington Place* established a template in 1970, but the only films to use it have been the deeply controversial *The Black Panther* (a scrupulously unsensational account of the Lesley Whittle murder) in 1977 and Fhiona Louise's 16mm *Cold Light of Day* (a chilling insight into the crimes of serial killer Dennis Nilsen) in 1989. Much more exploitational fare appears in the form of regular true crime 'drama docs' on television.

# References

Bryce, A. (2000) *Amicus: The Studio That Dripped Blood*, Liskeard: Stray Cat Publishing.
Conrich, I. (1998) 'The contemporary British horror film: observations on marketing, distribution and exhibition', in H. Fenton (ed.), *Flesh and Blood*, Book One, Guildford: FAB Press.
Dixon, W.W. (1991) *The Charm of Evil: The Life and Films of Terence Fisher*, Metuchen, NJ: Scarecrow Press.
Dixon, W.W. (ed.) (1994) *Reviewing British Cinema: Essays and Interviews*, New York: State University of New York Press.
Hill, J. (1999) *British Cinema in the 1980s*, Oxford: Oxford University Press.
Hunt, L. (1998) *British Low Culture: From Safari Suits to Sexploitation*, London: Routledge.
Hutchings, P. (1993) *Hammer and Beyond: The British Horror Film*, Manchester: Manchester University Press.
Hutchings, P. (2001) *Terence Fisher*, Manchester: Manchester University Press.
Murphy, R. (ed.) (2000) *British Cinema of the 90s*, London: British Film Institute.
Newman, K. (1988) *Nightmare Movies: A Critical History of the Horror Movie from 1968*, London: Bloomsbury.
Pirie, D. (1973) *A Heritage of Horror: The English Gothic Cinema 1946–1972*, London: Gordon Fraser.
Rigby, J. (2000) *English Gothic: A Century of Horror Cinema*, Richmond: Reynolds & Hearn.
Sangster, J. (1997) *Do You Want It Good or Tuesday? From Hammer Films to Hollywood! A Life in the Movies*, Baltimore: Midnight Marquee Press.
Sanjek, D. (1994) 'Twilight of the monsters: the English horror film 1968–1975', in Dixon (1994).
Trevelyan, J. (1973) *What the Censor Saw*, London: Michael Joseph.

# 2   The British censors and horror cinema

*Mark Kermode*

In 1960, Britain's then chief censor, John Trevelyan, decided that one of the most celebrated scenes of world cinema needed to be re-edited before it could be shown to the British public. His motives were twofold: first, the sequence, which depicted the hair-raising murder of a wet, naked woman had 'shots of blood all over the place' and was clearly 'sadistic' in intent; second, 'there had been much publicity in the press on two sensational killings, one in which a girl student had been decapitated' (Trevelyan 1973: 160). Although neither was the woman in the film a student, nor was she decapitated, Trevelyan felt that it would be best if he took a pair of scissors to the sequence 'to lessen the sadism' and generally take the sting out of the film's terrifying tale. And so it was that Mr Trevelyan sat down to re-edit the shower scene from Alfred Hitchcock's *Psycho* (1960), perhaps the finest sequence from one of the most influential movies ever made, and just one of the many victims of the British censors' undeclared war against horror films.

Like its literary antecedents, horror cinema has always focused upon fluctuating boundaries of taboo. It is, by its very nature, a genre of film-making which relies upon transgression. It demands that the audience's sensibilities be affronted, that decency be damned, and that (albeit temporarily) rules be broken. To censors the world over, however, horror cinema presents an insurmountable problem: How to make acceptable a brand of film-making which, at its very best, strives to be thoroughly unacceptable? In Britain, since the birth of cinema, the answer has been clumsily to neutralize and anaesthetize cutting-edge horror movies, blunting their very point and, more often than not, stripping them of whatever radical power they once possessed. Those few movies whose power stubbornly remains undiminished by the piecemeal hatcheting of key scenes are likely to find an outright ban slapped upon them. Ironically, the more inventive and effective a hard-core horror movie, the more likely it is to be butchered and banned.

The story of the British censors' strained relationship with horror cinema dates back to the beginning of the century. In 1920, The British Board of Film Censors (BBFC) seriously considered banning Robert Wiene's *The Cabinet of Dr Caligari* (1920) on the grounds that the asylum scenes could prove unnecessarily distressing to any members of the audience with relatives in mental institutions. (A proposed 1936 remake would later be opposed at script stage for including a parodic depiction of Hitler which might have been offensive to Germans!) In 1922, the Board did ban F. W. Murnau's genre milestone *Nosferatu*, although it has been widely suggested that this was done primarily to appease the notoriously litigious widow of Bram Stoker, who, fiercely protective of her late husband's copyright, didn't want any unauthorized version of Dracula showing up on Britain's screens. Since horror films were considered to be fairly debased fare anyway, the Board apparently had no qualms about blithely preventing the entire country from viewing what is now considered to be one of the greatest movies of all time in order to pacify one irate lady with a royalties claim who subsequently pursued the film-makers with destruction orders through the international courts.

In the early 1930s, both Tod Browning's *Dracula* (1931) and James Whale's *Frankenstein* (1931) suffered minor modifications before being allowed before the British public, the latter causing particular alarm for its eerie scene in which Karloff's monster accidentally drowns (off-screen) a little village girl with whom he has been floating flowers. Originally released with an 'A' certificate which allowed children to view if accompanied by an adult (as with the current American 'R' rating), *Frankenstein* provoked complaints from organizations such as the National Society for the Prevention of Cruelty to Children (NSPCC), whose impassioned entreaties to the Home Office led to the establishment of the new 'H' certificate, to be reserved for movies of a 'horrific' nature.

Although the 'H' category at least provided an official mandate for the exhibition of horror films in Britain, its reign was to be extremely uneven. Throughout World War II, the distribution of horror films was effectively suppressed, presumably on the assumption that such films were bad for the soul and would therefore undermine the collective war effort. In 1950 the Wheare Committee concluded its investigations into British film censorship by suggesting 'a single category of films, which should include the present "H" category from which children should be absolutely excluded' and that the category might be designated 'X' (quoted in ibid.: 52). The subsequent introduction of the adults-only 'X' rating in 1951 was perceived at the time as a long-term solution to the growing problems facing film censorship; surely, here was a system which would allow adults (initially meaning those over 16) to enjoy the more extreme elements of cinematic entertainment while protecting younger viewers from material for which they were not yet emotionally or intellectually prepared. It looked good on paper, but sadly, in practice, the 'X' certificate continued to treat adults as little more than advanced children, still blunting the sharpness of cutting-edge cinema, and therefore inevitably wreaking the worst damage upon that most extreme of genres, the horror film.[1] Whereas significant developments were made in the portrayal of screen sex throughout the 1950s, horror remained the subject of the censor's wrath, often inflaming the passions of the legendary John Trevelyan, whose published views on the genre perfectly reflect the predominant view that there was something innately vile about genuinely scary movies – a view which persists to this day.

Writing in his rip-roaring memoirs, *What the Censor Saw*, Trevelyan stated, for example, that:

> . In 1959 we had problems with a film called *Horrors of the Black Museum*, which was not a standard horror-film but which seemed to me to be both sadistic and nasty. It is a long time ago, but I can still remember a scene in which a girl who had been given a present of binoculars had her eyes spiked when she tried to use them; of course we had to see blood trickling down her face (ibid.: 159).

It is the final part of this statement which is the most telling – 'of course we had to see blood' – a phrase which clearly betrays both Trevelyan's view that there was no *need* whatsoever to see the blood in question, and his contempt for the film-makers who had opted to show it to us anyway, for no reason other than prurient pleasure. The fact that the sight of the blood is itself the dramatic pay-off to the scene in question – a scene of extreme tension followed by spectacular visceral release – carries no weight in Trevelyan's scheme of things. To the censor, the punch-line is simply both unnecessary and obnoxious, as opposed to crucial and climactic. Similarly, of Georges Franju's extraordinary *Eyes Without a Face* (1959), on which the BBFC duly performed their usual botched amputations, Trevelyan noted simply that 'Transplants of course provided film-makers with new opportunities' (ibid.: 167), that 'of course' once again leaving the reader in little doubt of the chief censor's view that opportunism was the order of the day throughout this misbegotten genre.

In 1960, Trevelyan found himself in the unusual position of being forced to grant a certificate to a horror film which he found 'really troublesome', but to which he had unfortunately given the go-ahead at script stage.[2] Michael Powell's visceral chiller *Peeping Tom* had initially been read by Trevelyan as a work which could 'contribute to a public understanding of mental illness', but the finished film seemed to him to be 'totally different' from the written draft (ibid.: 159). In fact, comparisons between the submitted script and its celluloid realization demonstrate very little deviation from what was originally approved by the Board. Indeed, even Trevelyan himself does not appear to be claiming that Powell had intended to deceive them by submitting one script and filming another. Rather, his outrage at the finished film seems to stem from the realization that the script itself could not encompass the weird magic created on screen by the mystical collision of sight and sound. Put simply, the censor seems to have been intrigued by the script, but actually scared by the film – a reaction over which he had no control, and for which he was thoroughly unprepared.

Panicked by his own response to the material, Trevelyan reacted in the only way he knew how: to cut hard and deep into the film in a desperate attempt to tear out

*Figure 4* 'We made extensive cuts and hoped for the best': Carl Boehm and Pamela
    Green scare the censor in Michael Powell's *Peeping Tom* (1960).

its dark heart, or at least wound it to the point that it could no longer exert any
power over an audience – or himself. 'We made extensive cuts and hoped for the
best' he blithely writes, finding his efforts vindicated when, upon release, 'the public
did not like the film, although it was well made' (ibid.: 160–1).

Once again, it is Trevelyan's off-hand asides which reveal the inherently
contradictory nature of the censorship of horror cinema, clearly demonstrating that
a horror film will be deemed acceptable only if it is either not horrific, or
(preferably) not aimed at a popular audience. Many years later, in 1999, the BBFC
president Andreas Whittam Smith and its secretary Robin Duval would announce
that Abel Ferrara's slasher classic *The Driller Killer* (1979) had been passed for
certification – albeit in a print which its distributors had taken the precaution
of heavily pre-cutting – since, according to their press release (available at
www.bbfc.co.uk), in its butchered form it was 'unexceptional', and, after twenty
years had 'lost much of its power to shock'. Prefiguring such decisions, and setting
the standard for future censors, Trevelyan seemed to believe that, ideally, horror
films should be silly rather than scary. In 1961, the Board under Trevelyan's
leadership banned Mario Bava's extraordinary Gothic shocker *Black Sunday* (1961)
on 'grounds of disgust' (ibid.: 166), concluding that its transgressive elements

(which were in fact visually fairly discreet, even by contemporaneous standards) were too provocative for public viewing. A mere seven years later, however, the Board duly granted the film an 'X' certificate, allowing it to play freely around the UK, under the new title *Revenge of the Vampire*, to the self-same adult audiences who had been so carefully 'protected' from it the first time around. The reason for this abrupt *volte-face* was simply that what once seemed horrifying now 'looked rather ridiculous' (ibid.: 166), and was therefore considered acceptable since it was more likely to provoke laughter than horror. 'One help to us', wrote Trevelyan, 'was that nobody took these films seriously'. Or, to be more precise, nobody was allowed to take these films seriously, for only when they had passed into the realms of ridicule were they finally considered acceptable for public viewing.

It was their potential for ridicule which seems to have underwritten the censors' relative tolerance of films from the Hammer stable. Trevelyan recalled a conversation with Hammer head Jimmy (later Sir James) Carreras in which the two agreed that Hammer films would 'avoid mixing sex with horror and would avoid scenes which people could regard as disgusting or revolting' (ibid.: 165–6). Since this agreement seems in principle to have effectively proscribed the entire basis of a large proportion of horror, it is hardly surprising that the censors were pleased with Carreras's tacit co-operation. Although Trevelyan went on to explain that changing sexual mores did in fact lead to the classification of films including nudity and overt sexuality by the early 1970s, he was also adamant that 'The second part of this agreement has continued to the present day' (ibid.: 166), thereby proving that home-produced British horror was forbidden from being 'disgusting or revolting' from the 1950s through to the early 1970s.

One film which singularly failed to live down to these bland standards was Michael Reeves's *Witchfinder General* (1968), of which David Pirie prophetically wrote in 1971 that it could be 'transferred into a pivotal position in the history of English cinema' (Pirie 1973: 105). Now widely regarded as perhaps the single most significant horror film produced in the UK in the 1960s, *Witchfinder General* was heavily censored at script stage by the BBFC, and then subject to considerable post-production cuts by the BBFC, despite Trevelyan's recognition that its creator was sincere in his condemnation of the atrocities portrayed. Once again, Trevelyan appears to have been torn between, on the one hand, appreciating the film-maker's skills, and, on the other, detesting the reactions which those skills provoked. Had the film been less well made, or less obviously aimed at a popular audience, the Board might well have been more lenient. Instead, they exacted more (and more damaging) cuts upon *Witchfinder General* than were usually inflicted on far less significant fare, with the result that a plainly heartbroken Reeves simply withdrew from the re-editing process and refused to co-operate with the massacring of his work.

Thus it was that, for a period of about twenty years, horror cinema in Britain was hamstrung by the demands of a censor board which insisted that it could be anything

*Figure 5* 'The single most significant horror film produced in the UK in the 1960s': Hilary Dwyer suffers at the hands of Robert Russell before submitting to the censor's knife in *Witchfinder General* (1968).

but horrific. Although this situation seemed entirely laudable to Trevelyan (who, let us not forget, failed to notice an erection in Andy Warhol's *Flesh* (1968), which the Board eventually passed uncut, while simultaneously insisting on trimming a relatively demure demonic fantasy from Polanski's *Rosemary's Baby* (1968)), it appeared somewhat ludicrous to his ill-fated successor. Stephen Murphy took over as new secretary at the BBFC in 1971, just in time to enjoy the storms of controversy which had been stirred up by the passing of films like *A Clockwork Orange* (1971), *Soldier Blue* (1970) and *The Devils* (1971) with an 'X' certificate, whose viewing age limit had been increased the year before from 16 to 18. Attacked on all sides by the press and politicians, Murphy retained a comparatively clear head throughout his brief and troubled reign, particularly in relation to the inherent extremities of horror cinema. According to the long-time regulator Guy Phelps:

> By early 1974, Murphy himself had become convinced that the repression of violence had been taken too far. In particular he felt that the Board's demands were tending to take the horror out of the horror film . . . it was apparent that

the Board was removing the whole point of the films by insisting that the horror be diluted.

(Phelps 1975: 123)

However, unfortunately for Murphy, who oversaw the passing uncut of such key works as William Friedkin's *The Exorcist* (1973), which would later be banned on video by his successor, such liberalism proved thoroughly unpopular not only with moral entrepreneurs such as Mary Whitehouse and their vociferous allies in the press, but also with a timorous film industry terrified of public controversy, contributing to his early downfall and making him the most unjustly lambasted chief censor in the entire history of the Board.

Yet, for all Murphy's apparent openness, he was still dismayingly inclined to draw a veil over some of the most important horror releases of the early 1970s. In particular, under his regime the BBFC banned two milestone horror films which changed the face of the genre and which are now accepted as major works of art throughout the rest of the world. Made in 1972, *Last House on the Left* was the directorial debut of the horror maestro Wes Craven, an extraordinarily visceral shocker which took the redemptive themes of Ingmar Bergman's *The Virgin Spring* (1960) and turned them into a nihilistic howl of rage about the corrupting power of violence. Depicting the rape and murder of two teenage girls by a 'family' of psychopaths who are in turn mutilated and mangled by the parents of one of their victims, the film straddled an uncomfortable divide between art-house angst and grind-house gore. Having been seen by the Board in a version already trimmed from its alleged original running time of ninety-one minutes, *Last House on the Left* was officially refused a theatrical certificate in July 1974, the distributors Oppidan being told in no uncertain terms that further cutting would not solve the problem. Nine months later, with Murphy by now heading for the door and soon to be replaced by the incoming secretary James Ferman, the Board refused to certificate Tobe Hooper's *The Texas Chain Saw Massacre* (1974), of which the deputy director Ken Penry commented that 'it did not have particularly outrageous visuals, but it was so well made it had this awful impact all the way through' (quoted in Mathews 1994: 252). Once again, excellence within the horror genre was to be rewarded with disapproval and ultimately dismissal in the corridors of the BBFC, where there seemed to be no greater crime than creating a truly effective film frightener.

Two years after having been first snubbed by the Board (but accepted by the Greater London Council and a number of other local authorities), *The Texas Chain Saw Massacre* found its way back to the BBFC, where Ferman spent some time attempting to dissect the movie's magical spell before concluding that extensive cuts made no difference at all to the 'awful' tone of the film. Paving the way for his subsequent reign of terror in relation to horror, Ferman promptly banned Hooper's masterpiece for a second time, concluding that since the film could not be made 'more palatable' (quoted in ibid.: 253), it must instead be rendered unwatchable.

While Ferman's savage treatment of *The Texas Chain Saw Massacre* in the 1970s was clearly indicative of the same general contempt for horror cinema which had underwritten British film censorship since its inception, the most sustained campaign against the genre was to be waged in the 1980s and 1990s. John Trevelyan had long recognized that what was considered unacceptable on British screens was wildly divergent from what was permitted elsewhere in the world. Thus, of his relationship with foreign distributors he noted that:

> While the audiences in the United States wanted their horror films stronger than we would accept in Britain, there were a few countries, notably Japan, that regarded the American versions as too tame for their audiences. . . . One European country, West Germany, seemed to want particularly nasty films of this kind, and their productions used to give us a great many problems.
>
> (Trevelyan 1973: 166)

Although Britain had been traditionally 'protected' from the 'stronger' traits of European and American cinema by the BBFC, the rise of unregulated videotapes in the early 1980s provided an opening for such material to enter the country on a large scale for the first time. The result was utter pandemonium.

Spotting a potentially lucrative business opportunity, a few industrious entrepreneurs took the opportunity to release on video movies which the BBFC would certainly not pass for theatrical distribution. Titles such as *The Driller Killer* (1980), *Cannibal Holocaust* (1979), *SS Experiment Camp* (1976) and *I Spit On Your Grave* (1981) suddenly became available in a country in which *Death Wish II* (1982) was still considered to be controversial. Yet the anarchic infancy of unregulated video was to prove extremely short lived, as tabloid newspapers mounted a campaign against the new 'threat' which they dubbed with the infantile label 'video nasties'. In a wave of government- and media-promoted hysteria, horror videos were promptly blamed for everything from inattentiveness at school to muggings and rapes, with teachers, clergymen, politicians and the usual moral entrepreneurs demanding drastic measures to protect the country from video dealers who were bizarrely branded 'merchants of menace'.

However, just as the film industry in Britain has always been among the strongest supporters of strict film censorship, so the video dealers themselves were as eager as anybody for some form of official regulation to be enforced, particularly since it was they (rather than the video distributors) who generally found themselves open to prosecution under the notoriously unpredictable Obscene Publications Act (OPA), which the director of public prosecutions had decided *could* be used to prosecute violent material, and not simply pornography – as had been the case in the past. Crucially, there were at that time no official guidelines indicating which videos were unacceptable to the authorities, and even videos of films which had been passed for theatrical release were not safe from prosecution under the OPA.

Although admittedly certain video versions of films contained scenes which had been cut for cinema showing (such as Tony Maylam's *The Burning* (1981)), other titles like Lucio Fulci's *House by the Cemetery* (1981) and Sam Raimi's *The Evil Dead* (1982) were considered impoundable on video in exactly the same format as the BBFC cinema-approved prints.

Between 1983 and 1985, the Director of Public Prosecutions drew up a list of around sixty titles (known affectionately by aficionados as the 'Big Sixty') which included such varied fare as *The Beyond* (1981), *Inferno* (1980), *Terror Eyes* (1980), *The Funhouse* (1981), *Madhouse* (1981), *EvilSpeak* (1981), *Nightmares in a Damaged Brain* (1981) and*Visiting Hours* (1982), all of which were considered prosecutable under the terms of the OPA. Finally, in 1984, following a landslide Conservative election victory, the government passed the notorious Video Recordings Act (VRA), under which the BBFC were officially empowered to classify and cut all video releases with 'special regard to the likelihood of video works in respect of which . . . certificates have been issued being viewed in the home'. This deceptively mild phrase was to have extremely serious consequences for videos in general, and for horror films on video in particular.

The VRA's stress on the home clearly implied that videos classified for adult viewing could be accessed by children, and thus should be judged more harshly than their cinematic counterparts. It also assumed that the malleability of videos would encourage miscreants to enjoy scenes of horror repetitively and 'out of context', something which it clearly regarded as dangerous and something to be discouraged as far as possible by the imposition of swingeing cuts on graphic scenes. Thus, after a few fleeting years in which hitherto starved UK fans were for the first time treated to the untrammelled delights of world-wide horror, British censors were able to clamp down upon the genre with more ferocity (and greater legal force) than ever before. At a single stroke, the so-called 'nasties' were removed from the British video shelves, and fines of £20,000 enforced for those who transgressed.

But it was not simply the more outré 'nasty' fare which was to suffer. In the years following the introduction of the Video Recordings Act, an average of one in four '18'-rated videos would be cut by the BBFC, many films suffering cuts in addition to those already made for their cinema release. In the case of *The Evil Dead*, which was officially acquitted of obscenity charges at a crucial hearing at Snaresbrook Crown Court on 7 November 1983, the BBFC simply refused to issue a video certificate despite the pre-cutting of forty-nine seconds which had already been lopped from the cinema print. This refusal was on the grounds that*The Evil Dead* had been successfully prosecuted at *other* courts around the country, and the BBFC – presumably in consultation with the Home Office – had established a self-imposed rule that no video found guilty under the OPA could subsequently be passed without cuts within a period of the first fifteen – and later ten – years. Although there is no good explanation as to why 'guilty' verdicts should always take precedence over 'not guilty' acquittals, *The Evil Dead* was to remain banned from video until 1990, when it was finally passed at '18' only after a *further* sixty-five seconds of cuts had been made, thus apparently making it in the eyes of the law a film 'substantially different' from that which had been prosecuted in the early 1980s. As Ferman said, neatly pinpointing the British censors' perennial problem with horror in general: 'the difficulty with *The Evil Dead* is that the name of the game is excess in the first place. To cut something that's meant to be over the top, so that it's no longer too far over the top, is very difficult' (quoted in Kermode 1995: 60). A decade later, Ferman's successors would finally remove all the over-sensitive censors' scissor-marks, proving once and for all that *The Evil Dead* was utterly unlikely to 'deprave and corrupt' *anyone*, even in the unexpurgated original format which had suffered so many indignities throughout the 1980s and 1990s.

More alarmingly, some mainstream horror titles such as *The Exorcist* (1973), which had never even been labelled a 'nasty' in the first place, were also banned outright in the wake of the VRA, Ferman declaring that such material was simply unsuitable for exhibition in the home. However, perhaps the most pernicious and cavalier mistreatment of a horror classic during Ferman's reign was that handed out to John McNaughton's savage gem *Henry: Portrait of a Serial Killer* (1990). Originally earmarked for an outright ban, *Henry* was finally passed for theatrical release in April 1991 with sixty-one seconds of cuts, and a firm promise that it would never be allowed to emerge on video. Two years later, in January 1993, the film was in fact granted an '18' video certificate, but by now the cuts had spiralled to one minute fifty-three seconds. But what was most distressing about the BBFC's tampering with *Henry* was that not only did Ferman choose to cut McNaughton's vision, he also surreptitiously re-edited it in order, quite deliberately, to change the very meaning of the film. In the movie's single most important sequence, McNaughton presents us with a degraded image of the murderers' crimes, before pulling back to reveal that the killers, Henry and Otis, are (like us) merely watching the atrocities on video-playback, for their own delectation. The whole point of McNaughton's scene was to implicate the viewer in the killers' crimes, and thus to make us question our own desire to watch such horrifying events. This was simply too much for Ferman, who radically restructured the scene, allowing the audience to watch Henry and Otis watching themselves, safe in the knowledge that these people have no connection with us. Once again, Ferman was striving with a vengeance to take the horror out of this purest of horror films. The result, as ever, was to deface and defile a radical work of art, to make it 'palatable' in a way which utterly negated its entire *raison d'être*. This re-editing of *Henry* remains an extraordinary testament to the UK censors' almost pathological fear and dislike of horror cinema, and the subsequent undoing of Ferman's re-editing jinx by his successors in 2001 merely confirms how muddle-headed his actions were in the first place.

Yet further damage was done to the reputation of horror movies in the UK in 1993–4 by the press coverage surrounding the conviction of two boys for the murder of the toddler James Bulger, their crime being irresponsibly (and insupportably) linked by the media to an alleged viewing of the anodyne horror comedy *Child's Play III* (1991). Although there was no proof that either boy had actually *seen* the film in question, the Liberal Democrat MP David Alton promptly demanded that new laws should be passed which would effectively have removed *all* horror videos from distribution in the UK. Aided by gutter-press headlines like the *Sun's* 'Burn Your Video Nasty', an amendment to the Video Recordings Act was duly inserted in the Criminal Justice Act which legally required the BBFC, every time that it classified a video:

> To have special regard among the other relevant factors to any harm that might be caused to potential viewers or, through their behaviour, to society, by the manner in which the work deals with: (a) criminal behaviour (b) illegal drugs (c) violent behaviour or incidents (d) horrific behaviour (e) human sexual activity.

Although (c) and (d) appeared to have considerable bearing on the censorship of horror videos, the Board's subsequent *Annual Report 1994–95* stated that: 'the possibility of harm had *always* been at the heart of BBFC policy, so the new clause did not require a fundamental shift in examining practice' (BBFC 1995: 1, my italics). The report further explained that the new criteria

> represent not a break with former policy, but a confirmation of it, since they put on the face of legislation factors which the Board has been taking into account for many years. The difference now is that the Board can be held to account, in court if necessary, for failing to apply these criteria with sufficient rigour. This, we said, would concentrate the mind. It has done.
>
> (ibid.: 3)[3]

Despite such calming words from the Board, the effects of this latter-day moral panic were to prove bizarre and far reaching for horror films in general. In the short term, low-budget British frighteners such as Vadim Jean's *Beyond Bedlam* (1993) or Ray Brady's *Boy Meets Girl* (1994) had their video certificates either severely delayed or denied entirely, thus badly damaging their ability to recoup their costs by making a profit in the crucial home-viewing market. In the long term, a spate of ludicrous OPA prosecutions in 1994 against classic 'video nasty' titles such as Dario Argento's *Tenebrae* (1982) and Lucio Fulci's *Zombie Flesh Eaters* (1979) were to cause ongoing problems for the new management of the BBFC as the turn of the century approached. Although an age of refreshing openness was declared by Andreas Whittam Smith and Robin Duval at the end of the 1990s, the Board found itself quite unable fully to re-evaluate such titles on account of the 'ten-year rule' mentioned earlier. It is thus expected that the year 2004 may be a significant watershed for those outstanding 'nasties' which are still snipped to comply with the law, but since it apparently only takes one moral panic per decade to take us all back to square one again, any optimism may well prove short lived.

When James Ferman retired from the BBFC in 1998, after a steady stream of press stories (allegedly inspired by hostile Home Office briefings) peddling the line that he had presided over an unacceptable degree of *liberalization* of the Board's standards, he was replaced by Robin Duval, formerly of the Independent Television Commission. A new president in the form of the *Independent*-founder Andreas Whittam Smith was already in place, and together they brought about the most thorough overhaul of BBFC guidelines since the introduction of the 'X' certificate. Declaring a progressive new dawn at the Board, the BBFC celebrated the millennium by organizing a series of road-shows and citizens' juries, at the end of which they unveiled a new series of classification guidelines. The main bene-ficiaries were undoubtedly in the 'R18' category, as licensed sex shops were finally allowed to sell a fairly wide range of hard-core porn videos, but even '18'-rated cinema films and videos, albeit art-house fare of limited appeal such as Lars Von Trier's *The Idiots* (1998) and Catherine Breillat's *Romance* (1999), had begun to reap the benefits of the Board's new-found liberalism towards representations of sexual activity.

But what of horror? At the time of writing it remains to be seen whether or not the BBFC intends to take a less censorious approach to the genre. The signs are somewhat mixed with, on the one hand, a number of gore classics finally being released uncut and, on the other, old attitudes prevailing. Thus Lucio Fulci's *The Beyond* is finally available in all its gory glory, but the same director's self-reflexive splatter extravaganza *A Cat in the Brain/Nightmare Concert* (1990) is banned outright on video, with the Board taking a by now wearyingly familiar line, and also, incidentally, underlining how damaging to horror movies is the now-statutory 'harm' test outlined above. Thus, its *Annual Report 1999* notes that it was

> potentially harmful to a significant proportion of its likely viewers, due to a profusion of gross sexual violence. Cuts were considered. However, the quantity of unacceptable material rendered such an approach impossible since it would be unlikely to change the general tone or approach of the work.
>
> (BBFC 2000: 22)

It is also worth pointing out that one of the reasons for finally passing *The Texas Chain Saw Massacre* uncut on film and video was that 'it was decided that the film's horrors were unlikely to be taken too seriously' (ibid: 22). *Plus ça change*. . . . Then, in February 2000, in the same press release which announced the passing, after a twenty-five-year ban, of Just Jaeckin's soft-core S&M romp *The Story of O* (1975) (in an abridged print which nevertheless contained *all* the explicit material which had originally prompted its rejection), the BBFC declared that *Last House on the Left* was still 'not suitable for cinema exhibition', nearly thirty years after its creation.

Whether the BBFC will ultimately prove itself the ally or enemy of horror in the twenty-first century only time will tell. One thing is for sure – whatever havoc it may wreak, the future could not be any more terrifying for lovers of the genre than the hundred-year reign of terror from which we are only now emerging.

## Notes

1  For a useful discussion of the advent of the 'X' certificate see Aldgate (2000).
2  At that time, the BBFC no longer insisted, as it once had, on vetting proposed film projects at script stage, but still liked to do so. Producers were, on the whole, happy to comply in order to avoid costly post-production censorship problems. This introduced a whole area of submerged and largely 'invisible' censorship into the system, with many films being vetoed at script stage. For a fascinating discussion of this process (of which, incidentally, *Witchfinder General* was a victim) as it affected the horror film in Britain, see Spicer (2000).
3  For a detailed discussion of the Alton affair and its aftermath see Petley (1994, 1995).

## References

Aldgate, A. (2000) '*Women of Twilight*, *Cosh Boy* and the advent of the "X" certificate', *Journal of Popular British Cinema* 3: 59–68.

British Board of Film Classification (1995) *Annual Report 1994–95*, London.

British Board of Film Classification (2000) *Annual Report 1999*, London.

Kermode, M. (1995) 'Horror: on the edge of taste', *Index on Censorship* 24, 6: 59–68.

Mathews, T.D. (1994) *Censored: What They Didn't Allow You to See and Why: the Story of Film Censorship in Britain*, London: Chatto & Windus.

Petley, J. (1994) 'Time for action', *Samhain* 45, July–August: 8–11.

Petley, J. (1995) 'Something nasty in the newspapers', *Social Science Teacher* 24, 2: 10–11.

Pirie, D. (1973) *A Heritage of Horror: The English Gothic Cinema 1946–1972*, London: Gordon Fraser.

Phelps, G. (1975) *Film Censorship*, London: Victor Gollancz.

Spicer, A. (2000) 'The BBFC scenario reports at the British Film Institute: the case of the macabre film', *Journal of Popular British Cinema* 3: 121–4.

Trevelyan, J. (1973) *What the Censor Saw*, London: Michael Joseph.

# 3 'A crude sort of entertainment for a crude sort of audience': the British critics and horror cinema

*Julian Petley*

It is the business of criticism not only to keep watch over the vagaries of philosophy, but to do the duty of police in the whole world of thought.

> T.H. Huxley, *Hume* (1879)

Will this wave of sensationalism die a natural death? Probably, but in the meantime it makes film-going a hazardous occupation, increases the number of customers who abstain from the cinema except on the rare occasions when 'there is something which, I hope, does not contain violence, sadism, lechery, torture, perversion, lust or cruelty' (I quote from one of the many letters on the subject.) Can't anything be done about it? Of course it can, if anyone in authority takes some trouble.

> C.A. Lejeune, reviewing *Dracula* in the *Observer*, 31 May 1958

Charming as were all Mrs Radcliffe's works, and charming even as were the works of all her imitators, it was not in them perhaps that human nature, at least in the midland counties of England, was to be looked for.

> Jane Austen, *Northanger Abbey* (1818)

The hostile British critical reception which greeted Hammer's early horror films, and horror-related titles such as *Peeping Tom* (1960) and *Straw Dogs* (1971), has already been well documented (Barr 1972, Christie 1978, Hutchings 1993). However, little has been done to put these negative critical responses into their wider cultural and literary-historical contexts, nor has there been much enquiry into the consequences, especially the long-term ones, of this tide of vituperation for horror cinema in Britain.

## Situations of torment, images of naked horror

In this chapter I want to show that the terms in which British horror films were routinely attacked by a significant number of British critics from the late 1950s to the early 1970s were remarkably similar to those employed by many of their predecessors against the Gothic novel in its heyday – which I take as stretching from the publication of Horace Walpole's *The Castle of Otranto* in 1764 to that of Charles Robert Maturin's *Melmoth the Wanderer* in 1820. It does need to be stressed from the outset, however, that the reception of the Gothic novel was by no means uniformly negative. Nonetheless, it attracted sufficient negative comments couched in strikingly similar terms to enable one to isolate a number of recurring themes and to suggest that a quite specific critical discourse was at work here – one so culturally deep-seated as to be able to be re-applied without much significant modification to a different medium around 150 years later. Furthermore, it can also be argued that this discourse did to some extent damage the Gothic novel in Britain – for example causing Matthew Lewis to self-censor *The Monk* (1796) – but had disastrous long-term consequences for horror cinema in Britain in the twentieth and twenty-first centuries. This well illustrates the fashion in which, as Chris Baldick has put it, censorship often acts as the 'armed wing' of criticism. He continues:

> The 'judgement' of literary works has a real extra-metaphorical equivalent in the fact that these works have always endured a degree of censorship and legal restraint upon their publication and dissemination. In casting themselves as 'judges' or as witnesses for the defence, critics habitually mimic the authority of more powerful assessors of literature . . . Criticism from Plato onwards has . . . presupposed censorship, banishment, and official persecution in the very language of its 'judgements' and in its images of its own authority.
>
> (1987: 8–9)

In Britain, as far back as the first half of the eighteenth century, the term 'Gothic' had already acquired distinctly negative connotations. As Fred Botting explains, it had become 'a general and derogatory term for the Middle Ages which conjured up ideas of barbarous customs and practices, of superstition, ignorance, extravagant fancies and natural wildness' (1996: 22). In other words, exactly the opposite of the then highly valued ideals of the Enlightenment, with its stress on harmony, order, rationality, symmetry, proportion and classical, rule-governed artistic forms. Romances were a particular target of many critics, who were concerned that they over-stimulated readers' imaginations, taught them nothing useful, and, worse still, threatened to corrupt their morals. John Cleland's review of Smollett's *Peregrine Pickle* (1751) neatly illustrates why, for such critics, novels based on real life were superior to works of pure imagination:

> For as the matter of them is taken chiefly from nature, from adventures, real or imaginary, but familiar, practical and probable to be met with in the course of common life, they may serve as pilot's charts, or maps of those parts of the world, which every one may chance to travel through; and in this light they are

public benefits. Whereas romances and novels which turn upon characters out of nature, monsters of perfection, feats of chivalry, fairy-enchantments, and the whole train of the marvellously absurd, transport the reader unprofitably into the clouds, where he is sure to find no solid footing, or into those wilds of fancy which go on for ever out of the way of all human paths.

(quoted in ibid.: 25)

This line of thought found its most extreme expression in Samuel Johnson, whom James Boswell's famous *Life* quotes as stating that: 'the value of every story depends on it being true. A story is a picture of either an individual, or of human nature in general: if it be false it is a picture of nothing' (1980: 165). There runs through Johnson a deep suspicion of all fiction, and indeed of all art, unless it is not only didactic, but also moral, in intent. As René Wellek has argued, he 'paves the way for a view which makes art really superfluous, a mere vehicle for the communication of moral and psychological truth' (1955: 79). Thus in the fourth edition of the *Rambler*, March 1750, which is devoted to 'The New Realistic Novel' he argues that the purpose of novels is:

To teach the means of avoiding the snares which are laid by Treachery for Innocence . . . to give the power of counteracting fraud, without the temptation to practise it; to initiate youth by mock encounters in the art of necessary defence, and to increase prudence without impairing virtue.

(reproduced in Greene, 1984: 175–9)

Great care must be taken in 'presenting life, which is so often discoloured by passion, or deformed by wickedness'. This does not mean that unpleasant things should not be represented at all, but that 'vice, for vice is necessary to be shewn, should always disgust; nor should the graces of gaiety, or the dignity of courage, be so united with it as to reconcile it to the mind'. At the same time, however, 'many characters ought never to be drawn'. Johnson's strictures on literature and its function provide the clearest evidence that, for many critics in the late eighteenth century:

Distinguishing between good and bad modes of writing was more than a merely aesthetic enterprise: it marked an attempt to supplement an assumed inability on the part of romances and their growing readership to discriminate between virtue and vice, and thus to forestall their seduction along fictional paths that stimulated antisocial passions and corrupt behaviour.

(Botting, op. cit.: 28)

For such critics, as the end of the eighteenth century approached, the importance of writing's social function – clearly an essentially conservative one in their view – was given added urgency by the spectre of revolution importing itself from France.

This, presumably, is at least partly what T.J. Matthias had in mind in 1796 when he argued in *The Pursuits of Literature* that 'literature, well or ill conceived, is the great engine, by which all civilised states must ultimately be supported or overthrown' (quoted in ibid.: 83).

From this kind of critical perspective, then, the Gothic represented an intensification of all that was wrong with the romance. Furthermore, as literacy increased in the late eighteenth and early nineteenth centuries, so the readership of novels grew. The fact that the Gothic became an extremely popular genre, and one which seemed to encourage a particularly intimate relationship between the text and its readers, many of whom were women, only increased many critics' fear and dislike of it. As Maggie Kilgour points out:

> To many early concerned critics, gothic novels were the unlicensed indulgence of an amoral imagination that was a socially subversive force. . . . The escapist imagination was denounced as corruptive of family values, as, when uncontrolled by reason, it rendered the vulnerable proverbial 'young person' unfit for real life. The art that is completely fanciful, an autonomous creation that does not refer to reality, offers a tempting alternative to the mundaneness of everyday life. It was feared that readers of fictions, seduced by the enticing charms of an illusory world, would lose either their grip on or their taste for reality.
>
> (1995: 7)

That this was indeed the case is proved by a quotation from a review of *Emmeline, the Orphan of the Castle* in the *Analytical Review*, July 1788, which complained that

> the false expectations these wild scenes excite, tend to debauch the mind, and throw an insipid kind of uniformity over the moderate and rational prospects of life, consequently adventures are sought for and created, when duties are neglected and content despised.
>
> (ibid.: 7)

From a different perspective, writers of the more extreme kinds of Gothic fiction also had to deal with the negative legacy of Edmund Burke's *A Philosophical Enquiry into the Origin of Our Ideas of the Sublime and the Beautiful*, which was first published in 1757 and in which he argued that: 'When danger or pain press too nearly, they are incapable of giving any delight, and are simply terrible; but at certain distances, and with certain modifications, they may be, and they are delightful, as we every day experience' (1987: 40). This suggests that certain potentially unpleasant and even painful experiences may actually become pleasurable under certain circumstances – if 'modified' and 'distanced' in the form of artistic representations, for example. Burke also suggested that 'to make anything very terrible, obscurity seems in general to be necessary' and praised Milton's depiction of Death in *Paradise Lost* for its 'judicious obscurity' (ibid.: 58–9). From here appears to have derived the idea that the subtle evocation of terror is greatly to be preferred, both aesthetically and morally, to the explicit depiction of horror.

For example, the influence of Burke is clear in the 1773 essay 'On the Pleasure Derived from Objects of Terror' by Anna Letitia Aikin (1773) in which she writes that:

> The more wild, fanciful, and extraordinary are the circumstances of a scene of horror, the more pleasure we receive from it; and where they are too near common nature, though violently borne by curiosity through the adventure, we cannot repeat or reflect on it, without an over-balance of pain.
>
> (quoted in Ellis 2000: 9)

Similarly, in *Literary Hours* (1800), Nathan Drake argues that terror requires the 'skills and arrangement' of art to 'prevent its operating more pain than pleasure'. He continues:

> No efforts of genius . . . are so truly great as those which approaching the brink of horror, have yet, by the art of the poet or painter, by adjunctive and pictoresque embellishment, by pathetic, or sublime emotion, been rendered powerful in creating the most delightful and fascinating sensations.

Ann Radcliffe's work is singled out for particular praise because, although it contains 'many scenes truly terrific in their conception' it is

> much relieved by the intermixture of beautiful description, or pathetic incident, that the impression of the whole never becomes too strong, never degenerates into horror, but pleasurable emotion is ever the predominating result.
>
> (quoted in ibid.: 10, 11)

Indeed, Radcliffe herself in her essay 'On the Supernatural in Poetry' (1816) was clearly drawing on Burke in her distinction between terror and horror:

> Terror and horror are so far opposite, that the first expands the soul, and awakens the faculties to a high degree of life; the other contracts, freezes, and nearly annihilates them. . . . Where lies the great difference between *Terror* and *Horror* but in the uncertainty and obscurity that accompanies the first respecting the dreaded evil.
>
> (quoted in Howells 1995: 40)

As both Devendra Varma (1987) and David Pirie (1973) have forcefully pointed out, this kind of approach has consistently privileged the tale of terror in the

Radcliffian mode of the Gothic over the tale of horror in its 'Schauer-Romantik' mode. (The German, *Schauer* translates as 'shiver', 'paroxysm' or 'thrill', and the German equivalent of the expression 'penny dreadful' is *Schauerroman*). This strategy, as we shall see, has been a remarkably persistent feature of the criticism of horror fiction both in literature and in the cinema. Indeed, the two modes have frequently been crassly confused by critics, with the tale of horror being criticized simply because it is not a tale of terror – and never mind the inconvenient fact that its author never intended it to be so in the first place. Yet the distinction between the two is perfectly clear, as Varma points out:

> Terror creates an intangible atmosphere of spiritual psychic dread, a certain superstitious shudder at the other world. Horror resorts to a cruder presentation of the macabre: by an exact portrayal of the physically horrible and revolting, against a far more terrible background of spiritual gloom and despair. Horror appeals to sheer dread and repulsion by brooding upon the gloomy and the sinister, and lacerates the nerves by establishing actual cutaneous contact with the supernatural.
>
> (1987: 130)

The critical bias against the tale of horror infected even those whose own writings contain some fine examples of the horrific. Thus Samuel Taylor Coleridge, the author of *Christabel* and *The Rime of the Ancient Mariner* no less, complained in a review of Matthew Lewis's *The Monk* that:

> Situations of torment, and images of naked horror, are easily conceived; and a writer in whose works they abound, deserves our gratitude almost equally with him who should drag us by way of sport through a military hospital, or force us to sit at the dissection table of a natural philosopher. . . . Figures that shock the imagination, and narratives that mangle the feelings, rarely discover *genius*, and always betray a low and vulgar *taste*.
>
> (quoted in Raysor 1936: 372)

Over-popular, lacking in morality, excessive, uncivilized, unrealistic, a bad influence: these are the charges laid against the Gothic, particularly at its most horrific, by a certain strand of English criticism in the eighteenth and nineteenth centuries. Thus, for example, even Horace Walpole's generally well-received *The Castle of Otranto* was criticized by some for its lack of a moral message, and one critic lamented that: 'it is, indeed, more than strange, that an Author, of a refined and polished genius, should be an advocate for re-establishing the barbarous superstitions of Gothic devilism' (quoted in Botting, op. cit.: 53). And later writers such as Matthias were quick to blame Walpole for being the progenitor of what went on to become what was, for them, a worryingly popular genre. Similarly, Radcliffe's *The*

*Mysteries of Udolpho* (1794) was not without its detractors, the reviewer in the *British Critic* complaining that 'the lady's talent for description leads her to excess' and that 'too much of the terrific' leads to a jaded sensibility (quoted in ibid.: 67). Again, it cannot be stressed too strongly that fears about popular literature in general, and the Gothic in particular, had a resolutely ideological and political base; as Botting himself points out: 'intensified by fears of radicalism and revolution, the challenge to aesthetic values was framed in terms of social transgression: virtue, propriety and domestic order were considered to be under threat' (ibid.: 21–2). In this respect it is worth remembering that *The Monk* was published only six years after the French Revolution, and that *Frankenstein* and *Melmoth* neatly bracket the Peterloo Massacre of 1819.

The criticisms of Walpole and Radcliffe, however, were as nothing compared to the furore which greeted *The Monk* (1796) and which led to its author expunging various passages for fear of being prosecuted. The *British Critic*, 7 June 1796, led the attack, describing the book as a collection of 'lust, murder, incest, and every other atrocity that can disgrace human nature, brought together, without the apology of probability, or even possibility for their introduction' (quoted in Botting op. cit.: 21), while the *Monthly Review*, August 1797, concluded that 'a vein of obscenity . . . pervades and deforms the whole organisation of this novel' (quoted in Ellis, 2000: 110). Even the most hostile reviewers, however, had to admit that the book had literary merits too, but this only further incensed them against its author, who stood accused of abusing and prostituting his talents. A good example of this kind of approach is provided by Coleridge in the *Critical Review*, February 1797 (reproduced in full, along with his reviews of other Gothic novels, in Raysor 1936: 355–82). Thus while finding elements to praise in the novel, Coleridge complained that Ambrosio's temptations 'are described with a libidinous minuteness', making the novel a 'poison for youth, and a provocative for the debauchee' (ibid.: 374). He also lamented that: 'the horrible and the preternatural have usually seized on the popular taste, at the rise and decline of literature. Most powerful stimulants, they can never be required except by the torpor of an unawakened, or the langour of an exhausted, appetite' (ibid.: 370). Meanwhile Matthias inveighed against *The Monk's* depiction of 'the arts of lewd and systematic seduction' and its 'unqualified blasphemy'. He also had to admit that it contained many 'poetical descriptions' but

> so much the worse again, the novel is more alluring on that account. Is it a time to poison the waters of our land in their springs and fountains? Are we to add incitement to incitement, and corruption to corruption, till there neither is, nor can be, a return to virtuous action and regulated life?
>
> (quoted in Botting, op. cit.: 82)

Finally, given the vituperation with which many British film critics would, as we shall see, greet Hammer's first Frankenstein film, it is important to note the critical reaction to Mary Shelley's original novel in 1818. Again, as one can judge from the contemporary reviews usefully reproduced in Hunter (1996), this was mixed, but the discourse with which we are concerned here clearly raises its head in the January issue of the *Quarterly Review*, which called it 'a tissue of horrible and disgusting absurdity'. While nonetheless being forced to admit that 'still there is something tremendous in the unmeaning hollowness of its sound, and the vague obscurity of its images' it concluded that:

> Our taste and our judgement alike revolt at this kind of writing, and the greater the ability with which it may be executed the worse it is – it inculcates no lesson of conduct, manners or morality; it cannot mend, and will not even amuse its readers, unless their tastes have been deplorably vitiated – it fatigues the feelings without interesting the understanding; it gratuitously harasses the heart, and wantonly adds to the store, already too great, of painful sensations.
>
> (Hunter, op. cit.: 189–90)

## Symptoms of a perverse and decadent imagination

Before examining British critical attitudes to horror cinema, and to British horror films in particular, it is important to note that, by the time the latter arrived on the scene, the critical discourse which we have been discussing thus far had been greatly augmented by the input of Matthew Arnold, the Leavises, T.S. Eliot and their followers. With their stress on the 'civilizing' mission of culture, on the importance of preserving and transmitting the cultural values of an educated elite, and on the moral function of both literature and criticism, it goes without saying that the 'culture and civilization' tradition which they represented was profoundly hostile to most forms of popular culture. Thus, for example, in 1930 F.R. Leavis in *Mass Civilisation and Minority Culture* criticized films because they

> involve surrender, under conditions of hypnotic receptivity, to the cheapest emotional appeals, appeals the more insidious because they are associated with a compellingly vivid illusion of actual life. It would be difficult to dispute that the result must be serious damage to the 'standard of living'.
>
> (1930: 10)

Meanwhile, two years later, in *Fiction and the Reading Public*, Q.D. Leavis dismissed the pleasures of Hollywood movies as 'largely masturbatory' (1978: 270). Of course, such views may now seem more than a trifle eccentric, but it simply cannot be emphasized too strongly that, given the way in which they drew upon already deeply embedded ways of thinking about literature and culture, and given the effective absence of any competing critical paradigms, they had an extraordinary influence which went way beyond the bounds of academic literary thinking.[1] Indeed, Terry Eagleton's remark on the impact of Leavisism is today much more true of English criticism than it is of academic English studies:

> There is no more need to be a card-carrying Leavisite today than there is to be a card-carrying Copernican: that current has entered the bloodstream of English studies in England as Copernicus reshaped our astronomical beliefs, has become a form of spontaneous critical wisdom as deep-seated as our conviction that the earth moves round the sun.
>
> (1996: 27)

Before discussing British critical attitudes to horror films from the late 1950s onwards we also need to know something about the dominant critical attitudes to cinema in general around the start of this period. Here there is no better guide than John Ellis's (1996) masterly reconstruction of the critical discourse of the 'quality' film in the 1940s. Admittedly this discourse pre-dates Hammer horror and its near relations by a number of years, but I would argue that it had changed little in the intervening period, and the key role played by the *Observer* critic C.A. Lejeune in both Ellis's analysis and the present one serves to emphasize this point. Indeed, as Ellis himself says:

> The critics of the 1940s defined middle-class conceptions about cinema for decades to come. The critics had more success in influencing British tastes than perhaps they realised. Decades of film appreciation have maintained the divisions that they initiated.
>
> (ibid.: 67)

I want now to examine briefly three elements of that discourse which are of particular importance to our understanding of British critics' negative reaction to the horror film. For the sake of both clarity and brevity I will not precisely reference each and every source.

First, cinema is seen as having a social purpose. Cinema has a key role to play as 'a medium of artistic expression and as a means of public information and education' according to the editorial in the first *Penguin Film Review* (August 1946). Films need 'realism, logic, truth' (Jympson Harman in *Sight and Sound*) if audiences are going to '*think* in the luxurious, hypnotic darkness of the cinema' (*Penguin Film Review*). Film-makers should be 'encouraged to make films about subjects which demand and deserve thought' (*Penguin Film Review*). Harman admits that he has been 'thinking of a quality in recent British films which can be most succinctly expressed as Truth. Alternatively it can be called Logic or Sincerity' (*Sight and Sound*). A *Sight and Sound* critic argued that audiences should be 'aided by every possible means to the contemplation of such things as exist in beauty, strength and, above all, truth. Isn't this the way to eliminate the tawdry and the gimcrack, to destroy dishonest doctrine and banish ugliness and evil?'

Second, 'the test of all good technique is unobtrusive service', as C.A. Lejeune put it in the *Observer*. A film's visual qualities are, of course, important, but Roger Manvell warns against the danger that 'visual eloquence becomes visual rhetoric, mere flowers of effect rather than active participation in the atmosphere and action of a story' (*Penguin Film Review*); worse still, images used wrongly may mean that audiences fall prey to 'symptoms of a perverse and decadent imagination' (*Sight and Sound*). Films whose style departs from the 'unobtrusive' rubric are apt to be met with incomprehension. Thus Powell and Pressburger's *The Red Shoes* (1948) left Joan Lester of *Reynolds News* with a 'slightly dazed sense of returning from some strange exotic nether regions. This is caused by the mixture of styles . . . and by the episodic nature of the story, but even more by the flamboyance of its spectacle, combined with the almost brutal insistence on backstage atmosphere.' Much to be preferred, according to Richard Winnington in the *News Chronicle* are 'discretion, discrimi-nation and taste' which flow from 'our native instinct for understatement'. Similarly Elspeth Grant in the *Daily Sketch* praises films which speak with a 'simplicity which is most satisfying and in all [their] admirable restraint [they are] far more moving than any picture deliberately designed as a tear-jerker'.

Finally, the job of the critic was seen as a firmly didactic, not to say nanny-ish, one. Thus John Sherman in the *Penguin Film Review* praises the critics for 'doing a first-class job now in making people critically aware of the content of films. Because of their efforts fewer and fewer people go to the pictures in a purely escapist mood.' Similarly, a *Sight and Sound* critic conceives of the audience as 'healthy adolescent, human, impressionable; but which needs a firm lead. It needs to be stimulated, too; it wants digging in the ribs, guidance, a sense of proportion and hope for the future.'

After the decline of the British 'quality' film project at the end of the 1940s and start of the 1950s, 'quality' was seen as residing largely abroad (though not, obviously, in Hollywood) as far as the critics were concerned; here, films still dealt with 'serious' issues in a 'realistic', adult and responsible fashion. But just how little mainstream film criticism developed in the 1950s and 1960s can be gauged from the diatribes against the critical establishment which issued forth from *Screen* at the end of the 1960s and early 1970s, many of which were couched in explicitly anti-Leavisite terms. Thus, for example, Alan Lovell argued that:

> At present the film critic seems to be in the position of a general practitioner studying the body without the aid of anatomy, physiology or neurology or anything but his own intuition and experience. Without any general framework he is not only trying to work out how the body operates but also trying to pronounce whether the body is a 'good' one or not.
>
> (1970: 78)

More specifically he complained that:

> Criticism is still principally a matter of expressing a personal taste that needs
> no other justification than that it is considered to be a superior taste; an
> impressionistic account of the critic's immediate response to a film is still the
> characteristic method; no critical vocabulary has been developed; amateurism
> is still a matter of pride. . . . There is no agreement as to who are the important
> artists, no consensus about critical method, no agreement about the crucial
> relationship between the artist and the industrial system of which he is a part;
> film critics even lack the social cement of a university community.
>
> (1969: 42, 45)

Similarly in 1972, from a perspective associated with *Movie*, V.F. Perkins in the then
ground-breaking *Film as Film* bemoaned the fact that:

> The weakness of much criticism is its insistence on imposing conventions which
> a movie is clearly not using and criteria which are not applicable to its form.
> Useful discussion of achievements within the popular cinema, in particular, has
> been obstructed by an insistence on the value of the films that are not made,
> and a corresponding insensitivity to the value of the actual product. Intelligent
> behaviour, sophisticated dialogue, visual elegance, profound investigations of
> character, sociological accuracy or gestures of compassion are demanded from
> pictures which quite clearly propose nothing of the sort.
>
> (188)

## 'There are no laughs in *Witchfinder General*'

These, then, were the various critical contexts within which *The Curse of Frankenstein*
(1957) and its successors would find themselves judged, and it is hardly surprising
that, as Peter Hutchings puts it: 'the critical verdict on British horror during the
time of its proliferation was overwhelmingly negative' (1993: 4). Of course, by no
means every review of every British horror film took violently against it; on the
other hand the sheer vituperation spewed out year after year was absolutely nowhere
offset by a positive engagement with these films in their own terms until the early
1970s, with the publication of Pirie's *A Heritage of Horror* and his reviews of horror
movies in *Time Out* and the *Monthly Film Bulletin* – by which time, of course, the
genre was about to decline in Britain. All that really balances the bucketfuls of bile
is the kind of light-heartedly patronizing and deeply irritating approach typified by
Paul Dehn's reviews in the *Daily Herald* and *News Chronicle*, as in his piece in the latter
on *The Stranglers of Bombay* (1959) in which he admitted that 'my readers know me
to be a sucker for the sort of Draculine horror film which is rooted in harmless
fairytale soil'. With friends like these . . .

I want now to isolate a number of recurrent themes in the 'critical verdict' on British horror movies and, in particular, to illustrate how closely they relate to the kinds of critical discourses discussed in the two previous sections of this chapter.

First, as in the manner noted above by Perkins, the films are judged by wholly inappropriate standards and roundly condemned for not being what they never set out to be in the first place. Thus R.D. Smith on *The Curse of Frankenstein* in *Tribune*: 'Character and story have faded into the background, suspense and surprise simply do not exist, plot has become a perfunctory filling-in of time between each macabre set-piece.' A similar line is followed by Derek Hill, also in *Tribune*, in his famous denunciation of *Peeping Tom*, who admits that: 'obviously there's a legitimate place in the cinema for genuine psychological studies. But this crude, sensational exploitation merely aims at giving the bluntest of cheap thrills.' And finally, David Wilson in the *Guardian* dismisses Michael Reeves's *Witchfinder General* (1968) on the grounds that it contains 'a not unpromising theme, but the film is less concerned with narrative than with exploiting every opportunity for gratuitous sadism'.

Second, the films are criticized for being too explicit in their depiction of physical details. In other words, horror films are condemned for being too horrific! This, of course, leads us directly back to our previous discussion of British literary critics' preference for terror over horror. Thus Dilys Powell in the *Sunday Times* on *The Curse of Frankenstein*: 'the infliction of pain becomes an entertainment, death-throes are elaborately examined and viciously prolonged. And I mean viciously.' Similarly C.A. Lejeune in the *Spectator* on *Dracula* (1958): 'we all know the vampire sucks blood and doesn't, on the whole, lose much sleep about it. But seeing a vampire sucking at its victim's neck, seeing the wound it makes in close-up, the blood round its teeth and lips, the exhaustion of its dying victim, etc. etc., is not my idea of a jolly evening.' Meanwhile Derek Hill, in his *Sight and Sound* article, 'The Face of Horror', which remains the key example of the kind of approach examined here and is usefully reproduced in Silver and Ursini (2000), treats this theme at some length. Explicitly contrasting contemporary horror films with the German silent ones which 'derived from legend, the supernatural and national mysticism' and the first Universal cycle which 'had strong literary origins and relied on stylized fantasy, with often remarkable qualities of atmosphere and suspense', Hill laments that in the 1950s a 'new sensationalism' crept into the American science fiction film, monsters became slimier and more repellent, and 'the power of suggestion, the greatest tool of the vintage horror film, was abandoned. Instead the screen began to concentrate on revolting close-ups' (ibid.: 54–5). Hammer simply took the process a stage further:

> Instead of attempting mood, tension, or shock, the new Frankenstein productions rely almost entirely on a percentage of shots of repugnant clinical detail. There is little to frighten in *The Curse of Frankenstein* or *The Revenge of Frankenstein*, but plenty to disgust.

*Figure 6* Not C.A. Lejeune's 'idea of a jolly evening': Christopher Lee goes for the jugular as *Dracula* (1958).

Hill complains that 'details immediately reminiscent of concentration camp atrocities are common' before concluding: 'the imaginative treatment of physical horror is one thing; but most of these new films merely attempt to outdo each other in the flat presentation of revolting details which are clearly regarded as their principal box-office assets' (ibid.: 56).

Third, certain critics appear to find particularly disturbing those horror films in which they feel that the director is not sufficiently 'distanced' from their material, with the result that the spectator becomes to an extent implicated in the horrors depicted on screen. Again, this reminds us that one of the familiar criticisms of Gothic literature was that authors were over-indulging in their own subject matter and in turn encouraging too intimate and complicit a relationship between the reader and the text.

The most famous example of this line of attack is provided by the 'scandal' of *Peeping Tom*, of which Nina Hibbin stated in the *Daily Worker* that 'it wallows in the diseased urges of a homicidal pervert, and actually romanticizes his pornographic brutality', while in the *Evening Standard* Alexander Walker dismissed it as 'just a clever but corrupt exercise in shock tactics which displays a nervous fascination with the perversion it illustrates. . . . It exploits fears and inhibitions for the lowest motives. It trades in the self-same kind of obsession that it relates' (ibid.: 56). But it was Isobel Quigley in the *Spectator* who finally pinpointed exactly what was so downright troubling about *Peeping Tom* for the critics. Noting that 'horror films are usually so crudely made that belief is never quite suspended' she contrasted the film with Franju's *Les Yeux sans visage* (1960) which

> didn't involve you, it made little attempt at direct emotional realism, as *Peeping Tom* does; you had the creeps, but remotely, and often with amusement. . . . We have had glossy horrors before (*The Fly*, for instance), but never such insinuating, under-the-skin horrors, and never quite such a bland effort to make it look as if this isn't for nuts but for normal homely filmgoers like you and me.

It is also tempting to speculate that similar concerns might well have accounted for the remarkable vehemence with which many critics rejected *Witchfinder General*. Was this why Dilys Powell in the *Sunday Times* found it 'peculiarly nauseating', one wonders? The film certainly angered the normally sensible Alan Bennett in *The Listener* to a degree which suggests that it certainly got under *his* skin:

> Of course, blood and guts is the stuff of Victorian horror films, though, as with Victorian melodrama, what makes them popular and even healthy are the belly laughs which usually punctuate them. For these one can generally rely on the film's star Vincent Price. But not here. There are no laughs in *Witchfinder General*. It is the most persistently sadistic and morally rotten film I have seen. It was a degrading experience, by which I mean it made me feel dirty.

As Charles Barr demonstrates in his seminal analysis of the critical savaging of *Straw Dogs* (which, significantly, remains banned on video in Britain), many British critics have severe problems in dealing with films in which the violence is not kept

*Figure 7*  'There are no laughs in *Witchfinder General*': Vincent Price fails to raise a smile
from Alan Bennett in Michael Reeves's 'sadistic and morally rotten film'.

comfortably remote and in which the audience, for perfectly valid and morally
defensible dramatic reasons, is encouraged to empathize with characters on screen
who are caught up in violent events and situations. Barr concludes that: 'what the
critics seem to fear is *contamination*; the director is involved: if we respond, we
become involved too. Violence is a vampire bite' (1972: 26).

It would seem abundantly clear that, quite apart from their individual elements,
these recurrent themes, when added together, betray a barely concealed dislike of
popular culture in general and popular cinema in particular. This being England, an
unpleasant vein of snobbery never lurks very far beneath the surface of this kind of
discourse, but occasionally it rises to the surface in an unashamedly naked fashion,
as I have pointed out elsewhere in some detail (2001). So, to illustrate the fourth
and final theme – class dislike – consider C.A. Lejeune in the *Spectator*: '*Dracula* is
clearly aimed at adults, as its "X" certificate proves. Without trying to make too
heavy weather out of it, I just murmur in passing that I hate to think what kind of
adults'; Lejeune, again, on *The Revenge of Frankenstein* (1958): 'the whole thing is,
to my taste, a vulgar, stupid, nasty and intolerable business; a crude sort of
entertainment for a crude sort of audience'; and finally Derek Granger, adding
sexism to snobbery, in the *Financial Times* on *The Curse of Frankenstein*:

Only the saddest of simpletons, one feels, could ever get a really satisfying frisson. For the rest of us they have just become a rather eccentric and specialised form of light entertainment, and possibly a useful means of escape for a housewife harrowed by shopping.

It is, of course, tempting to ascribe the critical denigration of British horror films to the overwhelming predominance of Conservative views within a press which, historically, has been heavily biased to the Right. However, this would be to ignore the fact that the criticisms cross the entire political spectrum, from the *Daily Worker*, *Tribune*, the *Daily Herald* and *News Chronicle* on various parts of the Left, the *Observer* in the liberal centre, and the *Spectator* on the Right. On the one hand this simply illustrates just how widespread among the educated elite were the kinds of views which we have been exploring in this chapter – and how papers on the Left were just as happy to draw upon this elite for their film reviewers as papers on the Right! More specifically, though, it also reveals a great deal about attitudes on the Left towards popular culture in the postwar period, in which a visceral anti-Americanism and a deep-seated hostility to what was perceived as the commercialization of culture was combined with a bitter disappointment that working class people were filling their heads with what Richard Hoggart memorably called a 'phantasmagoria of passing shows and vicarious stimulations' (1990: 246). As Martin Barker (1984) has pointed out in his detailed study of the campaign in 1950s Britain against American horror comics, such attitudes led many on the Left to adopt attitudes to popular culture which were not only highly nationalistic and woefully ill-informed but which also betrayed a remarkable lack of faith in the intelligence of ordinary people – in other words, attitudes which were the mirror image of many of those to be found on the Right.

## Poisonous weeds

Finally, we need to consider the consequences for horror cinema in Britain, and more specifically for British horror movies, of this vociferous and insistent critical clamour. On the one hand, of course, we could point to the fact that Hammer horror films generally performed well at the box office in spite of the critics; indeed, their chorus of disapproval undoubtedly helped to swell Hammer's coffers by giving their films shock value. Thus when the National Film Theatre eventually devoted a season to Hammer, Michael Carreras stated that 'I was horrified. I thought if they made us respectable it would ruin our whole image' (quoted in Hutchings 1993: 21).

On the other, and this brings us back to our opening discussion of critics as censors, there is not the slightest doubt that critical outrage over specific films, often wildly misleadingly described, has led to those films being banned by various local councils. This is confirmed by Guy Phelps, who at one time worked for the British Board of Film Censors (as it then was):

In a number of cases in recent years, coverage has been such that preconceived ideas have become firmly established before the films have even been seen. *Last Tango in Paris* was an extreme example of publicity reaching the stage when many local councillors felt able to deliver their verdicts on the film without the benefit of having seen it.

(1975: 276)

Horror-related victims of this game of Chinese whispers have included *The Devils* (1971) and *Straw Dogs*. Even more disturbing is the fact that, at certain moments, critics have effectively demanded even stricter censorship of horror-related titles, notwithstanding the fact that Britain has long had some of the strictest film and video censorship in the western world. Since journalists calling for curbs on media freedom might seem a trifle bizarre, even in the UK, this is usually done by nudges, winks and weasel words, as when thirteen critics[2] wrote to *The Times* on 17 December 1971 to complain about the BBFC passing *Straw Dogs*, stating that:

The use to which this film employs its scenes of double rape and multiple killings by a variety of hideous methods is dubious in its intention, excessive in its effect and likely to contribute to the concern expressed from time to time by many critics over films which exploit the very violence they make a show of condemning.

Just occasionally, however, the calls from critics for films to be banned become quite overt, as in the shrill and hysterical campaign by Chris Tookey of the *Daily Mail* and Alexander Walker of its sister paper the *Evening Standard* against *Crash* (1996), which is analysed in detail in Kermode and Petley (1997).

Most seriously of all, critical disdain for the horror film meant that when the 'video nasty' bomb dropped in the early 1980s, not one mainstream critic saw fit to defend in print any of the films in question, nor to take issue with the distorted and ludicrous nonsense that was appearing on the news pages and in the editorial columns of the papers for which they wrote. Admittedly critics such as Derek Malcolm in the *Guardian* and Alexander Walker in the *Evening Standard* and the *Listener* wrote various excellent pieces warning of the dangers inherent in the 1984 Video Recordings Act, but the only mainstream critic even to begin to attempt to discuss the *content* of some of the actual films themselves (and then in a barely helpful manner) was Nigel Andrews (1983) in the *Financial Times*. Significantly, it was not a film critic at all, nor even then a film expert, who wrote the only piece in a mainstream publication which examined a 'nasty' – *I Spit on Your Grave* (1978) – in an informed and serious manner: this was Martin Barker (1983) in *New Society*. As I pointed out at the time: 'this silence in the face of a campaign remarkable, even by British standards, for its level of ignorance about cinema, has allowed misconceptions to flourish unchecked like poisonous weeds' (1984: 351).

   The real pay-off, then, of the critical discourses examined in this chapter is the litany of horror films and videos cut and banned in the wake of the Video Recordings Act and subsequent bouts of hysteria over 'video nasties'. It may well also be the case that the seemingly endless moral panics over 'video violence' in Britain during the 1980s and 1990s discouraged the production of indigenous horror films, although this is much more difficult to quantify. However, in a culture better informed about popular cinema in general, and horror movies in particular, we might have been spared the dire spectacle of a hasty and ill-conceived law flushed through Parliament by legislators whose every utterance betrayed their total lack of knowledge and understanding of contemporary cinema, let alone the horror genre. But the stunted and doltish culture in which we actually live, and for which generations of critics must take their fair share of responsibility, is one in which the unfortunate Derek Malcolm, attempting at the Old Bailey to defend the video of *Nightmares in a Damaged Brain* (1981) as 'well executed', met with the unutterably crass and philistine response from the judge that 'so was the Nazi invasion of Poland'. As Malcolm himself concludes: 'there is no answer to this kind of ignorance and stupidity, and no way of conducting a logical argument in courts of law dominated by judges and magistrates who have scarcely heard of Hitchcock, let alone the shower scene in *Psycho*' (1984). But there again, it's difficult to conduct any kind of high-profile defence of horror films in a culture in which mainstream critics – Malcolm among them, unfortunately – have ganged up on a movie such as *Straw Dogs* and virtually invited its banning. Nor is it any coincidence that Peckinpah's much reviled movie remains banned by the BBFC on video – to critical indifference all round – while the much-lauded *A Clockwork Orange* (1971) was released uncut on both film and video once Kubrick's death rendered his own self-imposed ban on the film redundant. Even in these more liberal times, it seems, there is less of a gap between critics and censors than the former would like to have us believe.

## Notes

1  By an odd coincidence, the day after I wrote these words I read the *Guardian*'s obituary of the former *New Statesman* film critic John Coleman, which noted that 'beneath their bright surface, his reviews, especially of film, cut through fashion and pretentiousness to establish reference to longer-term human values. Ironically, the rigour of his analyses and the moral orientations of his criticism had a gravitas worthy of his Downing mentor'. And who was that mentor? No less than F.R. Leavis.

2  The signatories were Fergus Cashin, John Coleman, Nina Hibbin, Margaret Hinxman, Derek Malcolm, George Melly, Tony Palmer, Molly Plowright, Dilys Powell, David Robinson, John Russell Taylor, Arthur Thirkell and Alexander Walker. The letter is reprinted in full in Phelps (1975: 78–9).

# References

Andrews, N. (1983) 'The video nasty debate – sense and censorship', *Financial Times* 10 December.

Baldick, C. (1987) *The Social Mission of English Criticism 1848–1932*, Oxford: Clarendon Press.

Barker, M. (1983) 'How nasty are the nasties?', *New Society* 10 November: 231–4.

Barker, M. (1984) *A Haunt of Fears: The Strange History of the British Horror Comics Campaign*, London: Pluto Press.

Barr, C. (1972) '*Straw Dogs, A Clockwork Orange* and the critics', *Screen* 13, 2: 17–31.

Boswell, J. (1980) *Life of Johnson*, Oxford: Oxford University Press.

Botting, F. (1996) *Gothic*, London: Routledge.

Burke, E. (1987) *A Philosophical Enquiry into the Origin of our Ideas of the Sublime and the Beautiful*, J.T. Boulton (ed.), Oxford: Blackwell.

Christie, I. (ed.) (1978) *Powell, Pressburger and Others*, London: British Film Institute.

Eagleton, T. (1996, second edition) *Literary Theory: An Introduction*, Oxford: Blackwell.

Ellis, J. (1996) 'The quality film adventure: British critics and the cinema, 1942–1948', in A. Higson (ed.) *Dissolving Views: Key Writings on British Cinema*, London: Cassell.

Ellis, M. (2000) *The History of Gothic Fiction*, Edinburgh: Edinburgh University Press.

Greene, D. (ed.) (1984) *Samuel Johnson*, Oxford: Oxford University Press.

Hoggart, R. (1990) *The Uses of Literacy*, London: Penguin.

Howells, C.A. (1995) *Love, Mystery and Misery: Feeling in Gothic Fiction*, London: Athlone.

Hunter, J.P. (ed.) (1996), M. Shelley (1818) *Frankenstein*, Norton Critical Editions, New York: W.W. Norton & Company.

Hutchings, P. (1993) *Hammer and Beyond: The British Horror Film*, Manchester: Manchester University Press.

Kermode, M. and Petley, J. (1997) 'Road rage', *Sight and Sound* 7, 6: 16–18.

Kilgour, M. (1995) *The Rise of the Gothic Novel*, London: Routledge.

Leavis, F.R. (1930) *Mass Civilisation and Minority Culture*, Cambridge: Minority Press.

Leavis, Q.D. (1978) *Fiction and the Reading Public*, London: Chatto & Windus (reprint).

Lovell, A. (1969) 'Robin Wood: a dissenting view', *Screen* 10, 2: 42–55.

Lovell, A. (1970) 'The common pursuit of true judgement', *Screen* 11, 4–5: 76–88.

Malcolm, D. (1984) 'Stand up to the new censorship', *Guardian* 15 March.

Perkins, V.F. (1972) *Film as Film: Understanding and Judging Movies*, Harmondsworth: Penguin.

Petley, J. (1984) 'Two or three things I know about video nasties', *Monthly Film Bulletin* November: 350–2.

Petley, J. (2001, second edition) 'Us and them', in M. Barker and J. Petley (eds), *Ill Effects: The Media / Violence Debate*, London: Routledge.

Phelps, G. (1975) *Film Censorship*, London: Victor Gollancz.

Pirie, D. (1973) *A Heritage of Horror: The English Gothic Cinema 1946–1972*, London: Gordon Fraser.

Praz, M. (1970) *The Romantic Agony*, Oxford: Oxford University Press.

Raysor, T.R. (1936) *Coleridge's Miscellaneous Criticism*, London: Constable.

Silver, A. and Ursini, J. (eds) (2000) *Horror Film: A Reader*, New York: Limelight.

Varma, D.P. (1987) *The Gothic Flame*, Metuchen: Scarecrow Press.

Wellek, R. (1955) *A History of Modern Criticism 1750–1950: Volume One: The Later Eighteenth Century*, London: Jonathan Cape.

# 4    Screaming for release: femininity and horror film fandom in Britain

*Brigid Cherry*

Horror fandom in the UK takes a variety of forms. A number of groups and societies exist which are dedicated to horror, although there is a much larger number of fan groups based around related genres such as science fiction and fantasy in which horror fans participate. It is impossible to consider horror fandom as having distinct boundaries and there is a great deal of overlap with other fan cultures. As Reeves *et al*. argue in their work on fans of *The X-Files* (1996: 32): 'horror/dark fantasy fan groups . . . exist on the margins of sci-fi fandom.'

The results presented here derive from data supplied by female horror film fans from a number of such fan organizations, including the British Fantasy Society and various vampire groups, as well as the readerships of horror magazines and fanzines. As part of a research project on the female horror film audience,[1] an audience study of female horror fans was conducted during the 1990s, drawing participants from across the UK. Qualitative data were collected from a number of sources. A total of 109 participants responded to a questionnaire containing open-ended questions which was circulated to the female memberships of the British Fantasy Society and the Vampyre Society or who wrote in reply to a request for participants in horror magazines and fanzines (including *Shivers*, *The Dark Side* and *Samhain*). Additional written material in the form of letters and electronic mail messages on the participants' horror film tastes, viewing patterns and opinions was obtained from a further sixteen women. Fifteen further participants took part in focus groups held across the central belt of Scotland. These participants were recruited from local horror, science fiction and vampire societies, and people at a horror film festival and a science fiction convention running a programme strand on vampires, as well as by word of mouth contact. All participants were female.

There is every indication, however, that in general there is a low participation rate of women in traditionally organized fandom. Certainly this is true of literary science fiction fandoms (see Jenkins 1992: 48). As Jenkins has observed, female science fiction fans tend to congregate in specific areas of fandom dedicated to subjects of greater interest for women. One such horror fandom congregates around vampire films and fiction. Given the strong liking women have for vampire films (over 90 per cent of all female horror film viewers in this study liked all or most vampire films[2]), it might be expected that more women join these groups than others. The membership of the Vampyre Society confirms this with a 49 per cent female membership. This would seem to confirm, then, that, as with science fiction fandom, certain sections of horror fandom are more appealing or accommodating to female fans.

This situation of, on the one hand, women taking part in a specific area of horror fandom and, on the other, being diverted into other fandoms, may account (at least in part) for the seeming invisibility of female horror fans. A publicly professed liking for science fiction may be accompanied by a private taste for horror, to be seen to like science fiction being thought more acceptable. Several respondents stated that they had not made public their taste for horror. A 22-year-old stated that: 'People seem to find an interest in horror more disturbing in a woman, and I consider this most unfair.' Many of the respondents specified a liking for science fiction in addition to horror and several pointed out that they discovered their taste for horror through reading or viewing science fiction. It should be acknowledged, then, that many fans are nomadic (ibid.: 36), focusing their attention on a series of different fan objects including science fiction, fantasy and other related genres. Accordingly, there are large areas of overlap in the membership of fan cultures. Higher levels of active involvement in related fandoms, and in vampire fandom in particular, may be attributable to nomadic behaviour and to the social acceptability of science fiction, but many women have also experienced a lack of welcome in horror fandom. They are largely ignored by the mass market and fan-based horror publishing industry and, in addition, often derided by male fans. The female horror film fan, then, is doubly marginalized within horror fan culture.

## Models of fan behaviour

Since participation in horror fandom is thus not widespread among female horror film viewers, it is necessary to construct an alternative fan profile. Although the women who took part in this study viewed horror films frequently and habitually, as nomadic subjects, horror tended to form part of a group of genres which they watched and which may change over time. Many were isolated viewers with low rates of participation in fan culture, others were members of literary or multi-media fan organizations.

Despite the alienating environment and nomadic fan practices, many of the respondents did define themselves as fans in order to indicate a particular interest in a cultural product. Eighty-four per cent of participants were happy to describe themselves as horror fans. Only 12 per cent rejected this label, while 4 per cent were unsure about whether they were fans; this may indicate either an ambivalent attitude towards fans generally or doubt about whether they fit the typical horror fan profile.

There were two main differences in fan behaviour or consumption between those who would call themselves fans and those who would not. Those who considered themselves to be fans were significantly more likely to like slasher films than those who did not think of themselves as fans,[3] but there were few other differences between fans and non-fans in their preferences for horror film types. There was little indication, then, in the tastes of the respondents as to whether or not they classed themselves as fans. A liking for slasher films may be an indication of horror film viewers classing themselves as fans, but there may be another root cause for both these factors. Certainly, there was a strong correlation between the age at which the respondents first started watching horror films and whether they considered themselves to be fans.[4] Those who were under 12 years old when they first watched horror films were far more likely to consider themselves to be fans than to reject the label. The converse was true for those who started watching horror films at 16–18 years old. This indicates that the formation at an early age, certainly pre-teens, of an habitual liking for being scared is an indicator of classing oneself as a fan in later life. This could be related to adolescent gender socialization, in that female viewers who begin watching horror films in their teens may be discouraged by peer group pressure from admitting a liking for horror, as it is seen as unfeminine.

There are other possible reasons for not wanting to consider oneself a fan. Fans in general are depicted as other (Tulloch and Jenkins 1995), and terms such as 'nerd', 'geek' or 'anorak'[5] are often applied to fans. Some respondents did not wish to be too closely associated with such nerdish behaviour or labelled, as female fans often are, as kooky and associated with groupies, given that label's attendant implications about sexual behaviour. In addition, viewers of horror films are often equated with dangerous or insane criminals (rapists, mass or serial murderers) whose psychopathic behaviour is blamed on horror film viewing. Moral panics have led to the perception of horror films (and their viewers) as being a danger to society. This comes partly from the climate of censorship in the UK and the idea that 'video nasties' in particular have the potential to 'deprave and corrupt'. Such social pressures, in addition to the fact that it is considered unfeminine for women to like horror films, make it likely that many women would not willingly admit to a taste for horror. Those respondents who developed a liking for horror later in life may be more sensitive to these factors. A 32-year-old indicated that such sensitivity may fade with time: 'I used to watch them alone . . . because I didn't want people to know I watched them; now I watch as many as possible and don't care who knows.'

It is thus no surprise to find that female viewers do not wish to be labelled as fans, since this renders them abject on a number of counts – as fans they are geeks or nerds, as horror fans they are depraved, and as female horror fans they are unfeminine. It is solely for such reasons that some respondents did not consider themselves as fans – a 21-year-old, for example, stated that her self-image precluded such character traits. A 33-year-old, who had not publicly admitted to being a fan (although she did readily admit to participating actively in science fiction, fantasy and horror fandom by attending conventions), nevertheless considered her 'nerdish' behaviour to be like that of a fan:

> I don't know about being a horror fan, I'm very much in the closet so to speak. There's a big stigma attached to it. It's basically the spotty anorak type – I think I probably am a female version of that actually; you know, school swot and all that.

Such depictions are, according to Tulloch and Jenkins (1995: 15), exaggerated caricatures which allow ordinary viewers to reassure themselves that their own media consumption is on the normal side of 'the thinly drawn yet sharply policed boundaries between normal and abnormal audience behaviour'. As indicated by the above example, some respondents in this survey were quite keen to be seen to be on the 'right' side of that boundary, even to the extent that they thought of themselves as 'in the closet'. Certainly, the majority of female horror fans surveyed were keen to emphasize wide-ranging interests outside of horror, and many insisted that their behaviour and/or appearance was unlike that of a fan. This may partly account for female horror fans being invisible within large areas of fandom: many deliberately isolate themselves by not going to conventions and by not participating in fan consumption. The 27-year-old organizer of a horror film festival stated that female fans frequently asked her if it was okay for women to attend the festival since they had never dared to go to one before. A 20-year-old reported negative reactions from male fans:

> I think females who like horror are looked on as strange. I've had a lot of people come up to me and tell me I'm a bit strange because I'm female and I wear a leather jacket and I do vampire role playing and I run the science fiction society. They go 'oh, they're guy things' and I always think what does that make me, just because I like something different, am I supposed to be a man or something?

Other responses indicated different reasons why women might not wish to get involved in male-dominated fandoms. These ranged from not finding attractive the men involved (a 19-year-old student said: 'I had a look at the guys, I went: "oh no"') to not having the depth of knowledge required to participate in fandom. A 22-year-old said:

> I don't read horror books, I'm not interested in magazines or anything, I only watch films. I can't even remember what most of the things I've watched are called. 'Oh, is that the one in the London Underground: a boy and a girl and the girl had really great boots on and really cool hair and then she got caught by this monster . . . ?' But I hadn't a clue what it was called. That's what I think

of fans, like fans of football knowing every score for the last ten years. I don't know anything. Basically I just watch the films and I don't know who the actors are or whatever. I'm just not interested in all that in-depth knowledge in anything really.

The acquisition of trivial knowledge is considered a masculine attribute. A 20-year-old said: 'I guess men get more attracted to knowing, they enjoy knowing all the directors and then telling you he's made this film and did that.' The quote above also suggests that some female viewers might be interested in a different set of trivial details: here, fashions and hairstyles.

The respondents also differed from the accepted profile of the typical horror film fan in terms of age. The typical fan is often thought of as an adolescent who quickly 'grows out' of his (for it is most frequently assumed to be a male) liking for horror. However, the respondents' liking for horror did not fit the pattern of a passing adolescent fan interest. Many started watching or reading horror (or related genres) before their teens and their liking for the genre had persisted into adulthood. Those who considered themselves to be fans also dated their fan status from childhood. For these women, it is a life-long interest.

Given that neither the fans nor the non-fans among the respondents fitted the pattern of typical horror fans, different patterns of fan behaviour have to be considered in ascertaining the reasons behind the fan/non-fan split. In this respect it is interesting to note that Stuart Hall's 'preferred reading strategies' (1980) have been related by Reeves *et al.* (1996) to three levels of spectatorship identified in science fiction fans: casual viewers, devoted viewers and avid fans. It thus might appear likely that those who described themselves as fans in this study corresponded to avid fans, while the non-fans were more like devoted viewers. However, since horror film viewing patterns and fan behaviour did not seem to differ significantly between the two former groups, this division too may not be apt in this case. Several of the respondents who did not classify themselves as horror fans were members of fan groups and might, therefore, have considered themselves to be fans of other genres such as fantasy or science fiction. It is more useful, then, to examine other patterns of fan behaviour.

Lewis (1992) identifies four types of female fans: avid, intense, follower and hater. The avid fan is categorized by extreme behaviour, a high level of textual competence and is heavily involved in media interactions. There were a number of such fans in this study. They were very knowledgeable about horror and had seen large numbers of horror films which they were able to discuss in detail. These respondents could discuss films at length and could provide details on the making of films. A 35-year-old, for example, demonstrated a high level of textual competency when discussing the work of Clive Barker. She could name the novels from which Barker adapted his films, as well as the characters in them, and also demonstrated a detailed knowledge of the special effects team that worked on his films. She also related the films to other works in the horror genre. However, such avid fans constituted the smallest group among the respondents and avid fan behaviour was something many respondents criticized as being a negative feature which they associated with masculine fan behaviour. The rejection of male-dominated fandom led some respondents to less formal fan groups, as with the small group of women who formed their own women-only club, Women in Favour of Movies with Mindless Violence.

The behaviour of many respondents matched that of intense fans, identified by a distanced perspective and linked to life goals. Many respondents were themselves involved in the writing of horror fiction or other material, often for fanzines or on the Internet, and hoped one day to be published professionally. Such writing is often strongly linked to horror film viewing. A 38-year-old said of her horror film viewing: 'I like to examine the way things are done – and make note of the things I think best not to do.' A 29-year-old stated that:

> As a writer I need to keep abreast of changes in the genre. A friend once asked why I wrote horror/fantasy fiction as opposed to writing about 'real life'; my answer was that I have to live 'real life', why should I have to write and read about it too?

It may be, however, that female horror film fans and followers are seeking goals or pleasures in their participation in fandom which have thus far been accorded little recognition. One area of horror fandom in which female fans participate in large numbers is that centred around vampire films and fiction. The high participation rates in vampire fandom reflect the strong liking for vampire films, but there are other reasons for the high levels of participation by female fans, and these will be explored later in this chapter. In particular there are links to patterns of fan consumption described by Stacey (1994), especially commodity purchase and fashion.

## Fan consumption: magazine and fanzine readership

For horror fans, one of the largest areas of fan commodity purchase is magazine and fanzine publishing. There is a large number of professional titles on sale in the UK, a number of American imports, and a substantial number of fanzines. Despite the fact that many respondents in the study wrote horror fiction and others wrote reviews of horror, very few women were frequent readers of the mass-market horror publications. Of the UK magazines, only 13 per cent of all respondents read all or most issues of one leading title, *The Dark Side*, and 12 per cent all or most issues of another, *Shivers*. Sixty per cent never read *The Dark Side* and 57 per cent never read *Shivers*. Regular consumption of imported American magazines was even lower (most probably due to their limited availability, usually in specialist SF/comic shops not frequently visited by women). Nine per cent read all or most issues of the effects and make-up oriented *Fangoria*, while only 2 per cent regularly read the science fiction and horror title *Cinefantastique*.

If regular readership of horror publications was clearly low, many women did read the magazines on an irregular basis: 25 per cent read *Cinefantastique* occasionally, 34 per cent *Fangoria*, 20 per cent *Shivers* and 26 per cent *The Dark Side*. This appears to be because the respondents were choosy about which issues they bought, purchasing a magazine only when it had something of particular interest to them in it. A 35-year-old reported: 'I tend to buy issues related to specific films or topics such as design/special effects I'm interested in.' This suggests that the respondents may have been interested in special effects not in their own right but in association with particular films.

Of those respondents who read horror magazines only infrequently, they were just as likely to read an American import as a British title. This may have been because they were interested in specific films, which are covered earlier in the American publications than in UK ones due to earlier release in the US. The respondents were also particularly interested in Hammer films and this explains the popularity of the short-lived UK magazine *Hammer Horror*, which reflected their tastes and interests more than other titles.

Regular consumption of any particular horror magazine by the respondents was, by and large, absent, with 33 per cent of respondents never reading any horror magazines at all, and a further one-third reading one or more titles only irregularly. Of the one-third who did read one or more horror magazines regularly, less than half of these read more than one title regularly. Fanzine readership was similarly low. Rather than women being unrecognized consumers of horror magazines, it would seem that they often do not read these publications at all, and, indeed, the editor of the UK fanzine *Samhain* has confirmed that women rarely subscribe.

While the low female readership of magazines and fanzines may be due to the fact that the respondents did not like these publications, or bought them only selectively, it might also be that such magazines are simply unavailable, especially outside of the major metropolitan centres. Some respondents indicated that they were not aware of some or all of the titles. A few had never heard of the magazines, others found that they were just not available in the area in which they lived. Access to horror magazines, then, is restricted and this was undoubtedly compounded by women's low rates of participation in horror fandom or association with other fans: knowledge of these titles is unlikely to be handed down by word of mouth to the isolated viewer. Often the magazines are available only in specialist shops which women tend not to frequent in large numbers; where they *are* available in high street stores, they are unlikely to be with traditional women's titles and, therefore, may be overlooked by this group of viewers. There is also a possibility that they are deliberately overlooked, either because it is not thought socially acceptable for women to read them, or because they are aimed at a young male readership with an attendant emphasis on gore, sex and trivial facts. In fact, several respondents found many of the titles

*Figure 8* 'Lots of little interesting bits', stitched together in the pages of the short-lived *Hammer Horror* magazine: genre stars Peter Cushing and Christopher Lee feature on the cover of its 'first issue' (March 1995), which was actually preceded by a 'collector's edition'.

distasteful. A 46-year-old did not like most professional horror magazines 'as they seem to lay an emphasis on gore, which I'm not fond of.' A 42-year-old thought they were 'appalling', adding: 'I do not read most because they aim for the lowest common denominator and I find them rubbish.' The emphasis on gore as the reason for disliking most horror magazines reflected the tastes of the participants and, in particular, the dislike of gory, special effects-driven horror films. Some respondents also perceived an obsession with trivia in the magazines, repeating one of the main objections to male-dominated fandom. A 20-year-old stated: 'I did once see a *Hammer Horror* magazine and although I was tempted – I flicked through it – I thought it seemed quite sad to enthuse about horror in a fanatical way.'

Many more respondents took exception to the objectification of the female body that some titles reproduce. The contents of some horror magazines were seen as near-pornographic and as perpetuating negative female stereotypes or representations of violence against women. For example, a 26-year-old said:

> I look through things like *Fangoria* to see what's coming up but most fanzines spend too much time on 'tits and arse'. They seem to have concluded that all horror fans are sex starved adolescent males who will drool over any naked female body, so cram the issues with glossy photos of scantily clad women.

This is not restricted to the American titles. The UK title *The Dark Side* comes in for particular criticism in this area. A 23-year-old stated:

> I used to read *The Dark Side* but got disillusioned with the continual coverage of sado-porn videos in which I have no interest. I understand that the editor also edits a magazine devoted to the porn video industry and I think he may get a little confused as to which films should be discussed in which magazine!

Many of the respondents found this approach offensive. A 19-year-old felt 'its attitude and coverage of certain subject matter deeply sexist.' The 42-year-old quoted above, who had children, disliked seeing 'naked babes' in the magazines and found the photos 'frankly embarrassing'. This attitude was not related solely to feminist arguments about pornography. Some respondents felt that the coverage of horror in such magazines was not representative of their definitions of the genre. The 19-year-old again: 'One reason that I stopped buying *The Dark Side* was that it concentrated on the worst examples of sexism in the horror genre when the vast majority of horror films are not like this at all.' Although *The Dark Side* did come in for most criticism over its representations of women, it was, paradoxically, the most widely read magazine among this group of viewers – as reported above. This may indicate that some women are prepared to overlook sexist or pornographic content in their desire to find out more about particular films or subjects (as they may indeed do in certain horror films).

Reasons given for reading horror magazines were varied, but the patterns do seem to conform to those of fan consumption existing elsewhere, particularly among women. Notable reasons given were the coverage which magazines give to favourite horror films, stars or characters. A 19-year-old read *Hammer Horror* magazine because:

> I . . . really like the actors in those films. I think the magazine has good pictures, is very informative and has lots of little 'interesting bits'. . . . I also hope (although he didn't do much work with Hammer) to get more info about Vincent Price!

Such respondents were searching for pictures of their favourite stars – this particular respondent was looking for 'coverage of vampire films, pictures of good films, stories on horror actors like Vincent Price, Peter Cushing', For one 18-year-old this involved cutting out the pictures. Another, a 26-year-old, collected *Hammer Horror* magazines: 'I have a habit of buying them for a few months without looking at them. Then when I get some time to myself I read the lot from cover to cover.' This is similar to forms of fan behaviour commonly associated with fan adoration of actors and popular music stars, particularly among teenage girls.

From this evidence, the low rate of horror magazine and fanzine purchase and consumption by female fans seems to be attributable to the fact that they are predominantly written, edited and published by men for men. Like female science fiction fans, who are ghettoized into 'feminine' forms of fanzine publishing (Tulloch and Jenkins 1995: 12), female horror fans are excluded from male-dominated horror fan commodity purchase and production.

## Vampire fandom

Fan cultures surrounding the vampire film, by contrast, have high rates of participation by female fans. There is nothing to suggest that vampire fandom is dominated by women, but female fans do seem to play a more active role in this area than in other sectors of horror fandom. Women such as this 23-year-old fan do seem to be more comfortable with participating in vampire fandom; as she put it: 'I started a fanzine . . . to give me an opportunity to explore my interest [in vampires] and share my ideas more widely.' Aside from a strong interest in vampire films and fiction, a more equal female-to-male ratio in the vampire societies (than in, say, the British Fantasy Society) may be one of the main reasons why women are active participants in this area of fan culture. They are encouraged and supported by fellow female members and not subject to the negative remarks made by male fans in male-dominated fan groups.

Female participation in vampire fandom illustrates the attraction of vampire films for many fans. The wearing of vampire costumes – often consisting of period, usually

Victorian, dress – is popular (and there is also a concomitant interest in the Gothic and historical costume drama). Dressing up and fashion are the principal forms of commodity purchase associated with vampire fan culture. Fans often make their own period costume and purchase garments such as opera cloaks and Victorian or Elizabethan corsets. In keeping with the Goth subculture, to which many vampire fans also belong,[6] they dress in predominantly black clothing, wear their hair long, black or vibrantly dyed and crimped, and wear white or very pale makeup with black or blood red lipstick, heavily black-lined eyes and black nail polish. Typical clothing is remodelled on Victorian, Georgian and other historical fashions (frock coats, poet's shirts, cloaks and capes, fans, ornate walking sticks and top hats) as well as punk and fetish clothing, velvet, lace, leather and PVC being predominant materials. Styles borrow heavily from funerary, religious, pagan or vampiric imagery, including crucifixes, coffins, skulls and bats. The 23-year-old quoted above is typical:

> My enjoyment of horror films used to be evident in that I adopted a Gothic style based primarily on my envy of those beautiful vamps in horror films and their exotic glamour. I began to feel ridiculous like this as I got older and grew out of it, but my interest in horror is as strong as ever.

For many of these women, their liking for horror and vampires was a reason for them being attracted to the Goth movement. A 21-year-old respondent stated that:

> When I was 14 I started getting interested in Gothic music. So that's what happens when your parents buy you horror stories. The Gothic scene watches horror movies so you get even more attracted to it. You have all this music and then you read ghost stories together and it goes on and on.

This dual attraction to vampires and to the Goth subculture seems to be strongly linked to an expression of femininity and the female masquerade. The vampire look adopted by some vampire fans appears to be an aberrant form of the feminine masquerade (Rivière 1929). Vampire costumes conform to (historical) extremes of femininity, particularly according to Victorian standards, and are predominantly black which, although symbolic of mourning or death, is also associated with a fetishistic (and dangerous) sexuality. This impression is reinforced by the wearing of underwear as outerwear (corsets over dresses, sheer or lacy fabrics exposing underwear or the body) and the use of fetishistic materials. Basing their appearance on images of predatory female vampires, these fans adopt extremes of femininity in opposition to contemporary social norms. Long, sharpened finger nails, exaggerated lips, eyebrows plucked into extreme arches, excessive amounts of jewellery, Victorian styles of dress and the wearing of corsets all mark this look as aberrant. The wearing of vampire fangs and abnormally coloured contact lenses also renders the wearer as a figure of monstrosity or danger, emphasizing the lack of conformity

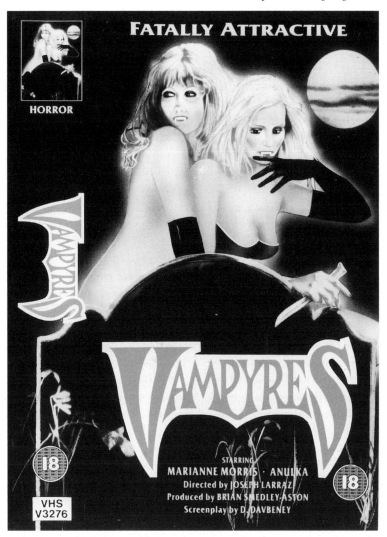

*Figure 9* Vampire chic: a video cover for Larraz's erotic shocker *Vampyres* (1974) illustrates one source of inspiration for 'an aberrant form of the feminine masquerade'.

to current ideals of femininity. This parallels a reversal of the Gothic role of victim which Gallafent (1988) has called the anti-masquerade.

The vampire masquerade forms, in many instances, an outward sign of the respondent's identity. Although the masquerade takes place largely within fandom, several stated that they had worn vampire-style or Goth clothing on an everyday basis at some point in their lives. This was not uneventful for some: one 21-year-old, for example, complained about people calling her Morticia[7] in the street. For a few, the appropriation of vampire imagery spread to other areas of their lives, influencing how they decorated their homes or named of their pets. A 23-year-old reported:

> Horror films influence my taste in clothes, objects and literature and give my imagination scope to roam. The clothes that vampires [wear] have influenced my dress sense, as the sets have influenced my taste in decor. I have named my black cat Louis (after the vampire of course), he has small sharp white teeth and I love him.

It would appear that, for many vampire fans, participating in fan culture allows them to dress up and to act out a fantasy. As Baert (1994) states, this contains the potential for destroying the dominant codes of gender. The 'bad girl' look of the vampire masquerade, like the punk street fashions discussed by Evans and Thornton (1989: 42), mangles sexual codes, confounds given meanings, valorizes 'bad taste', advocates an unpretty look of menace and threat and subverts the mask of femininity. The Goth vampire costume thus works as subversive anti-fashion, but for the respondents it is a glamorous image which embodies femininity, albeit a differently articulated one. Such clothing may, as Baert suggests, offer the woman a partial means to 'play her way out of . . . the impasse of femininity' (ibid.: 143). The adoption of the vampire masquerade seems related to a desire for a more extreme form of femininity (or, at least, style of dress) than that currently fashionable in contemporary society; a yearning 'for bygone days of opulence and elegance' that reveals 'hidden passions and [a] sensual nature', as one maker of vampire costumes put it. A 28-year-old explained that: 'It was a hobby before I went to college as I used to make elaborate ball gowns for my dolls when I was 11, which progressed to making all my own clothes.' Thus, a traditional feminine childhood interest had been subverted by an attraction to horror but, nevertheless, can still be coded as feminine. For female vampire fans, the pleasure in dressing up could be seen as an extension of the young girl's desire to dress up in adult or fairy tale costumes. However, here it has developed into an aberrant form of dress (dark and vampiric, often highly sexualized or fetishistic) which lasts into adulthood and frequently spills over into everyday life; as one 26-year-old commented: 'Prance around in pink dresses all day? Huh. I don't think so.'

The adoption of the vampire masquerade is a way of coding allegiance to a subculture (the Goth movement or vampire fandom), but such behaviour might also be read as subversive. Adoption of the vampire masquerade may provide the female horror fan with a 'liminal moment outside the time and space of the dominant order' (Mulvey 1987: 16). It may even allow entry into the language of politics for, as Cosgrove (1989) says, the adoption of subcultural fashions can be 'an inarticulate rejection of the straight world and its organisation'.

These fan activities, then, can be related to rituals of resistance against social norms of femininity, as well as to other forms of feminine consumption such as the romance, historical novel and Gothic fiction. This offers further evidence that female horror film spectatorship, although complex and possibly contradictory, might be feminine in nature, yet aberrant. The adoption of the vampire masquerade and the acting out of vampire fantasies in real life are important forms of appropriation of horror film texts and a source of pleasure. This can also be seen as a form of cultural resistance against accepted ideals of femininity, but, again, does not break away entirely from patterns of feminine behaviour. This is linked to the relationship between style, fashion and beauty and female spectatorship. In particular, it can be seen as a form of commodification which links a film or star with a specific product (Doane 1989). As a form of consumerism this is connected to extra-cinematic identification as described by Stacey (1994: 138–70). Transformation of the self occurs not just as a viewing fantasy but to various extents in real life, including an extension of dressing up into the realms of play-acting through the adoption of a vampire persona.

## Fan practices

In conclusion, then, it should be noted that female horror fans follow patterns of practice similar to other types of fans, particularly in the areas proposed by Stacey for female fans of classic cinema. There are some notable differences, however, between male and female horror fan practice, most notably in the consumption of horror merchandise such as magazines and fanzines. In this respect, the respondents in this study who were active fans practised a form of behaviour similar to other groups of female genre fans, specifically, female science fiction fans – for example, in the area of fan fiction. Although these respondents – like many other fans – can be described as nomads, the findings here suggest that female horror fans seek out spaces where feminine fan practices can be exercised without attracting negative comments from male fans in particular and society in general. In addition, many respondents go through a process of incorporating the vampire appearance, mannerisms and behaviour into everyday life 'as if they were aspects of the fan's private sectarian world' (Eco 1987: 198).

A significant proportion of the respondents did not participate at all in horror fandom. They hid their liking for horror, watched horror films alone on television or video, did not mix with other fans or followers, and were not able to talk about it with friends or family, who did not understand the liking for horror. This was not necessarily through choice. Some simply did not know any other women who like horror. One 28-year-old lamented that: 'If I'm the only female horror buff out there, I'd like to know.' The following quote from a 34-year-old demonstrates why many women might view alone:

> One reason I watch some horror on video is that I have no female friends who like this and it can be awkward going to the cinema on your own at night, when

this is on the programming. Therefore, for purely practical reasons, video makes things easily accessible.

Some did reject certain forms of fandom, but most found some area in which they could indulge their interest. It may be that a broad-based, literary-oriented and long-established fan organization is more acceptable to some women, while others find fandoms organized around sub-genres which are popular with women more accommodating to female fans. Within horror fandom, an 'us and them' mentality operates along similar lines to the general population's view of fans as other (Jenkins 1992), in this case working along gender lines.

Obviously, much of what has been said about extra-cinematic identification in this chapter will not apply to the respondents who did not participate in fandom to any great extent. Nevertheless, it would be wrong to ignore this group entirely. It may be that such female horror film viewers are representative of a 'silent majority' whose primary form of fan consumption is to view horror films in the privacy of their own homes, either alone or with a trusted viewing partner, often a close friend or husband or other family member. It may be that, for these fans, the main source of pleasure from such fan consumption is an enrichment of their fantasy lives, but that it may be a guilty pleasure, like romance reading or soap opera viewing. Some fan practices may then act as a form of reassurance that there are others out there with similar interests and that the fan is not abnormal in her tastes, as the following 32-year-old indicated:

> I . . . read the magazines just to see why others make/write/like horror. I like to hear about how an idea got started, why it was done instead of another idea. I like to know about the people behind the horror . . . somehow, it makes me feel not quite so weird.

Female horror film viewing may have been rendered invisible in the same way that soap opera and romantic fiction has at times been devalued and denigrated. This study has revealed that female horror fans and followers have found areas of support among fellow fans and developed ways of expressing resistance against social norms. The areas of fan practice and commodity purchase explored here need to be reviewed in the context of popular pleasures and feminine subjectivity within cinema studies.

## Notes

1  Undertaken as research for the author's PhD thesis (Cherry 1999a).
2  See Cherry 1999b for an account of the female viewers' horror film tastes.
3  The chi-square value indicates a probability above 95 per cent confidence that there is a relationship between liking slasher films and thinking of oneself as a fan ($\chi^2 = 5.86$, $p = 0.00$).

4  The chi-square value indicates a probability above 95 per cent confidence that there is a relationship between age at which horror films are first viewed and thinking of oneself as a fan ($\chi^2 = 32.78$, p $= 0.00$).

5  The term 'anorak' – first applied to trainspotters (after the item of clothing which they wore as protection against the elements while standing on train platforms) – is now widely used to refer dismissively to other groups of fans and hobbyists.

6  Although the interest in vampires is strong, it should be pointed out that not all vampire fans would consider themselves to be Goths, nor indeed do all Goths have a liking for vampires. Indeed, there is evidence that this leads to frequent splits and heated debates in both camps. One member of the Vampyre Society participating in this research expressed her dislike of the fact that many active members of the society were Goths and that it had been said to her that one had to be a Goth in order to have a strong liking for vampires and be in the society. From the evidence of this research, this is obviously not the case, and some respondents are unaware of the Goth subculture. Conversely, discussion of vampires in Goth circles is frequently met with disapproval.

7  In reference to the character from the American comic strip, TV comedy and films of *The Addams Family*.

## References

Baert, R. (1994) 'Skirting the issue', *Screen* 35,4 : 354–60.

Cherry, B. (1999a) *The Female Horror Film Audience: Viewing Pleasures and Fan Practices*, PhD thesis (unpublished) University of Stirling.

Cherry, B. (1999b) 'Refusing to refuse to look: female viewers of the horror film', in M. Stokes and R. Maltby (eds) *Identifying Hollywood Audiences: Cultural Identity and the Movies*, London: British Film Institute.

Cosgrove, S. (1989) 'The zoot suit and style warfare', in A. McRobbie (ed.) *Zoot Suits and Second-hand Dresses: An Anthology of Fashion and Music*, London: Macmillan.

Doane, M.A. (1989) 'The economy of desire: the commodity form in/of the cinema', *Quarterly Review of Film and Video* 11: 23–33.

Eco, U. (1987) *Travels in Hyperreality*, London: Picador.

Evans, C. and Thornton, M. (1989) *Women and Fashion: A New Look*, London: Quartet.

Gallafent, E. (1988) 'Black satin: fantasy, murder and the couple in *Gaslight* and *Rebecca*', *Screen* 29, 3: 82–105.

Hall, S. (1980) 'Encoding/decoding', in S. Hall, D. Hobson, A. Lowe and P. Willis (eds) *Culture, Media, Language*, London: Hutchinson.

Jenkins, H. (1992) *Textual Poachers: Television Fans and Participatory Culture*, London: Routledge.

Lewis, L.A. (1992) 'Something more than love: fan stories on film', in Lewis (ed.) *The Adoring Audience: Fan Culture and Popular Media*, London: Routledge.

Mulvey, L. (1987) 'Changes: thoughts on myth, narrative and historical experience', *History Workshop Journal* 23: 3–19.

Reeves, J.L., Hague, A. and Cartwright, M. (1996) 'Rewriting popularity: the cult files', in D. Lavery, M. Rodgers and M. Epstein (eds) *Deny All Knowledge: Reading* The X-Files, London: Faber & Faber.

Rivière, J. (1929) 'Womanliness as a masquerade', reprinted in V. Burgin, J. Donald and C. Kaplan (eds) (1986) *Formations of Fantasy*, London: Methuen.

Stacey, J. (1994) *Star Gazing: Hollywood Cinema and Female Spectatorship*, London: Routledge.

Tulloch, J. and Jenkins, H. (1995) *Science Fiction Audiences: Watching Doctor Who and Star Trek*, London: Routledge.

# 5 Horrific films and 1930s British cinema

*Ian Conrich*

The horror film was established in the American cinema of the 1930s. The monster movies of this period, most notably the productions of Universal, have since become regarded as representing the genre's golden age. In contrast, British horror cinema is often absent from the historical discourse of 1930s film, and it is not until the productions of companies such as Hammer in the late 1950s that it is acknowledged genuinely to exist.

If British horror films of the 1930s are determined by their correspondence to the Hollywood monster movies, then there are only examples of a fragmented genre: *Castle Sinister* (1932), *The Ghoul* (1933), *The Unholy Quest* (1934), *The Man Who Changed His Mind* (1936), *Dark Eyes of London* (1939) and *The Face at the Window* (1939). The staple figures of the Hollywood horrors – the Mummy, Frankenstein, Dracula and the Wolf Man – were owned by the Hollywood studios, leaving British cinema to depend on the depiction of alternative villains, fiends, psychopaths and mad scientists. Moreover, British film censorship, with its disinclination to pass images of horror, impeded the development of a British genre. As I have argued elsewhere, this led to film-makers importing 'horror into comedies and thrillers rather than attempting to make outright horror films' (Conrich 1997: 228).

So concerned about horrific images was the British Board of Film Censors (BBFC), that it introduced a new form of film classification – the 'H' rating (which existed 1933–51) – and this grouped together films deemed 'horrific', including the Hollywood monster movies among others. Subsequently 'horrific films', as opposed to 'horror films', was the dominant term. Distributors of films released in Britain, hoping to distance themselves from the label 'horrific', employed promotional campaigns that variously marketed the productions as 'uncanny', a 'mystery', or a 'melodrama'. This chapter will suggest that there was in fact no British horror cinema of the 1930s. There were, instead, British productions of a 'horrific' nature; comedies, thrillers and melodramas with 'horrific' elements; and American horror films which were frequently referred to in Britain as 'horrific' films.

# Rated 'H' for 'horrific'

The 'H' rating – initially an advisory classification, later a certificate – is crucial to understanding the horrific film in British cinema. In 1932, there existed in Britain a two-point film certification system – the 'U' certificate, which indicated films to be especially suitable for children, and the 'A' certificate which indicated films to be generally suitable for public exhibition. The third, 'H' (for 'horrific'), classification applied to 'any films which are likely to frighten or horrify children under the age of 16 years', was introduced in January 1933, largely to deal with the influx of American horror films that had begun in 1931–2 with Universal's *Dracula* and *Frankenstein*. *Bioscope* had warned that *Frankenstein* would 'initiate a whole riot of "creepy films" which in point of horrors, are designed by Hollywood to out-do the stickiest of gangster films' (6 January 1932: 33). Not yet a formal certificate, the 'H' did not alter admission procedures but simply required films to carry the warning that they were unsuitable for children. With those under the age of 16 still allowed into screenings if accompanied by a *bona fide* guardian or parent, there were purportedly situations in which children hoping to gain entrance to a film approached strangers to act as their 'guardian'. Hugh Loudon remembers that 'implementation of the rules at grass-roots level was flexible – birth certificates were not required and one could shop around for sympathetic commissionaires' (1991: 179).

The 'H' rating did not abate concerns about the horrific film. In a paper given at the annual summer conference of the Cinematograph Exhibitors' Association (CEA), the president of the BBFC, Edward Shortt, stated that:

> [A]lthough a separate category has been established for these [horrific] films, I am sorry to learn they are on the increase, as I cannot believe such films are wholesome, pandering as they do to the love of the morbid and the horrible. . . . Some Licensing Authorities are already much disturbed about them, and I hope that the producers and renters will accept this word of warning, and discourage this type of subject as far as possible.
>
> (*Kinematograph Weekly* 4 July 1935: 14)

American film producers did listen. Aware of the need for good relations with a nation regarded as a significant film market, in 1936 they reduced the number of Hollywood horrors. Universal expunged horror from its production schedule for a period of at least a year after the release of *Dracula's Daughter* (1936). The trade paper *Variety* reported:

> Reason attributed by U[niversal] for abandonment of horror cycle is that European countries, especially England, are prejudiced against this type product [sic]. Despite heavy local consumption of its chillers, U[niversal] is taking heed

to warning from abroad. . . . Studio's London rep has cautioned production exec to scrutinise all so-called chiller productions, to avoid any possible conflict with British censorship.

(Quoted in Dello Stritto 1995: 26)

Soon after, on 24 June 1936, at the annual conference in Eastbourne of the CEA, Lord Tyrell, the newly appointed president of the BBFC, declared that: 'I am given to understand that the "horrific" film has gone.' He therefore announced the cessation of the 'H' classification:

It was never considered desirable by the Board, although we gave way to the determined pressure of the few that it should be inaugurated and given a trial. It is gratifying to find that those who advocated this innovation have come to the conclusion that it was wrong in principle.

(*Kinematograph Weekly* 25 June 1936: 7)

The BBFC had been established in the first place to centralize and harmonize the potentially diverse censorship decisions of Britain's many local councils. These local governing bodies have the legal authority to act as the primary regulators of film content within their district or area, and it has always been in the interests of the film industry that a good working relationship is maintained between them and the BBFC. Yet, contrary to the BBFC's announcement, the cessation of the 'H' classification did not have the complete support of the local councils. Regional authorities such as Huddersfield, Oldham and Margate had never accepted the 'H' films and, despite a major studio such as Universal announcing a temporary abandonment of horror film production, previously released films remained in circulation, albeit limited. Three county councils – London, Middlesex and Surrey – had publicly challenged, during 1935 and 1936, the decisions of the BBFC regarding the 'H' films. They then took a lead when the 'H' was removed by instigating their own 'H' certificate, which this time prevented the admission of children. The London County Council (LCC) was particularly active. They introduced their 'adults only' 'H' on 1 January 1937, decreeing that such films must be accompanied by a notice outside cinemas which read: 'Children under 16 not admitted to see this film.' The LCC had the support of education officials, which it revealed in a letter to *Today's Cinema*:

During the earlier part of 1935, representations were made to the Council as to the character of 'horrific' films. . . . We accordingly inspected, in conjunction with the Education Committee and representatives of the Middlesex and Surrey County Councils, two typical 'horrific' films (*The Invisible Man* and *The Bride of Frankenstein*), which had been classed as such by the British Board of Film Censors. As the result, the Education Committee have expressed to us the general view that films of this character are unsuitable for exhibition to children in any circumstances.

(2 November 1936: 1)

Other local councils began to follow the actions of London, Surrey and Middlesex. The BBFC needed to re-centralize classification decisions, so the 'H' was re-introduced in the second half of 1937, but now as an official BBFC certificate, and the first 'adults only' one. This certificate was not adopted simultaneously throughout the country, taking up to two years to be accepted in places such as Bristol.

Of the fifty-five films rated 'H', thirty-eight can be recognized as American horrors. All of these productions would have consequently suffered some loss of exhibition at British cinemas, since certain local authorities and cinema chains consistently barred 'H' films. Moreover, authorities such as St Helens in north-west and Birmingham in central England not only banned many of the 'H' films but they also restricted the showing of 'A' certificate films such as *King Kong*. Both the St Helens and Birmingham magistrates made *King Kong* 'adults only', a classification that exceeded the advisory status of the 'H' rating (*Kinematograph Weekly* 7 September 1933: 18; 16 November 1933: 43).

Since local councils acted independently of each other, film regulation varied between neighbouring bodies. This can be observed in the case of *Son of Frankenstein* (1939), which was rated 'H' and immediately banned by both Birmingham and Walsall councils. But a cinema such as the Beacon in Great Barr was in a neighbouring district that had not banned the film and this was duly emphasized on the promotional handbills distributed by the cinema for its one-week screening of the film in September 1939. These proudly announced the showing of 'The Screen's Most Sensational Thriller – Can Only be Seen at the Beacon. Will not be Shown in Birmingham or Walsall.'

## Initial British experiments

Exeter was a local council with a reputation for banning 'horrific' films, but in nearby Torquay at the Empire cinema, viewers could see, for one week only, *The Ghoul* (1933), the first British production to be rated 'H'. Both David Pirie (1973: 22) and Marcia Landy (1991: 390) are incorrect when they write that the film was never distributed in Britain. Certainly the film remained for many years unseen, and, as the film historian and archivist William K. Everson wrote in 1974:

[It] has been the most elusive and mysterious of all the 'lost' horror films. Elusive because, until 1969, it had never shown up once since its original release, and even in England it disappeared from distribution within a very few years. No prints are known to have survived in this [Northern] hemisphere . . . Mysterious because little was ever really known about the film; no reputable historians appeared to have seen it, only a handful of mouth-watering but not very informative stills seemed to have survived.

(118)

A print of the film is now in circulation, and the British press book is interesting as it suggests six poster designs for possible employment by exhibitors, with only one referring to the film as 'horrific'. The other posters variously promote the film as 'a gripping mystery story', and 'a weird and exciting mystery'. Torquay's Empire cinema advertised the film as a 'Weird and Uncanny Thriller!'. The 'H' classification received by *The Ghoul* would have severely reduced its exhibition prospects, even more so in a climate of mounting moral concern following the first wave of Hollywood horrors. The press book for *The Ghoul*, which would have been distributed to exhibitors, takes care to reassure that the content of the film is suitable: '*The Ghoul* is thrilling and uncanny without being "horrific"', adding that 'while perhaps it is not exactly the type of film which a very sensitive person should see, it most decidedly is not on the horrific plane of other mystery thrillers.' A similar concern about the wrong sort of publicity was also occurring in America where Paramount attempted to alter the reception of *The Island of Lost Souls* (1932), a film which the BBFC had banned outright: 'Admittedly a horror picture, Paramount is trying to find a selling angle for *Island of Lost Souls* that will eliminate reference to it as such . . . [the] studio is afraid *Lost Souls* will do a dive unless the creepy angle is eliminated', reported *Variety* on 8 November 1932 (quoted in Dello Stritto 1995: 23).

*The Ghoul* starred Boris Karloff and was his first production in Britain. The film concerns an Egyptologist who returns from the dead, and was an attempt by Gaumont-British to create a version of the American horrors and reproduce aspects of recent Karloff productions – *The Old Dark House* (1932) and, especially, *The Mummy* (1932) – for which he had received excellent reviews (see Bojarski and Beals 1976: 78, 86).

Karl Freund, the director of *The Mummy* and previously the cinematographer for the German films *The Golem* (1920), *The Last Laugh* (1924) and *Metropolis* (1926), was one of a number of German-Austrian émigrés, including Curt Siodmak and Edgar G. Ulmer, who found initial employment in the American motion picture industry producing horror films. *The Ghoul* similarly drew on the skills of German film-makers. Tim Bergfelder writes that the 'economic imperatives' of the 1920s compelled 'European film industries to combine forces against the market hegemony of Hollywood' (1997: 45). Discussing the work of German designers at the studios of Gainsborough, Bergfelder notes that they were 'employed by British producers primarily for their technological expertise, and it is in this respect, the innovations in production and studio design and, to a lesser extent, in cinematography, that the continental influence was strongest' (1997: 45; see also Bergfelder 1996: 20–37).

Michael Balcon was head of production at Gaumont-British and he continued to benefit from his connections with German film producers – Erich Pommer and the Ufa studios at Neubabelsberg, and the Emelka studios in Munich – established while he was working at Gainsborough. The German film-maker Gunther Krampf was employed as the cinematographer for *The Ghoul*, Alfred Junge was the art director, and Heinrich Heitfeld supervised make-up. The film's director was T. Hayes Hunter, an American who had previously filmed the British shocker *The Frightened Lady* (1932).

I disagree with James Chapman that *The Ghoul* is 'just as easily located' in terms of its 'Britishness' as it is as an imitation of American horror (1998: 87). *The Ghoul* as a manifold production is just not that simple. It is exploitative, in the manner in which it aimed to capture both the popular subject matter of Egyptology – Lord Carnarvon and Howard Carter had discovered the tomb of King Tutankhamen in 1922, and the final sarcophagus was not opened until 1926 – and in the atmospheric style of the American horrors. Yet the film moves beyond exploitation and imitation, and it has an appearance that is, at times, design-dominated, displaying a continental European influence. Junge's set of vast bookcases towers over the characters in the office of the lawyer Broughton (played by Cedric Hardwicke). Other parts of the set submit to the cinematography and are closed by areas of darkness which are then punctuated by pockets of light from candles and fires. Heitfeld was brought from Germany in order to achieve the high standard of special make-up effects that were being produced in Hollywood by, most famously, Jack Pierce. Heitfeld gave Karloff's face a heavy and 'bloated' look, a protruding forehead and a crusty and parched skin. It has the effect of making Karloff seem undead even before he has died, and combines well with his exaggerated and unrefined mannerisms. Karloff's character, the fanatical Egyptologist Professor Morlant, is buried, as he requests, with the ancient Egyptian jewel of 'The Eternal Light' bandaged tightly into the palm of his hand. At his burial, with Wagner playing on the film's soundtrack, torchbearers light the way to an immense mausoleum containing a statue of the Egyptian god Anubis and fronted by a colossal door bearing hieroglyphics on its inside. The impressive set is menacing and it is well established as a location of impending horror. Later, when Morlant's jewel is stolen, he rises from his sarcophagus and staggers to the door of the mausoleum, the unwrapped bandage hanging from his hand. This image references Karloff's *The Mummy*, and the scene combines elements of expressionism with the Gothic, continental European stage design, Egyptology and Egyptian superstition.

Mythology and mummified bodies were also part of *The Unholy Quest*, a film to be considered in conjunction with *Castle Sinister*. Widgey R. Newman directed the former and produced the latter, for which the director was credited as R.W. Lotinga. But what no historian has realized is that Newman and Lotinga are actually the same person. For instance, Denis Gifford writes that 'Newman failed to direct a good film. He failed again with *The Unholy Quest*, despite letting R.W. Lotinga direct'

(1974: 200). Widgey Raphael Lotinga Newman occasionally employed the name R.W. Lotinga while making around twenty quota quickies in the 1930s, each lasting barely more than fifty minutes. It is unfair of Gifford to judge the films so harshly as hardly any reviews exist, there appear to be no stills, posters or press books to which to refer, and both films remain lost. Their subject matter is unusually gruesome for British productions of the period, and thus their apparent lack of censorship is surprising. *Castle Sinister* concerns a mad doctor who, while searching for the secret of longevity, attempts to exchange the brains of a woman and an ape. A mad doctor also appears in *The Unholy Quest*, and his experiments are to enable him to revive the mummified body of a Crusader. Both films appear to be in the tradition of the Hollywood horrors, and one possible reason why they escaped the type of censorship which *The Ghoul* received is that they lacked a distinct genre star such as Karloff, whose presence drew immediate attention to the more notorious films, like *Frankenstein*, in which he had appeared.

## British horrific films

Following *The Ghoul*, five more British films were rated 'H': *The Tell-Tale Heart* (1934), the short film *The Medium* (1934), *The Man Who Changed His Mind*, *Dark Eyes of London*, and *The Fall of the House of Usher* (1948). *The Medium* and *The Tell-Tale Heart* were the directorial debuts of the film-makers Vernon Sewell and Brian Desmond Hurst respectively. Both films were produced for little money and reflect the independence and determination of their directors. *The Medium* was made by the Bushey-based Delta Pictures, the small production company behind *Castle Sinister*, and was from the play *L'Angoisse*, by Pierre Mills and C. de Vylars. Sewell had bought the rights to the play and was to revisit the story – of haunted properties, murdered wives and lovers, and spiritualism – in his later films *Latin Quarter* (1945), *Ghost Ship* (1952) and *House of Mystery* (1961).

The quota quickie *The Tell-Tale Heart* was made for £3,200 and financed privately by an acquaintance of Hurst, Henry Talbot de Vere Clifton (Harry Clifton). Hurst chose the Edgar Allan Poe short story as 'it was sensational film material, and was in the public domain . . . and would call attention to me', and his account of the production suggests that it was crude and artless – '[t]here were no professional actors . . . detectives were played by two electricians, the old man by a painter . . . [and] I used for music records . . . as we could not afford composer or musician' (quoted in McIlroy 1994: 27). But the film, as Brian McIlroy notes, was technically competent and the review in *Variety* declared it to be 'photographically a gem' (quoted in McIlroy 1994: 27). McIlroy had to judge the film by autobiographical accounts and contemporary reviews as he writes that it is unavailable for viewing; Jonathan Rigby (2000: 23) and Andy Boot (1996: 33) make the stronger claim that the film is lost.

The film, however, does exist and was shown at the National Film Theatre, London, in August 1992. It is a striking production, not just for the photography but also for its visual design. Because of budgetary restraints the film's sound and dialogue are minimal, so the effect of the old man's heart beating under the floorboards is repeatedly supplanted by visual emphasis on the old man's Evil Eye. In Poe's story, his narrator tells how the eye 'resembled that of a vulture . . . [w]henever it fell upon me, my blood ran cold . . . I made up my mind to take the life of the old man, and thus rid myself of the eye forever' (1960: 173). Significant parts of Hurst's film are set in an asylum where the narrator of the tale, the old man's murderer, declares he is sane. Yet he appears terminally haunted by multiple images of the Evil Eye and these pictorial and photographic flashes recall the drawings of single eyes and detached heads by the symbolist painter Odilon Redon.

Interestingly, Poe was an inspiration for Redon, who drew a series of charcoal images of his Gothic tales in the early 1880s. For the charcoal *The Tell-Tale Heart* (1883), Redon replaced the beating heart with the visual metaphor of a single eye peering through a slit in the wooden boards of a floor. Hurst's depiction of the Evil Eye has a similar metaphorical impact, but it is difficult to comprehend fully why the film was rated 'H', even after it had undergone revisions requested by the British censor. It is possible that British producers were targeted by the film censor to deter other indigenous film-makers from adding to the trend for the 'horrific'. Though such is the film's artistic inclination and the surrealist effect of the hallucinatory style of narration that it is unlikely it would have appealed to a mainstream audience.

Gaumont-British was sure that it had an audience for another Karloff production. In 1936, Karloff returned to Britain for *The Man Who Changed His Mind*, the second of his three British films which, like *The Ghoul*, was modelled on the Hollywood horrors, although this time on the growing popularity of the deranged-scientist theme. Sidney Gilliat co-wrote the film with John L. Balderston, who had written the screenplays for the American productions *The Mummy* and *The Bride of Frankenstein* (1935). The British film censor was concerned about the depiction of the misuse of modern science – and in particular of eugenics – and *The Man Who Changed His Mind*, with its story of longevity and the transposition of minds into healthy bodies, was regarded as 'horrific' material, despite the attempts of the producers to avoid the rating.

The previous year Bela Lugosi had also been in Britain filming *The Mystery of the Marie Celeste* (1935). Lugosi's career was by now in decline; there was a gradual falling-off in the production of horror films by the main studios, and he was increasingly being offered acting roles in 'B' movies. By contrast, the film's producer, Hammer, was a new company which had previously made just one film. It had succeeded in convincing Lugosi that they were capable of creating a production that would exploit the then widespread interest in the Marie Celeste myth. As with other British-made maritime murder-mysteries – *The Phantom Light* (1934) and *Tower of Terror* (1941) – *The Mystery of the Marie Celeste* contained the horrific within melodrama and an expressionistic style.

Lugosi returned to Britain in 1939 to film *Dark Eyes of London*, an adaptation of the Edgar Wallace novel. Whereas *The Mystery of the Marie Celeste* had been promoted on the image of Lugosi, *Dark Eyes of London*, for its British campaign, was publicized with an emphasis on Lugosi as Dracula. One British advertisement displayed above the film's title: 'BELA (DRACULA) LUGOSI'. Above is a letterboxed close-up of Lugosi's staring eyes, reminiscent of his acclaimed role in *Dracula*. Despite the fact that the film was made nine years after *Dracula*, Lugosi's association with an original Hollywood horror was a key attraction and *Dark Eyes of London* exploited this where possible.

The film's grisly story of bodies drowned in vats, victims of an insurance scheme run by Dr Orloff (Lugosi), constructs a London that is murky and oppressive. The bodies are hauled out of the vat and tossed into the Thames below in order to disguise the original cause of drowning. Deception and concealment are themes central to the film, with Dr Orloff also revealed to be Mr Dearborn, a supposed philanthropist operating a home for the blind. Here, the blind inmates unwittingly provide a respectable 'front' for Orloff's activities and serve his wicked plans by carrying messages typed in braille. In view of its scenes of brutality, torture and

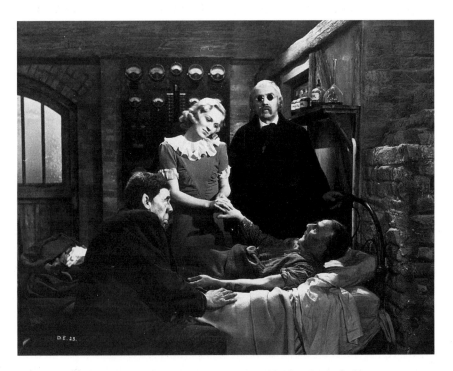

*Figure 10* 'H' for horrific: a bespectacled Bela Lugosi displays his bedside manner to (from left) Wilfred Walter, Greta Gynt and Arthur Owen in *Dark Eyes of London* (1939).

misappropriated electrotherapy, the British censor required 'extensive' cuts before even applying an 'H' certificate.

Orloff's obedient servant, Jake, a blind and hideous hulk who murders on his master's instructions, dominated the publicity for the film's American release. Acquired for US distribution in 1940 by Monogram Pictures, and retitled *The Human Monster*, the film's images of Lugosi, along with its Gothic emphasis, were replaced by 'B' movie techniques for horror film exploitation. Any references to the British origins of the film were also removed. The narrative images of many of the US posters isolated the grotesque features of Jake and a scene in which he clutches the helpless heroine in one arm. Some posters asked 'MAN or BEAST?', and, although this appeared to be equally pertinent to both Orloff and Jake, the publicity could most likely be read as promoting Jake as 'The Human Monster', a Frankenstein-like creature. Whereas *Dark Eyes of London* drew on an association with Dracula, *The Human Monster* drew on the success of *Son of Frankenstein* (1939), a film which had recently resurrected the genre and which starred Lugosi. One American poster makes the association explicit declaring: 'FRANKENSTEIN WAS A SISSY! Compared to this half-beast half-man who kills at the command of a vengeful maniac!' The American press book contained exploitation tips and imaginative foyer display suggestions: a 'Lobby Grave' with the inscription 'Here Lies a Victim of The Human Monster', provision of artificial nails and an invitation to audiences to 'ask usher for a free set . . . to replace the ones you've chewed off', and 'full-length woolen hose' for audiences with 'the chills' and 'cold feet'.

## Melodramas, comedies and thrillers

The press book accompanying the American release of the Tod Slaughter film *The Face at the Window* suggested similar extra-theatrical promotional activities. But whereas the promotion of *The Human Monster* was exploiting a 'horrific' film, *The Face at the Window* promised a bygone frolic. Cinema managers were encouraged to organize the audience to 'hiss the villain' and were advised that 'Victorian costume for the theatre staff, and bally hoo in the 19th century manner will intrigue patrons'. The press book also contains suggested reviews for local publication and one proposes: 'This is good old-fashioned melodrama of the kind that sent shivers of fright and thrills down the backs of our grandparents.' Similarly, British publicity announced the production to be 'old-time melodrama'.

Norman Carter 'Tod' Slaughter worked largely in the theatre as an actor and manager. He had, purportedly, a repertoire of 340 plays, including *Dr Jekyll and Mr Hyde* and *Burke and Hare*, which he often performed in the provinces, at the Theatre Royal, Chatham, and the Elephant and Castle Theatre, south London. The melo-dramatic nature of Slaughter's productions is stressed by Jeffrey Richards (1998: 139–59), but this monomorphic approach obscures recognition of secondary influences. Slaughter's specialism in crime dramas and a British variety of Grand

Guignol combined the 'penny dreadfuls' with Victorian theatre and the innocent fun of Edwardian music hall for his portrayal of playfully demonic larger-than-life villains.

Certainly Tod Slaughter is an important figure within the British tradition of horror. With the director and producer George King, he filmed several 'Strong Meat' melodramas, screen adaptations of his popular stage performances: *Maria Marten* (1935), *Sweeney Todd, the Demon Barber of Fleet Street* (1936) and *The Crimes of Stephen Hawke* (1936). *The Face at the Window*, complete with a hideous half-brother, a criminal known as 'The Wolf' who stabs his victims in the back, and the galvanization of a corpse, contains distinctly 'horrific' moments. In a contemporary review, Graham Greene wrote that *The Face at the Window* 'leaves the American horror films far behind' (Parkinson 1993: 333). However, the films and plays of Slaughter were intended as melodramas: highly theatrical, mischievous and pantomimical.

Horrific elements also emerged in the British comedy, which, like the musical, was a prevailing cinematic genre of the period. A tradition of American spook-spoofs has been observed, but the British equivalent is still largely ignored, although notable examples include *Excess Baggage* (1933), *Forging Ahead* (1933) and *Ask a Policeman* (1939). Exhibiting filtered versions of the Gothic, these uncanny tales were established within a popular interpretation of myth and the supernatural.

Similar characteristics functioned within the many mystery-thrillers that were produced in the 1930s, and the Chamber of Horrors in Madame Tussaud's was on

*Figure 11* 'Hiss the villain': Tod Slaughter enacts another larger-than-life performance in *The Curse of the Wraydons* (1946).

occasions employed as a convenient location. The film *Chamber of Horrors* (1929) was followed by *Midnight at Madame Tussaud's* (1936). Both are tales of murder and an ill-fated night spent in the London museum. The British press book for the latter milked the fact that, between midnight and six in the morning, when the attraction was closed, the subterranean Chamber of Horrors was used for the shoot. It provided a genuine location, but it had also, supposedly, challenged the crew of the production:

> although none of them would now admit it, the experience eventually began to tell on them, and they were not at all sorry when the scene of their activities transferred to Highbury Studios for the completion of the film.

The Chamber of Horrors is an interesting metaphor for British horrific productions of the period. A manufactured attraction displaying figures operating death-dealing devices and re-enacting moments of true crime, it is where the horrific could appear authentic, contiguous and menacing, yet frozen, distant and secured. Many British horrific films of the period fell between these values as they struggled within the constraints laid down by the British censor.

## References

Bergfelder, T. (1996) 'The production designer and the Gesamtkunstwerk: German film technicians in the British film industry of the 1930s', in A. Higson (ed.), *Dissolving Views: Key Writings on British Cinema*, London: Cassell.

Bergfelder, T. (1997) 'Surface and distraction: style and genre at Gainsborough in the late 1920s and 1930s', in P. Cook (ed.), *Gainsborough Pictures*, London: Cassell.

Bojarski, R. and Beals, K. (1976) *The Films of Boris Karloff*, Secaucus, NJ: Citadel Press.

Boot, A. (1996) *Fragments of Fear: An Illustrated History of British Horror Films*, London: Creation.

Chapman, J. (1998) 'Celluloid shockers', in J. Richards (ed.), *The Unknown 1930s: An Alternative History of the British Cinema 1929–39*, London: I.B. Tauris.

Conrich, I. (1997) 'Traditions of the British horror film', in R. Murphy (ed.), *The British Cinema Book*, London: British Film Institute.

Dello Stritto, F.J. (1995) 'The British "ban" on horror films of 1937', *Cult Movies* 14: 26.

Everson, W.K. (1974), *Classics of the Horror Film*, Secaucus, NJ: Citadel Press.

Gifford, D. (1974) *A Pictorial History of Horror Movies*, London: Hamlyn.

Hanke, K. 'Tod Slaughter', *Films in Review* 8, 4 (April 1987): 206–17.

*Kinematograph Weekly* 7 September 1933: 18.

*Kinematograph Weekly* 16 November 1933: 43.

*Kinematograph Weekly* 4 July 1935: 14.

*Kinematograph Weekly* 25 June 1936, 'Censor on improved standards': 7.

Landy, M. (1991) *British Genres: Cinema and Society, 1930–1960*, Princeton, NJ: Princeton University Press.

Loudon, H. (1991) *My Hollywood*, Worcestershire: Forest Books.

McIlroy, B. (1994) 'British filmmaking in the 1930s and 1940s: the example of Brian Desmond Hurst', in W.W. Dixon (ed.), *Re-Viewing British Cinema, 1900–1992: Essays and Interviews*, New York: State University of New York Press.

Parkinson, D. (ed.) (1993) *Mornings in the Dark: A Graham Greene Film Reader*, Manchester: Carcanet.

Pirie, D. (1973) *A Heritage of Horror: The English Gothic Cinema 1946–1972* London: Gordon Fraser.

Poe, E.A. (1960) *The Fall of the House of Usher and Other Tales*, New York: New American Library.

Richards, J. (1998) 'Tod Slaughter and the cinema of excess', in J. Richards (ed.), *The Unknown 1930s: An Alternative History of the British Cinema 1929–39*, London: I.B. Tauris.

Rigby, J. (2000) *English Gothic: A Century of Horror Cinema*, London: Reynolds & Hearn.

*Today's Cinema* 2 November 1936: 1.

# 6 Psycho-thriller, qu'est-ce que c'est?

*Kim Newman*

Before examining the British psycho-thriller, it is necessary to attempt a definition of this sub-generic grey area. An overlap between the crime film and the horror film, the psycho-thriller is something of a pendant to both and, as such, often slips through the cracks in studies of either form.

Considered as a sub-genre of horror, the psycho-thriller (as opposed to the psychological thriller, which is something else again) deals with the horror of madness. The pure mystery is uncomfortable with homicidal mania, since a motiveless criminal sabotages the essential puzzle element of a whodunnit. A murderer driven by a lust to kill, rather than by something deducible like financial gain or revenge, renders the final revelation of guilt entirely arbitrary. Anyone could secretly be the psycho.[1] The likes of Sherlock Holmes or Hercule Poirot wisely stay away from cases like this in favour of crimes in which contested inheritances or insurance policies are deciding factors.[2] Similarly, the traditional horror film deals with supernatural menace rather than a 'human monster'[3] and there is, quite rightly, a certain unease about the presentation of the mentally ill as literal monsters in the mad-killer-on-the-loose variety of horror epitomized by the various Jack the Ripper-derived foggy melodramas and the flood of masked slashers from John Carpenter's *Halloween* (1978) to Wes Craven's *Scream* (1996).[4]

Nevertheless, it is a long-established tradition in horror, especially at the most disreputable margins of an already-disreputable genre, that human evil or madness can substitute for the supernatural if horrific and gruesome enough. In these cases, some attempt is often made to equate a human villain or villains with the supernatural: for instance, ordinary people, some not even clinically insane, are literally demonized in titles like *The Flesh and the Fiends* (1959), *The Fiend* (1971) and *The Doctor and the Devils* (1986). A particularly British strain of proto-psycho-thriller is the blood and thunder melodrama practised (indeed, monopolized) by the star Tod Slaughter between *Maria Marten, or Murder in the Red Barn* (1935) and *The Greed of William Hart* (1948). Slaughter's villains are all-too-human, but rate fiendish metaphors in the titles (*Sweeney Todd, the Demon Barber of Fleet Street* (1936), *Sexton Blake and the Hooded Terror* (1938)) or symbolic fates (*Sweeney Todd* and *Crimes at the*

*Dark House* (1940) both wind up with Slaughter falling through a stage trapdoor into a literal inferno). Given the amount of cackling Slaughter manages in each role, not to mention the often outrageous nature of his misdeeds (in *The Crimes of Stephen Hawke* (1936) 'the Spine-Snapper' is introduced breaking the back of an obnoxious child who has said 'my father doesn't keep a garden for common people like you'), it would be a brave psychologist who ruled that Slaughter's villains were *not* insane – though his all-round dastards are invariably motivated as much by avarice and lechery as sheer sociopathic glee. Only budget and subtlety of writing and performance separate Slaughter from Anton Walbrook as the icy husband of Thorold Dickinson's *Gaslight* (1940), based on the Patrick Hamilton play, who tries to drive his wife (Diana Wynyard) mad but himself succumbs to insanity. Walbrook's tyrant in the home is as intent on profit as one of Slaughter's swindlers, searching his cluttered house for secreted jewels, but his climactic 'mad scene' reveals that his motive is not financial gain but an unhealthy fixation ('the rubies, the rubies') bordering on fetish.

As *Gaslight* demonstrates, the madness at the centre of the psycho-thriller is not solely or even necessarily an attribute of the villain. The device of baddies conspiring to drive the heroine (or, rarely, the hero) out of their minds was popularized by John Willard's often-filmed play *The Cat and the Canary* (1922) but really became a staple of the field with both the British and Hollywood (1944) versions of *Gaslight*. Henri-Georges Clouzot's *Les Diaboliques* (1954), from a novel by Boileau-Narcejac, is an influential development[5] of the 'it's-all-a-plot' plot: a situation is contrived to suggest to the heroine-victim that a supernatural curse is persecuting her in order not to snap her mind but to induce a fatal heart attack. Though the victim (Vera Clouzot) questions her sanity when her supposedly dead husband seems to return from the bottom of the swimming pool, there are no mad people in the film; it is nevertheless a key psycho-thriller, importing an icy, calculating sadism to the sub-genre that suggests baroque suspense is enough to tip a mystery over the genre borderline into horror.

The term psycho-thriller (or *Psycho*-thriller) did not come into wide use until Alfred Hitchcock's extraordinarily successful *Psycho* (1960), from the novel by Robert Bloch. Though it put the murderous madman at the centre of the screen, *Psycho* was at least in part an explicit 'answer' to *Les Diaboliques* and an attempt to up the horror stakes so that Hitchcock could reclaim his 'Master of Suspense' title from the French usurper that some critics had hailed as his replacement: a body rising from the bath is trumped with a stabbing in the shower, a weed-choked swimming pool is bettered by an entire swamp. In *Psycho*, the most-imitated film in its genre, Hitchcock celebrates the wedding of the horror film and the psychological thriller, using the Gothic trappings of the former to emphasize the extreme mental states of the latter. After 1960, everyone knew what a psycho-thriller was, if only because it could be defined as a film like *Psycho*, a horror movie with a madman as a monster and a combination of modern and Gothic trappings.

Hitchcock had experimented with psychopathic killers in his British work. *The Lodger* (1926), from Marie Belloc Lowndes's Jack the Ripper-inspired novel, is set during a murder spree on the part of a homicidal maniac known as The Avenger, who preys on flighty blondes (another lifelong Hitchcock theme), but the protagonist Ivor Novello is not the killer – just an amateur detective who excites the wrong sort of suspicion. *Young and Innocent* (1937) features a great 'reveal' of the mad murderer with a distinctive facial tic, at the end of a long slow track across a nightclub full of dancers to close on the blacked-up face of a minstrel drummer whose eye twitches. It was only in Hollywood, in a run of films from *Shadow of a Doubt* (1943) through *Strangers on a Train* (1951) and *Vertigo* (1958) to *Psycho*, that the director came to grips with the psycho as at least co-protagonist, dark double of the sympathetic lead and (ultimately) hero, despite himself, of plots constructed like Norman Bates's private traps. Late in his career, Hitchcock returned to the United Kingdom for a last psycho hurrah, the remarkable *Frenzy* (1972), but his specific obsessions (Jack the Ripper, dominating mothers) and general insights (the family as cradle of psychosis) made him the dominant shaping influence in the sub-genre in Britain and abroad.[6]

Before *Psycho*, British films we might now tag as psycho-thrillers were necessarily half-formed (though that is often their interest), not neatly fitting onto the genre grid. Arthur Woods's *They Drive by Night* (1938), from a novel by Arthur La Bern (author also of the book that became *Frenzy*), begins as a social-realist drama with Emlyn Williams as an ex-convict adrift in a lorry-driving milieu of transport cafés and lonely pick-ups but takes a detour into full-blooded psycho horror when the real murderer turns out to be James Whale's favoured madman Ernest Thesiger, a pompous and prissy amateur criminologist who murders young girls so he can put one over on the pub cronies he looks down his long nose at. The film winds up, of course, in one of the old dark houses traditionally used as a setting for film homicidal mania, the shadowed and decayed Gothic trappings providing an externalization of the killer's elaborate but cracked mental processes.

Similarly, Leslie Arliss's *The Night Has Eyes* (1942) deploys the trappings of the Brontës' moorland Gothic – a crumbling castle, a family curse that may be mental or supernatural, a hidden room, quicksand, sinister servants – before revealing calculating human agency behind the plot against neurotic scion James Mason. On the thriller side of the border is Harold Huth's *East of Piccadilly* (1940), with Niall MacGinniss as a Ripper-like Soho strangler apprehended at the end of a plot that is more akin to detective-procedural than horror. An outwardly meek Mervyn Johns flashes a terrifying grin and makes an unusually threatening mad killer in Basil Dearden's *My Learned Friend* (1943), trembling with desires that can't possibly be slaked within the rigid British genre confines of a Will Hay comedy, and playing a deadly game of hide-and-seek with Hay and chums as they scale Big Ben. An impulse to kill without reason is there, but these films all take the approach of depicting the madman as a fiend, almost (or outright) comical in the Tod Slaughter mode, and often take the trouble of contrasting him with supposedly 'proper' criminals, the familiar, comforting low-lifes of the well-established British crime or comedy-crime genres.

Just before *Psycho*, but shortly after the revival of Gothic horror by Hammer Films, the British cinema flashed back to the likes of *East of Piccadilly* and unloosed a few notable homicidal maniacs, establishing what are now called serial killers as fit horror subjects. Michael Powell's *Peeping Tom* (1960) was perhaps a development of the 'glueman' of Powell and Emeric Pressburger's *A Canterbury Tale* (1944), though the film-obsessed murderer is clearly far more antisocial than Eric Portman's cultivated justice of the peace (who pours glue into the hair of girls who walk out with GIs).

One of the first films told from the skewed viewpoint of the psychopath, *Peeping Tom* is as vital a shaping influence in the sub-genre as *Les Diaboliques* or *Psycho* and, in its immersion in the world of a murderous yet semi-sympathetic madman, easily as transgressive of then-accepted values. Previous British psychos, like Valentine Dyall's Ripper redux in Hammer's early *Room to Let* (1950), were stern, remote, black and white figures, as implacable as Dracula and as unlike identification figures as could be. Powell's Mark Lewis (Carl Boehm) is an Eastmancolor killer in a duffel coat, visually indistinguishable from an ordinary or sympathetic hero, inhabiting a world of shifting realities and illusions that we are forced to share, hauling in the audience – as Hitchcock would do when Norman cleans the bathroom – as an accessory after (and eventually before) the fact.

It is no coincidence that companies desperate to imitate the Hammer formula reached back to Tod Slaughter's gaslit grue for the likes of Robert Day's *Grip of the Strangler* (1958), John Gilling's *The Flesh and the Fiends* (1959) and Baker and Berman's *Jack the Ripper* (1959). The Ripper, an archetype who is at once a classic monster (stalking the same foggy London as Mr Hyde and even Dracula) and an avatar of a modern ill (the first true serial murderer), is a recurrent figure in the sub-genre, whether in historical recreation/fantasy or in contemporary-set re-runs of his criminal pattern. Yet Mark Lewis was not alone, and there were a number of other serial killers who carried out their night-work in contemporary settings, emerging from Hammer-style old dark houses to stalk victims in modern pubs, alleyways and villages. British cinema of the late 1950s unloosed the impotent, sadistic mystery writer (Michael Gough) of Arthur Crabtree's *Horrors of the Black Museum* (1959), the sex-obsessed puritan (Harry H. Corbett) of Terry Bishop's *Cover Girl Killer* (1959), the plastic surgeon-cum-ringmaster (Anton Diffring) of Sidney Hayers's *Circus of Horrors* (1960), the sweetie-proffering child molester (Felix Aylmer) of Cyril Frankel's *Never Take Sweets from a Stranger* (1960)[7] and, perhaps most subversive of all, the murderous rapist pervert ('a cup of tea and a suggestive biscuit') who turns out (in a scene that evokes *Young and Innocent*) to be a pantomime dame (John Salew) in Alfred Shaughnessy's *The Impersonator* (1961).

All these films – even *Peeping Tom* – have one foot in the crime genre, with footage-eating police investigations to provide relief from psychotic behaviour and a wallowing in peculiarly British sleaze (note the homey 'glamour' pornography common to *Peeping Tom* and *Cover Girl Killer*) or merely to add a bluff sense of tea-drinking normality that serves to isolate and render freakish the fascinating but deplorable murderers (*Never Take Sweets from a Stranger* makes its killer pathetic, but stops just short of crossing the line into sympathy, which got *Peeping Tom* into such trouble). What is interesting for against-the-grain readers is that these British maniacs are not estranged from the familiar world of cosy British cinema, but are nestled in its very heart. The murder-strings of Robert Hamer's *Kind Hearts and Coronets* (1949) and Alexander Mackendrick's *The Ladykillers* (1955) are treated with Ealing delicacy, but behind the chintz and good manners lurks a flamboyant ruthlessness that would emerge into dementia in the traducing of British popular entertainment in the lurid depths of *Horrors of the Black Museum* (crime writing), *Circus of Horrors* (the big top), *Peeping Tom* (British cinema), *The Impersonator* (pantomime) and the Punch and Judy-themed short *That's the Way to Do It* (1980).

In the early 1960s, as the British horror scene settled into a pattern of overlapping and complementary cycles (Gothic, science fiction, anthology, etc.), the psycho-thriller became an accepted genre strand. The key film is Seth Holt's *Taste of Fear* (1961), the first of Hammer's attempts to keep up with a genre that had been as changed by *Psycho* as by their own *The Curse of Frankenstein* (1957).[8] Scripted by Jimmy Sangster, who would return to and rework the material many times, *Taste of Fear* (more blatantly retitled *Scream of Fear* in the US) is not a true *Psycho* imitation but a riff on *Les Diaboliques* (even to the extent of being set in France), its heroine Susan Strasberg the victim of a plot to drive her mad or to death, and involving the Clouzot staple of a body appearing and disappearing under water. Despite *Psycho*-esque titling (and advertising images), Michael Carreras's *Maniac* (1963) and Freddie Francis's *Paranoiac* (1964), *Nightmare* (1964) and *Hysteria* (1965) are also 'it's-all-a-plot' films (*Maniac* reuses the French setting). *Paranoiac*, based on Josephine Tey's novel *Brat Farrar* (1949), was originally scheduled for a 'straight' adaptation before Hammer hit big with horror. The film straddles influences by imposing upon Tey's imper-sonate-the-missing-heir plot an outrageously insane rich-kid-gone-wrong villain played at full throttle by the young Oliver Reed, the closest Hammer would come to Norman Bates, complete with mummified choirboy brother.

The company stuck with the sub-genre just as they stayed with their Gothics, though they absorbed new influences by evoking the 'ageing actress' modern Gothics of Robert Aldrich's *What Ever Happened to Baby Jane?* (1962) and *Hush . . . Hush, Sweet Charlotte* (1965),[9] and employing Bette Davis for Seth Holt's *The Nanny* (1965) and Roy Ward Baker's *The Anniversary* (1968), Tallulah Bankhead for Silvio Narizzano's *Fanatic* (1965) and Joan Fontaine for *The Witches* (1966). When this cycle ran its course, Hammer fell back on sexed-up reworkings of earlier styles, as in Alan Gibson's *Crescendo* (1970), which retains *Fanatic*'s heroine Stefanie Powers for yet another tale of a family secret (a mad twin in the attic) set in France, and the 'Women in Terror' double-bill of Peter Collinson's too-late-to-be-trendy *Straight on Till*

*Figure 12* A 'full throttle' Oliver Reed in Hammer's *Brat Farrar*-inspired *Paranoiac*
(1964).

*Morning* (1972), in which new-to-the-sinful-city Rita Tushingham is stalked by a
blonde Peter Pan obsessive Shane Briant, and Jimmy Sangster's *Fear in the Night*
(1972), which has Judy Geeson being prodded in a deserted school to murder one-
armed Peter Cushing. In the 1980s, when the company name was attached to a run
of TV movies ('The Hammer House of Mystery and Suspense'), the whole thing
started up again, with more plotted-against heroines and conspirators posing as
homicidal maniacs in the likes of Peter Sasdy's *Last Video and Testament* (1984) and
Gabrielle Beaumont's *The Corvini Inheritance* (1984).

Hammer's psycho-thrillers tend to revolve around the theme of trouble within
the family, often harking back to *The Old Dark House* (1932)[10] by using decaying
mansion settings (and, not incidentally, sets from their period Gothics) to represent
a decadent, inbred milieu that harbours scheming, calculating evil (plots to usurp
the inheritance or get rid of the inconvenient spouse) and psychotic, random
violence (Bankhead's plan to sacrifice her dead son's fiancée to his memory, Reed's
childhood murder of his elder brother). The world of these films is essentially that
of Agatha Christie, preserving the values and cruelties of the classic country house
whodunnit while the rest of Britain is getting on with the 1960s.

Only *Fanatic*, with its contrast between the modern heroine (her boyfriend drives
a sports car and works in television) and the Gothic-stereotype household (with
sinister servants Peter Vaughan and Donald Sutherland and a splendid study in

imperious puritan tyranny from la Bankhead), makes much of this theme, though *Straight on Till Morning* tags along with an unhappy mix of social comment and psychosis. The films stay trapped in the house on the hill, and rarely come down to the antiseptic Bates Motel or even the symbolic swamp. Indeed, Hammer's most thoroughgoing explorations of the psycho theme are dressed up with their traditional period Gothic costumes – Peter Sasdy's *Hands of the Ripper* (1971) and Peter Sykes's *Demons of the Mind* (1971) examine familial legacies of violent madness that can be read as supernatural curses or psychological conditions and present early Freudians (Eric Porter, Patrick Magee) as dangerous tinkerers on the Hammer Frankenstein model.

Even *The Nanny*, the most rooted in reality of all Hammer psycho movies, is about a wealthy diplomatic family – though it represents the most elaborate development (Joseph Losey's 1963 film excepted) of the obviously intriguing 'servant' theme, as the deferential but resentful nanny (Davis) who has favoured other people's children over her own takes it upon herself to tidy up the house through murder of her grown-up or child charges. Away from Hammer, and a step or two down the social class scale, other films found more embattled families (often childless couples) victimized by the changing times as incarnated by various psycho menaces, who were often screwed up by the same trends that put such a strain on the heroes and heroines. Cyril Frankel's *The Very Edge* (1962) is about a housewife (Anne Heywood) left at home ('see you in nine and a half hours') in her ideal suburban home by her struggling husband (Richard Todd), stalked by a youth (Jeremy Brett) who remembers her former career as a cover-girl model. Shot on anonymous locations in Ireland, it is an intriguingly discontented drama about broken promises: Heywood misses her exciting old life, Todd is driven to an affair (with a French co-worker) by his wife's traumatized frigidity after a rape attempt, and Brett (disguised in the fetish leathers of an RAC motorcyclist) looks from the outside at a perfect but empty home and thinks Heywood is wasted on Todd.[11] The film – like everything from *Beat Girl* (1961) to *The Damned* (1963) – assesses postwar prosperity, concludes that something is dangerously wrong with the picture, and deems psychotic violence as likely a frame-breaking solution as any other.

Apart from Hammer and Amicus, the British psycho movie presents a run of films that weirdly crossbreed the 'angry young man' of *Room at the Top* (1959) and *Saturday Night and Sunday Morning* (1960) with that 'nice young man', Norman Bates. Director Karel Reisz and star Albert Finney followed up the seminal *Saturday Night and Sunday Morning* with a remake of Emlyn Williams's *Night Must Fall* (1964), casting Finney as the plausible charmer who carries a victim's head around in a hatbox. At once a rebel and a creep, Finney's Danny Boy is merely a homicidal extension of Arthur Seaton or Billy Liar, and the type became common in British movies from the mid-1960s through to the 1970s: to whit, the well-spoken but mad-eyed likes of Terence Stamp (*The Collector* (1965)), Mark Wynter (*The Haunted House of Horror* (1969)), Hywel Bennett (*Twisted Nerve* (1968), *Endless Night* (1972)), Patrick Mower

*Figure 13* 'An inside-out rewrite of *Psycho*': Judy Huxtable recoils from mamma's boy
　　　　　John Standing in Freddie Francis's *The Psychopath* (1966).

(*Incense for the Damned* (1970)), Martin Potter (*Goodbye Gemini* (1970)), a whole class
of public schoolboys (*Unman, Wittering and Zigo* (1971)), Shane Briant (*Demons of
the Mind, Straight on Till Morning*), Nicholas Clay (*The Road Builder/The Night Digger*
(1971), Paul Nicholas (*What Became of Jack and Jill?* (1971)), Mark Lester (*Night Hair
Child* (1972)) and Ralph Bates (*Persecution* 1974)).

　These are mostly subtly conservative backlash fantasies about how dangerous
rebellious or 'swinging' youth can be, discovering more violence and cruelty in
well-spoken, clean-cut young men than in the obvious bikers, drop-outs or hippies.
For preference, these psychos pick on older rather than younger women as victims:
Clay is plotting against Patricia Neal, Nicholas is trying to murder his gran (Mona
Washbourne), Bates is out to rid himself of Lana Turner. Quite a few are unworthy
aspirants (like Stamp's pools-winner or Clay's handyman) to a lifestyle that is
naturally the birthright of the middle-aged or middle-class. The parade of pretty
boys also suggests an ambiguous sexuality (most obvious in *The Haunted House of
Horror* and *Goodbye Gemini*) inevitably seen as twisted into misogyny, impotence and
murder. Michael Reeves's use of Ian Ogilvy in *The Sorcerers* (1967) is an interesting
deconstruction of the myth of the killer youth, who exists in this film only as the
fantasy puppet of a clucking old woman (Catherine Lacey) and her ineffectual
husband (Boris Karloff). Reeves, who always sees youthful violence as a reaction to
geriatric oppression, attacks the underlying assumptions of late 1960s/early 1970s

psycho movies in which smiler-with-a-knife killers are let loose in decadent worlds that see-saw between psychedelic parties and stately homes.

Another cycle harks back to the days of *Cover Girl Killer* (as the film's central character puts it: 'surely sex and horror are the new Gods in this polluted world of so-called entertainment'), with psychopathic killers (often rapists as much as or more than murderers) preying on miniskirted birds who follow such sexually tantalizing professions as modelling or prostitution, or happen to incarnate British porn stereotypes of the teasing schoolgirl, the provocative barmaid or Susan George. Though these films can be accused of an even more exploitative attitude to youth, which tends to be stripped naked and cut into pieces, than the murderous-young-man movies, it is notable that a great many of them present authority figures as monstrous psychopaths, suggesting their murderous activities are logical extensions of perverted crazes for power. Witness: patriarch Michael Gough (*The Corpse* (1970)), matriarchs Ursula Howells (*Mumsy, Nanny, Sonny and Girly* (1970)) and Sheila Keith (*Frightmare* (1974)), judges Jack May (*Night, After Night, After Night* (1969)) and Patrick Barr (*House of Whipcord* (1974)), ex-husband Ian Bannen (*Fright* (1971)), doctor Anthony Ainley (*Assault* (1971)), security guard Tony Beckley (*The Fiend* (1971)), publican Barry Foster (*Frenzy*), Santa Claus (Oliver MacGreevy) (*Tales From the Crypt* (1972)), priest Anthony Sharp (*House of Mortal Sin* (1975)), policeman Christopher Cazenove (*The Fantasist* (1986)) and dentist Peter Firth (*White Angel* (1993)).

Though depicting these establishment professionals as murderous madmen is in tune with the disenchanted, questioning tone of the times in which they were made, it is also true that the convention of the pious hypocrite who is secretly a fiendish villain goes back as far as Wilkie Collins and the eighteenth-century Gothic novel, and our old friend Tod Slaughter was often found living a double life as a respectable banker or philanthropist by day and sadistic master criminal by night. Some of his filmed melodramas even carry over nineteenth-century penny-dreadful message-mongering. *It's Never Too Late to Mend* (1937) is an exposé of prison conditions with Slaughter as a prison governor even more flamboyantly nasty than the villain of *House of Whipcord* (he winds up chained to his own torture wheel); and *The Ticket-of-Leave Man* (1937) contrasts the hard row hoed by an ex-convict who wants to stay straight with the easy life of the apparent do-gooder who wants to suck the hero back into a life of crime. Like these films, Pete Walker's efforts have an undeniable social charge, and certainly play to audiences predisposed to distrust respectability and cant, though they indulge in their own brand of hypocrisy by striking condemnatory poses while revelling in sadistic sleaze. The virtuous figures of Slaughter and Walker films are equally stiff and ridiculous, though by the 1970s mores had changed to the extent that Walker was able to demonstrate the unfairness of society by having villains who usually triumph over ineffectual good guys.

Comparatively few films fall back on the *Cover Girl Killer* image of the powerless, resentful outsider (Kenneth Griffith in *Revenge* (1971), Dudley Sutton in *The Playbirds*

(1978), Alan Lake in *Don't Open Till Christmas* (1985) or the almost-unseen stalker (*And Soon the Darkness* (1970), *Blind Terror* (1971)), though there are isolated instances of inbred degenerates (*Tower of Evil* (1972), *Death Line* (1972)) existing Sawney Beane-like in overlooked corners of modern Britain. British psychos are over-whelmingly people we know: cheerful character actors usually found as lovable characters in television sit-coms or police dramas: Jack May is quite a sight in leathers and a curly wig, stalking Soho for tarts to slice in *Night, After Night, After Night*, though Harry H. Corbett in *Cover Girl Killer* now strikes audiences as equally unsettling. These degrading murder romps feel almost like betrayals of the public trust: if Nelson Gabriel, Harold Steptoe, Van der Valk, or Oliver Twist are serial killers, then nobody is safe. This gives these mostly grotty films a real charge that occasionally, as in the use of Rupert ('Maigret') Davies as the ineffectual husband in *Frightmare*, even seems deliberate. When Hitchcock essayed a film (*Frenzy*) based on this model, he cast the engagingly bluff Barry Foster as the real killer and the boozily unlikeable Jon Finch as the ex-officer in the frame for the necktie murders. Hitchcock knows exactly what he is doing as he makes withering observations about class between the murders, but the often-underrated Pete Walker and David McGillivray sometimes achieve an even greater charge with uninhibited, cartoonish attacks on establishment figures who are also drooling, merciless nutters.

As both R.D. Laing and Alfred Hitchcock suggested in their different spheres, the prime arena of psychosis is the family – witness the shifting balances of incestuous cruelty in *The Corpse, Mumsy, Nanny, Sonny and Girly* and *Frightmare*, or even *The Ruling Class* (1971) and *The Homecoming* (1973). Since J.B. Priestley's *Benighted* (1927) – source novel for *The Old Dark House* (which ditched most of the politics) – used an extended family of mad people to represent a cross-section of post-World War I Britain on the brink of moral and intellectual collapse, there has almost always been a national element to the analysis.[12] Just as the House of Usher is a building, a family and also America, the British psycho movie presents a crumbling national self-image, bitterly reacting to all manner of social change with killing strokes that more often represent the forces of reaction than revolution, intensely suspicious of the new-fangled but morbidly trapped in the stately homes of the past (American villains are after the cash, but British schemers more often want the property or the title), and clinging desperately to the detritus of high culture (British psychos are often artistically or musically inclined) while their misdeeds (raped schoolgirls, throttled tarts, squandered inheritances) are the stuff of the *News of the World* end of the newspaper market.

## Notes

1  'That's the trouble with sex crimes,' says police inspector Alfred Marks in *Scream and Scream Again* (1969), 'the only motive is the sex.' The same goes for the 'werewolf break' in *The Beast Must Die* (1974) – any of the characters could be suffering from a curse, so the whodunnit gimmick is unfair.

2 In this, Arthur Conan Doyle knew better than subsequent hands who have had Holmes track the archetypal homicidal maniac, Jack the Ripper. Notably, the two film versions of this theme – James Hill's *A Study in Terror* (1965) and Bob Clark's *Murder by Decree* (1978) – add revenge and conspiracy elements, which *can* be unpicked by deductive reasoning, to the psychosis.

3 *The Human Monster* is the US release title of the British *Dark Eyes of London* (1939), which straddles genres by capitalizing on the thriller source material (an Edgar Wallace novel) and a horror movie superstar (Bela Lugosi).

4 There are almost no British slasher movies. George Dugdale, Ezra Martin and Peter Litten's *Slaughter High* (1987), a rare example, harks back to Arthur Crabtree's *Fiend Without a Face* (1958) by faking an American setting for an imitation American genre movie.

5 British films that borrow (or plagiarize outrageously) from *Les Diaboliques* include *Taste of Fear* (1961), *Nightmare* (1963), *The Corpse* (1970), the 'Method for Murder' episode of *The House that Dripped Blood* (1970), *Fear in the Night* (1972), *Night Watch* (1973) and *Dominique* (1978).

6 The American Robert Bloch, made famous by *Psycho*, became an Amicus mainstay, scripting or inspiring a run of anthology films or psycho-thrillers – including Freddie Francis's *The Psychopath* (1965), an inside-out rewrite of *Psycho*, and *The Deadly Bees* (1965), from H.F. Heard's Holmesian novel *A Taste for Honey*.

7 One of the rarest of all Hammer films, *Never Take Sweets from a Stranger* (1960) preceded the company's official entry into the psycho-thriller genre with *Taste of Fear*. Based on a play by Roger Caris and impressively shot by Freddie Francis, it makes some slight attempt to distance its subject by setting the story in small-town Canada rather than rural England. Guy Green's *The Snorkel* (1958) and Val Guest's *The Full Treatment* (1961) also predate *Taste of Fear* and find Hammer making sketches for the sub-generic cycle they would shortly launch.

8 Sir James Carreras, Hammer's chairman, explicitly referred to *Taste of Fear* and its follow-ups as 'mini-Hitchcock'.

9 *Hush . . . Hush, Sweet Charlotte* is yet another rewrite of *Les Diaboliques*. Its theme song was an unlikely British single for Bruce Forsyth.

10 Hammer and William Castle produced a remake of this property in 1962, but it's among no one's favourite films – despite a good supporting cast.

11 Todd, stalwart hero of many British war films, has a similar peacetime struggle in *Never Let Go* (1960), where he is crippled by hire-purchase payments when the vehicle he needs for his travelling salesman job is stolen by Peter Sellers' hot-car gang.

12 Jonathan Coe's novel *What a Carve-Up!* (1994), constructed around an obsession with the 1962 film of the same name, is an explicit and successful variation on this theme.

# 7   Necromancy in the UK: witchcraft and the occult in British horror

*Leon Hunt*

Ninety-eight percent of so-called Satanists are nothing but pathetic freaks who get their kicks out of dancing naked in freezing churchyards and use the devil as an excuse for getting some sex. Then there's the *other* two percent.

John Verney (Richard Widmark), in *To the Devil a Daughter* (Peter Sykes, 1976)

Dana Andrews pursued by the fiery footprints of Professor Karswell's demon. The Duc de Richleau preparing his companions for a night in the pentagram, during which '*something* will come'. The eye of some unholy 'fiend' found in a freshly ploughed field, waiting to return, waiting to be worshipped once more.[1] Some of the British horror film's most memorable images deal with the occult, 'black magic', witches and warlocks. But while *Night of the Demon* (Jacques Tourneur, 1957) and *The Wicker Man* (Robin Hardy, 1973) have established cult reputations, the films overall have not been seen as constituting a distinct sub-genre in the manner of either the British vampire film or 'demonic' films made elsewhere (*Rosemary's Baby* (Roman Polanski,1968), *The Exorcist* (William Friedkin, 1973), *The Omen* (Richard Donner, 1976)). Certainly this is a stylistically and thematically diverse group of films, encompassing the 'Lewtonesque' *frissons* of *Night of the Demon* and *Night of the Eagle* (Sidney Hayers, 1962), the bleak cruelty of the witchfinder films, the fleshy covens of *Virgin Witch* (Ray Austin, 1971) and *Satan's Slave* (Norman J. Warren, 1976) and the pagan ethnography of *The Wicker Man*.

The British occult film falls roughly into two periods. Initially, from 1957 to 1964, it emerges as a counter-tradition to the dominant Hammer Gothic in its play on the unseen and the unrepresentable. Moreover, films like *Night of the Demon* and *Night of the Eagle* are often seen as being only nominally 'British'. Not only were writers, directors and stars imported from America – Tourneur, Richard Matheson, Charles Beaumont, Dana Andrews – but, by implication, the films' aesthetics, too. *Demon*, in particular, has been linked to Tourneur's films for Val Lewton in the 1940s:[2] black-and-white 'expressionist' photography, mobile camerawork, an emphasis on 'mood' and 'suggestion' over exposition and graphic horror. Peter Hutchings goes so far as to call *Demon* and *Eagle* 'British "Lewton" films' (1993: 92), while William K. Everson describes *Demon* as 'the last genuine horror "classic" that we have had' (1974: 184) in contrast with the 'shock, sensation and speed' of the colour Gothics (ibid.: 206). *City of the Dead* (US: *Horror Hotel*, John Moxey, 1960) has the most 'imported' look of all, with its New England setting and dry ice-shrouded Lovecraftian atmosphere, looking for all the world as though Mario Bava made it during an exchange visit to Shepperton. It would be tempting to detect here a disavowal of the occult as a part of British life, but a second look at *Night of the Demon* complicates matters. The film has an American star, producer, director and narrator, and a British émigré writer (Charles Bennett). But the first thing we see on screen is Stonehenge, accompanied by a portentous reminder that 'man, using the magic power of the ancient runic symbols, can call forth these powers of darkness, the demons of hell'. In contrast with *Eagle*, *City of the Dead* and *Witchcraft* (Don Sharp, 1964), these powers are at least partly indigenous and Dana Andrews' imported scepticism is not entirely welcome – 'Take it easy on our ghosts,' pleads one minor character, 'we English are very fond of them.' There's certainly much pleasure to be had from fire demons materializing on the 8.45 to Southampton. Most importantly, Professor Karswell (Niall MacGinnis), the leader of a 'devil cult', is British cinema's first allusion to Aleister Crowley, the prototype for the genre's charismatic Satanist.[3]

The sub-genre found new life in its second phase, from 1966 to 1976,[4] which saw the occult take its place more securely in British horror's imaginary. *The Witches* (Cyril Frankel, 1966), in particular, brought witchcraft 'home' with its rural setting and its combination of pagan belief and esoteric 'expertise'. Magic's prime locale was now the countryside, the site of superstition, savagery and puritan cruelty (the witchfinder films) or a more 'authentic' and liberating set of cultural practices and beliefs (*The Wicker Man*). By the late 1960s, one thing was clear: the occult = sex. Tigon studios, in particular, were not slow in exploiting the occult as a link between horror and sexploitation. *Curse of the Crimson Altar* (Vernon Sewell, 1968) is laced with sex, bondage, S/M, some nominal inverted deities (Herne, Pan – 'Hm, eroticism' murmurs Boris Karloff sagely) and undigested references to drugs and psychedelia. The end-credits' cast list is particularly indicative of Tigon's priorities – '1st Virgin', '2nd Virgin', 'Woman with whip'. The film acknowledges the hypocrisy of the witch-hunts but can't resist including a full-blown vengeful witch (horror icon Barbara Steele). *Witchfinder General* (Michael Reeves, 1968) is equally important to subsequent 'witch' films, even if it is not itself concerned with magic. Rather, its 'monster' is the witchfinder himself, Matthew Hopkins (Vincent Price), the model for numerous corrupt and/or psychotic authority figures, the enemy of permissiveness (see Hunt 1996 and 1998). The film also explores a 'gynocidal' narrative that is not dissimilar to some feminist accounts of the witch-hunts, 'the story of how perfect our lives would be . . . if it were not for patriarchy and its violence' (Purkiss 1996: 8). Yet the film is not interested in witches – Hutchings

(1993) argues that its real conflict is between men – and Diane Purkiss cautions against a 'myth that portrays women as nothing but the helpless victims of patriarchy' (1996: 17). *Cry of the Banshee* (Gordon Hessler, 1970) and *Blood on Satan's Claw* (Piers Haggard, 1970) retain the vicious witchfinder, but bring witches back into the frame, so that the films play more as a conflict between the 'old' (pagan) religions and the 'new' (Christian) one. Again, end-credits are particularly telling, with *Banshee*'s demarcating the film's protagonists into 'The Establishment', 'Witches' and 'Villagers'.

Crowley's 'Sex Magick' had considerable potential for co-option into counter-cultural and 'permissive' discourses – both saw sex as a liberating, boundary-dissolving force. The publishing blurb for Mayflower's 'Masterworks of the Occult' series suggests how these ideas were passing from the 'counter culture' into broader popular consumption:

> a new list of the finest in Occult Non-fiction, the occult being all sciences concealed or "covered over" by the mechanical straightness of society, particularly Western, that hide from the senses and from understanding the more liberating facts and fantasies of our cosmos.[5]

This is punching all the right buttons – would you rather be 'liberated' or mechanically 'straight'? The years 1966–8 mark a particularly significant turning point for popular understandings of the occult and these cultural shifts are contemporaneous with the horror genre's gradual break from a Judaeo-Christian dualistic framework. There was a growing interest in pre-Christian pagan cults allegedly representative of a more 'authentic', prelapsarian national culture.[6] In 1967, Crowley was one of the cultural icons to appear on The Beatles' *Sergeant Pepper* album cover, and the Rolling Stones' *Their Satanic Majesties Request* appeared the same year. Across the Atlantic, Anton La Vey opened the first Satanic church in California in 1966 and was technical adviser on *Rosemary's Baby* in 1968. As John Symonds (1951/1973: 9) put it in his Crowley biography, revised in 1973:

> the tide has turned in Crowley's favour. The doctrine of 'Do What Thou Wilt', with its encouragement to trample the gods under foot and to take one's fill of love, wine, and 'strange drugs', has seized the imagination of this restless world. Crowley's philosophy . . . invites one 'to do one's thing.'

One legacy of this is a non-generic one – it includes Kenneth Anger's 'Magick Lantern' cycle and *Performance* (Donald Cammell, Nicolas Roeg, 1971). In the latter, 'Do What Thou Wilt' is echoed in the words 'Nothing is true. Everything is permitted' (see Wollen 1995: 20–3).

Of course, 'swinging' witchcraft co-existed with more traditional representations in popular culture, even if the prurient efforts of Dennis Wheatley and others

*Figure 14* A more 'authentic' and liberating set of cultural practices and beliefs? Christopher Lee and *The Wicker Man* (1973).

literally to demonize magic(k)al practices were starting to look a little rearguard. Wheatley was enjoying a revival in the early 1970s and novels like *The Devil Rides Out* (1934) were reprinted in a choice of formats – paperbacks with 'sexy' covers or red-bound book-of-the-month volumes for the 'connoisseur'. Wheatley also launched his 'Library of the Occult', in which Stoker's *Dracula* and Guy Endore's *Werewolf of Paris* rubbed shoulders with Crowley's *Moonchild* and Helena Blavatsky's *Studies in Occultism*.

Within the British occult film, there are three strands of particular significance: first, the way the figure of Crowley translates into popular representations of the libertine and 'black magician'; second, the figure of the female witch; and third, the conflict between 'old' and 'new' religions suggesting some recognition of the counter-cultural capital of paganism. Two broader distinctions are worth making along the lines of gender and geography. In the 'Crowley' films, the occult is more likely to be identified as a 'masculine' realm of *knowledge* and *experience*. Its semantic designation is a 'science', but it also involves a will to power – 'the science of causing change to occur by means of one's will', as Mocata puts it in *The Devil Rides Out* (Terence Fisher, 1968). By contrast, where magic is referred to as a religion – 'the oldest religion in the world' – it is more likely to be coded 'feminine'. Sometimes this draws on a notion of woman-as-mystery – *Curse of the Crimson Altar*'s Lavinia is 'Mother of the mysteries, keeper of the black secret' (shades of Dario Argento's

'Three Mothers') – sometimes closeness to nature (*Blood on Satan's Claw*) or what Diane Purkiss calls an 'originary matriarchy' (1996: 8). The latter underpins *Cry of the Banshee*, as witch-mother Oona (Elizabeth Bergner) laments the massacre of her 'children' by witch-persecuting magistrate Edward Whitman (Vincent Price). Oona's sect give the impression of frolicking, harmless flower-children until the new (masculine) order intervenes, whereupon it is time for avenging demons to be summoned. There are exceptions to both rules. Stephanie (Kay Walsh) in *The Witches* is very clear about magic's status as a 'science' and about her own transcendent will – her academic study of the 'art' distinguishes her from the more instinctive 'old religion' of the locals. On the other hand, Father Dominic (Donald Pleasence) in *Eye of the Devil* (J. Lee Thompson, 1967) and Lord Summerisle (Christopher Lee) in *The Wicker Man* participate in and encourage the locals' return to the 'old gods'. The second distinction brings us back to the 'Britishness' of the occult. In one group of films, magic is found elsewhere (often with colonialist implications) – in Jamaica (*Night of the Eagle*), Greece (*Incense for the Damned*), Haiti (*Plague of the Zombies*), France (*Devils of Darkness*, *Eye of the Devil*), the Middle East (*Hellraiser*), even Mars (*Quatermass and the Pit*). But increasingly, by the early 1970s, it is firmly located in the (primarily English) countryside. *Blood on Satan's Claw* contains the most irresistible version of this mythology – its hairy demon is in the soil itself waiting to return. This Green and Pleasant Land forever resists the onset of an Age of Reason.

## Snakes and ladders

> Snakes and ladders – an English game. . . . Funny thing – I always preferred sliding down the snakes to climbing up the ladders. You're a doctor of Psychology, you ought to know the answer to that.
>
> (Professor Karswell, *Night of the Demon*)

It never seems to be possible to describe Aleister Crowley without hyperbole as: the 'Wickedest Man in the World', Beast 666, 'poet, painter, chess master, lecher, drug addict and magician' (Wheatley, introduction to Crowley 1929/1974), 'the Picasso of the Occult . . . bridges the gap between Oscar Wilde and Hitler' (Cyril Connolly, *Sunday Times*), 'the unsung hero of the hippies' (*International Times*).[7] Few people could live up to such descriptions, but Crowley had the advantage of not really needing to. For generic purposes, his main importance is as the 'model for Satanist villains considerably less flamboyant and more powerful than he actually was' (Newman 1996: 83). He is to the 'black magician' what Byron is to the vampire – polymorphous fop translated into libertine *Ubermensch*.[8] Symonds's description already points to some perverse Gothic villain – jewelled serpents on his rings, 'cold, staring eyes set in his fat, feminine face . . . shaved head, oddness of dress . . . sweet, slightly nauseous smell' (Symonds 1951/1973: 412). Best of all, there's

His Satanic Majesty's Haircut – a 'horny' lock which could be worn 'erect', or parted into twin horns. His fictional counterparts pick up on these connotations – uncanny and magnetic, hysterically phallic, queer in the broadest sense of the term. These Satanic lords owe considerably less to Crowley's philosophy or writing than they do to the scandal, the hyperbole, the myth of the Great Beast. Crowley was reportedly delighted by his thinly disguised representation in Somerset Maugham's *The Magician* (1908) as 'an atrocious scoundrel', declaring it 'an appreciation of my genius such as I had never dreamed of inspiring' (Symonds 1951/1973: 150). In British horror, the Crowleyan prototype is, variously, a self-hating mother's boy (*Night of the Demon*), a hypnotic predator (*The Devil Rides Out*), libertine-philosopher (*The Wicker Man*), heretic-visionary (*To the Devil a Daughter*) and a nomadic figure exploring the boundaries of experience (*Hellraiser*).

Crowley's bisexuality seems to loom large in the 'scandal'. In H.R. Wakefield's 'He Cometh and He Passeth By' (1928), Crowley *manqué* 'Oscar Clinton' is likened to 'the *other* Oscar' (Parry 1974: 58).[9] Stephen Bourne notes the 'clues' surrounding Karswell in *Night of the Demon* – 'he lives with his mother in a large mansion in the country . . . a "feminine" household . . . surrounded by porcelain', and his mother comments that 'he really ought to be married, but he's too fussy' (1996: 129). Wheatley's Mocata (*The Devil Rides Out*) is a bloated, lisping queen with 'limp hands' and a weakness for chocolates – he is likened by the Duc de Richleau to a 'large

*Figure 15* Snakes and ladders: Niall MacGinnis's black magician is beaten at his own game by Dana Andrews's sceptic in Tourneur's *Night of the Demon* (1957).

white slug' (Wheatley 1934/1986: 11). Matheson and Fisher's filmic Mocata (Charles Gray) is more urbane, 'handsome in appearance, precise in diction' (Hutchings 1993: 153), but just a little too interested in Simon Aaron (Patrick Mower) who, the novel tells us, has a 'sensual mouth' (ibid.: 13). He also has designs on Tanith (Nike Arrighi), but she is paired off with square-jawed Rex, while unattached Simon can still be led down the 'left hand path'.

In his introduction to *Moonchild*, Wheatley tells the tale of meeting a disappointingly innocuous Crowley, 'charming to talk to and a gifted intellectual', but making 'no attempt to draw me into any occult circle' (Crowley 1929/1974: 9). But the Great Beast had an excuse – a friend later told Wheatley that Crowley's invocation of Pan in Paris left him a shadow of his former self (ibid.: 10). This is not far from the conception of Karswell, the Satanist most mindful of the cost of consorting with 'dark forces', notwithstanding the material wealth it has brought him:

> You get nothing for nothing. This house, the land, the way we live – nothing for nothing. My followers, who pay for all this, do so out of fear, and I do what I do out of fear also. It's part of the price.[10]

Karswell's cult is investigated not for moral reasons but 'scientific' ones – Holden (Dana Andrews) wants to expose him as a charlatan. From the beginning, Karswell is trapped between the 'cold light of reason' and those forces who will not welcome his practices being dragged out of the shadows. His fear gives him a licence to be articulate, and even sympathetic – the 'bachelor' stereotype (as Bourne puts it) allows him to at least care about someone (namely his mum, who advises: 'If it makes you unhappy, stop it').

Mocata is never allowed this amount of space – there is nowhere near enough of him in *The Devil Rides Out*, allowing Christopher Lee's Duc de Richleau to dominate proceedings. The film's preferred doctrine is as far away from 'Do What Thou Wilt' as possible – 'Only they who love without desire shall have power granted to them in their darkest hour.' It took younger talent to rethink Wheatley. Christopher Wicking's script for *To the Devil a Daughter* notes the novel's debt to *Moonchild* – the creation of *homunculi*, and of a 'magickal' child. Father Michael Rayner (Christopher Lee, never better) wants to reincarnate Astaroth through a complex process of sacrifice and rebirth. His avatar is to be Christine (Nastassia Kinski), pledged to Rayner at birth in a pact made with her father. Now eighteen, she's ready to *become* Astaroth. 'The youth of this world has lost its way,' she explains to occult novelist John Verney (Richard Widmark), 'They need something to believe in, to follow, something new and powerful. We will provide it very soon.' In the novel, one of the villains is named the Marquis de Grasse, and the film seems to spot the connection to *another* marquis – Lee's defrocked priest has a Sadean investment in chaos. He was excommunicated for his belief in 'the absolute capability of man', the bishop suggesting that 'man' is 'programmed for catastrophe'. Rayner's agenda is 'terminal chaos presided over by . . . Astaroth'. Like Crowley's Sex Magick, Astaroth worship is resolutely phallic, and, as in Sade, the defiance of nature happens at the expense of the female body (gory, womb-tearing births). The film seems to spot the latent fascism in this quest for a 'God' who will 'renew the vital spirit of the world', but its jigsaw plotting makes it hard to tell where it's coming from. As Tanya Krzywinska (2000: 26) points out, the film deploys inverted/perverted Christian imagery – 'Astaroth . . . crucified by the legs on an inverted cross . . . (his) open legs imply a sexual invitation on the cross of the S/M dungeon'. But the chilly, bleak tone suggests less of an investment in the divine than its commercial inspiration, *The Exorcist*. Moreover, the film's ambitions were partly curtailed by money running out. Verney's warning that 'the demons hate you . . . they're waiting for you' hints at a more epic finale than the film's anticlimactic denouement.

*Hellraiser* (Clive Barker, 1987) may seem to have a less direct connection to Crowley, but it is the British horror film which most embraces the logic of Sex Magick. The Cenobites, 'Demons to some, angels to others', offer extreme but potentially liberating experiences. Frank Cotton (Sean Chapman) is a Crowleyan nomad, exploring the 'further regions of experience', which take the form of spectacular sadomasochistic imagery. The 'cost' (or reward) is implicit in the box he acquires, a Rubik's Cube of self-endangering *jouissance* and Pandora's Box in one – 'What's your pleasure?' is the film's first line of dialogue. He's literally in pieces after his first night at Club Cenobite, but sister-in-law/lover Julia (Claire Higgins) is so besotted with him that she aids his reconstitution, picking up male victims to put flesh back on his bones. His pinned, flayed and scarified deities are after him, but it's hard to punish a true masochist – 'Je-sus wept!' he laughs ecstatically, licking his lips as the Cenobites' hooks pull him apart a second time. *Hellraiser* is a gift to 'transgression' buffs, but it is firmly conventional in its division of occult labour – it is the male again who is defined by knowledge and experience, while Julia is left to represent desire.

## Witchworld

> If we were to investigate all the strange rituals performed by women based on their so-called intuition, half the female population would be in asylums.
> Professor Norman Taylor (Peter Wyngarde), *Night of the Eagle*

There is a large body of (particularly feminist) writing devoted to female witches that extends beyond the limits of the horror film into literature, theatre, art and, of course, history. The witch has been studied as a focal point for the logic of misogyny (historical persecutions), as 'implacable enemy of the symbolic order' in the horror film (Creed 1993: 76), as representative of male anxiety (Russell 1984) and/or female power (Purkiss 1996: 8). In British cinema, the 'witch' movie falls roughly into two groups. The first deals with vengeful witches returning from the dead. Vanessa Whitlock (*Witchcraft*), Elizabeth Selwyn (*City of the Dead*), Lavinia Morley (*Curse of the Crimson Altar*), Camilla Yorke (*Satan's Slave*) and Dolores Hamilton (*Terror* (1978)) are all burned at the stake, and all but Camilla have bestowed a curse on the ancestors of their persecutors. Lavinia, we are told, was unfairly accused, but this is not a distinction that the film dwells on. The cinematic referent here is Italy – Mario Bava's *La Maschera del Demonio* (1960) and other vehicles for Barbara Steele, who plays Lavinia – but there is one feature which sets these British witches apart from Steele's all-powerful Asa. Sharon Russell notes how often the witch narrative retains the 'male as the dominant, controlling the witch' (1984: 118). In *Curse of the Crimson Altar* Lavinia is ostensibly controlling her ancestor (Christopher Lee) and he seems to be possessed by her in the final scene. But the structure of the film implies the opposite: it is Lee's obsession which has brought her back and she is an insubstantial figure without him. *Satan's Slave* is more blatant – Camilla is barely represented at all, and the cult surrounding her is firmly under the control of Alexander Yorke (Michael Gough). He wears a goat-headed mask to remind us that Satanism is best left to the boys, and sacrifices various family members in his efforts to resurrect his ancestor. The film climaxes with the sacrifice of heroine Candice Glendenning, but one infers that Camilla will be just as much an instrument of Alexander's Satanic authority.

The second group of films deals with a cult or community consisting of or led by women. *Night of the Eagle*, *The Witches* and *Virgin Witch* each uncovers a 'secret matriarchy' within a nominally masculine space in which male authority has, in fact, been overthrown. While Hempnell Medical College (*Eagle*) is ostensibly a stage for Professor Norman Taylor (Peter Wyngarde) to flex his intellectual muscles, it is in fact ruled by 'middle aged Medusa(s)' – jealous faculty wives and, in particular, the formidable Flora (Margaret Johnston), doubly threatening because she is both academic and competitive wife. This mixture of authority and thwarted ambition finds an outlet in practical voodoo, designed to inhibit Norman's career trajectory and, by the end, his lifespan. Her counterpart in *The Witches* is another scholar, the wealthy Stephanie Bax (Kay Walsh) who is ostensibly researching an essay on witchcraft as a hobby. Her brother Alan (Alec McCowen) is an almost parodic embodiment of disempowered masculinity, a failed would-be priest in a town which no longer has a church. Alan wears a minister's collar 'for security' and listens to tapes of the organ from Salisbury Cathedral – the symbols of male authority can only be simulated, the clerical equivalent of playing with model trains. Wychworld (*Virgin Witch*) is owned by the wealthy Gerald, the nominal head of a 'white' magical cult. But Gerald is as ill-equipped for the role of mystic *roué* as Alan is to join the cloth. His academic 'authority' compromises him here – he has 'the knowledge but not the power' and is 'High Priest in name only'. Witches are *born*, not *made*, in *Virgin Witch* – and born *female* – and magic is embodied by svelte lesbian photographer Sybil (Patricia Haines) and ambitious bad-twin Chris (Ann Michelle).

According to Pennethorne Hughes (1952/1965: 216), in his testy history of witchcraft, contemporary magical practice is:

> the play of lonely minds, miserably seeking power . . . the pre-occupation of the over-sophisticated and the pervert. It germinates away in suburban covens and among the incense-ridden flats of the wealthy irreconcilables of every society.[11]

This is exactly the conception of witchcraft promoted by *Night of the Eagle* and *Virgin Witch*. Witchcraft is synonymous with bitchcraft, the province of bitter, over-ambitious women. Jeremy Dyson refutes any charge of misogyny against *Eagle*, but he is strangely confident that Flora's unexplained limp 'says so much about (her) twisted nature' (1997: 222). Each witch finds a younger nemesis. Tansy (Janet Blair), in *Night of the Eagle*, is firmly on the side of the boys – casting counter-spells to protect husband Norman and tutored in the arts by an (unseen) Jamaican warlock. 'A *male* witch', scoffs Norman, as though it is the most emasculating image he can think of, but it aids the film's project to give Tansy a male initiator. Chris, in *Virgin Witch*, is the bad half of two twins lured to Wychworld for a modelling assignment – 'I'm a career girl . . . I don't want to be tied down', she tells Sybil, who has a more than professional interest in her. Chris allows herself to be seduced, but her sights are set on the role of high priestess – she, too, has natural powers – and she deploys some impromptu voodoo to supplant Sybil. Good sister Betty (Vicky Michelle) is up for initiation but, tellingly, 'saved' by abruptly losing her virginity to her charmless boyfriend. Both films pursue fairly conservative agendas, but some of the pleasures they offer suggest that they have fallen under a spell of their own – Chris's empowerment through witchcraft (an extension of a permissive appetite for new experiences) and Norman's boorish scepticism dissolving before Flora's arcane powers.

*The Witches* is conspicuously absent from most accounts of British horror, and in some ways one can see why. It's rather flatly made until its climactic rituals, and Joan Fontaine's performance seems designed to act as an audience repellant. With her disconcerting Thatcher bouffant and constipated demeanour, her Gwen Mayfield is a distinctly unappealing figure – when she has a breakdown midway through the film, at least her hair relaxes a little. But this only helps to showcase Kay Walsh's magnificent performance as Stephanie – she is, quite simply, the best witch in British cinema. Gwen has had bad experiences with witchdoctors and tribal uprisings at an African mission school, and sets out to rebuild her life as a teacher in the village school at Heddaby. In contrast to Stephanie, Gwen represents hysteria and repression, Stephanie uses her scholarly credentials to accumulate arcane knowledge. 'It's a sex thing deep down,' she tells Gwen disingenuously about contemporary witchcraft, 'mostly women go in for it – *older* women.' At another level, however, she is dropping some confidential hints. Stephanie has discovered the cruel paradox of the ageing process – the accumulation of true knowledge runs parallel with time's corruption of the body and its attendant faculties. Her solution is to possess the 'skin' of local girl Linda – a child 'has no value at all', whereas 'if I could live a second lifetime, just another fifty years . . .'. This motif of the old preying on the young becomes more insistent in British horror in the late 1960s and early 1970s in films like *The Sorcerers* (Michael Reeves, 1967), *Countess Dracula* (Peter Sasdy, 1970) and *Frightmare* (Pete Walker, 1974). But there is an energy and vitality about Stephanie that sets her apart from the often grotesque and pathetic 'bad parent' figures who followed her. In addition, the wording of her spell suggests that this isn't *all* about intellectual accumulation:

> Grow me a gown with golden down
> Cut me a robe from toe to lobe
> Give me a skin for dancing in!

In an earlier scene, Linda sulks when she is cast as Galileo in the school pageant. Gwen is amused by her reluctance to drag up and helpfully explains the gendering of history to her – 'There are hardly any girl parts because hardly any girls invented anything.' It is, of course, Gwen's role to keep things that way, to ensure that Linda herself isn't 'played' by a woman (Stephanie) who can make her mark on history. Unlike Sybil or Flora, magic for Stephanie is a 'science' not a religion (she likens her power to an atom bomb), as much a matter of will as for her satanic male counterparts.

## Occult heritage

> The earth has to have sacrifice.
>
>               Alain Demonfaucon (Emlyn Williams), *Eye of the Devil*

In *Quatermass and the Pit* (Roy Ward Baker, 1967) it transpires that human culture (in particular its collective image of the demonic) was implanted by visiting Martians during Earth's pre-history. The local specificity of the film (and Nigel Kneale's TV series which preceded it) suggests that for 'Earth' we might read 'Britain' – an occulted (hidden) Britain which returns in phantasmatic form. This link between national identity and the occult is revisited in the 1960s and early 1970s through the conflict between Christianity and various 'old' religions which predate it. There are two determinants here. First, the growing popular interest in paganism was partly bound up with uncovering a more 'authentic' national identity and culture, what Krzywinska calls a 'psycho-geography of Britain in which the landscape and cultural practices of the land were imbued with pre-Christian paganism' (2000: 74). Second, the conflict between 'old' and 'new' faiths was a way of talking about the relationship between the upheavals of the late 1960s – the emergence of youth and 'counter' cultures, permissiveness, the possibility of revolution – and the backlash of the 1970s represented, in particular, by the 'law and order' agenda of the new Heath government. In *Cry of the Banshee*, *Blood on Satan's Claw* and *The Wicker Man* we find a puritanical male authority figure (a magistrate, a judge, a policeman, respectively) pitted against a Dionysian cult, and losing in two cases out of the three. Apart from *The Wicker Man*, which works slightly differently, the films hedge their bets about which horse to back – they seem as fearful of orgiastic abandon as they are of repressive authority. *Banshee* tries to have it both ways. The vengeful Oona dies, insisting that 'hatred and revenge brought us nothing' and advising her followers to 'find back your ways of peace'. But her avenging demon (Patrick Mower) is not so easily deterred and dispatches both good and bad members of the Whitman family with undiscriminating efficiency.

   *Blood on Satan's Claw* is an intoxicating, if not entirely coherent, blend of rural horror, generational conflict and *fin de siècle* bleakness. David Taylor's excellent retrospective reveals that the film was very much a product of conflicting agendas. For the writer Robert Wynne-Simmons, the film was about 'the inherent evil of children and the overt sexuality of evil' (Taylor 1996: 86), but also about 'the stamping out of the old religions . . . by an atheistic belief that all sorts of things must be blocked out of the mind . . . a dogged enlightenment' (ibid.: 88). For the former, Wynne-Simmons had in mind such contemporary referents as Altamont,

*Figure 16*  Occult heritage: hairy-eyebrowed cult leader Linda Hayden addresses her
   flower children in *Blood on Satan's Claw* (1970).

the Manson cult, and the 11-year-old killer Mary Bell, which suggests a reaction against the 'fallout' of the 1960s. But Patrick Wymark's Judge (he has no other name) is clearly a backlash figure, even after Tigon attempted to make him more conventionally heroic – the film's resurrected demon, according to Wynne-Simmons, 'was somehow more "alive" than the Patrick Wymark character, whose viewpoint is essentially a dead one' (ibid.: 88). Add to this the fact that the script was initially constructed as a portmanteau of tales only linked by their period and setting and it is little wonder that the film is such a fascinating mess.

*Satan's Claw* has another apparent reference point, Margaret Murray's *The Witch-Cult in Western Europe* (1921). Murray argued that witchcraft *did* exist and was the remnants of a matriarchal fertility cult. This cult worshipped a hairy, horned god and engaged in ritual sex with him. Purkiss notes that Murray's book reinvents the chief deity as a male, but also manages to 'instal women as active worshippers and desiring subjects' (1996: 37). *Satan's Claw* is about the return of such a horned god and of his worship by a female-led cult, both set against the onset of the Enlightenment. As the film opens, the remains of this creature are uncovered in a ploughed field – a skull, an eyeball, some fur, later, a claw. In the village, the children have turned to cruel 'games' which soon turn into sacrifices and other rituals. This cult is led by Lolita-from-Hell Angel (Linda Hayden), who grows hairier as the cult (and its deity) gets stronger and youthful hormones run amok. The motif of children-on-the-turn can also be found in films like *Taste the Blood of Dracula* (Peter Sasdy, 1970) and *Hands of the Ripper* (Peter Sasdy, 1971), but in *Satan's Claw* their violence is turned against each other rather than on literal or figurative parents. They are shown to be ecstatically nihilistic rather than directly engaged in generational struggle, as though the film is keen to deter any potential identification with them.

On the other side stands the Judge, initially sceptical – 'witchcraft is dead and discredited' – but gradually persuaded by events in the village. Once convinced, however, his strategy is to allow things to get worse before acting:

> I shall return when the time is right. But you must have patience. Even while people die, only thus can the whole evil die. You must let it grow.

When he finally returns, it is with the warning that 'I shall use undreamed of measures.' The film is being unusually eloquent here about the genre's negotiation of repression and the permissive: establish the existence of 'evil', allow it to grow and thus provide a certain amount of pleasure for the audience, and then come down hard in a violent climax partly facilitated by giving the forces of anarchy a limited licence. But it arguably speaks also to the backlash of the 1970s – for the Festival of Light, Mary Whitehouse, Conservative politicians and all the others for whom 'permissiveness' was an evil which had been allowed to spread much too far. 'Only the most strict discipline will save us', insists the Judge, unmoved by the caveat that 'innocent folk may be hurt'. The law acts only for its own preservation rather than claiming to represent an imagined 'public'. Wynne-Simmons's original script apparently ended with a massacre, making the planned climax sound not dissimilar to *Night of the Living Dead* (George Romero, 1968). Instead, the film opts for a more conventional struggle between Wymark and the reconstituted demon – the restoration of the phallic is represented through the penetration of both Angel (with a pitchfork by an angry mob) and the sexually ambiguous 'god' (with a crucifix-sword).

Some of the themes and concerns of *The Wicker Man* are anticipated by a film which stands apart from the other British occult films of the late 1960s, *Eye of the Devil*. *Eye*, too, deals with regenerative sacrifice and crop failure, pagan practices in a seemingly isolated community and the responsibilities of a feudal 'Lord'. Marquis Phillipe Demonfaucon (David Niven) must return to the town of Bellenac when the vineyards fail – it is his responsibility to be sacrificed (shot with an arrow) in order to make them fruitful again. This failure is implicitly linked to the refusal of Phillipe's father Alain (Emlyn Williams) to be sacrificed when it was his time – all other male heads of the family have traditionally given up their lives for the land. This pagan community hides behind Christian trappings – the church is a 'fortress of heresy' presided over by Father Dominic, the ritual of twelve men (the apostles) dancing around the one (Christ) a disguise for a ritual which existed 'long before Christianity' in which the twelve dancers will invoke the appearance of the Old God (the One) through the sacrifice of the Lord. But the film implies a blurring of old and new religions – Phillipe is heavy-handedly symbolized as a dove in the film's visual imagery and he insists that 'it is our belief in something that makes that thing, for a moment or forever, divine'. *Eye* is a mixture of generic ingredients. First, its uncovering of 'old' religions clearly predates *The Wicker Man*, but it is less concerned with getting details right – it draws heavily on conventional representations of 'black magic' (hooded figures, references to the black mass, burning crosses, candles-a-go-go). Second, the figure of Catherine (Deborah Kerr) links the film to those Hollywood thriller-melodramas of the 1940s (*Rebecca* (1940), *Suspicion* (1941), *Secret Beyond the Door* (1948)) in which a female protagonist investigates her husband's dark secret – she is even slipped a diabolical, milky-looking drink (containing belladonna) in one scene. It is through Catherine that we learn the secrets of Bellenac and the fate of the Demonfaucon men, and it is her (unsuccessful) mission to save Phillipe. Third, this is a film concerned with another notion of sacrifice, that which cohabits with terms like duty and responsibility – 'I have a great responsibility here', explains Phillipe, 'and it can't be shared'. While he is nominally French, at another level he clearly isn't – Niven is the model of British masculine stoicism, and another example of an occulted national identity. He must restore male responsibility and honour as well as the crops and compensate for the failure of his father. The film ends with his young son Jacques accepting this duty as father-to-son heritage.

*The Wicker Man* dispenses with so many of the dynamics of the horror film that it starts to resemble a pagan musical with an equal opportunities take on Christianity and the 'old gods'. Lord Summerisle declares the Christian God dead – 'Can't complain. He had his chance and, in modern parlance, blew it' – and himself 'a heathen . . . but not, I hope, an unenlightened one'; nor is he an unpragmatic one. As in *The Witches* and *Eye of the Devil*, it is the aristocracy who really keep the old religions going, even if all three films depict a 'whole community' practice. This isn't just a preservation of nature, but (benign) feudalism too. The story takes place on an island off the coast of Scotland, bought by Summerisle's 'free-thinking' grandfather in the nineteenth century. This pagan revival begins as a matter of expediency, as a way of encouraging the islanders to make the land fruitful again, exploiting the volcanic soil and warm Gulf Stream. But this culture has become bigger than its ostensible patron. When the crops fail, Summerisle (like Phillipe) puts his faith in the regenerative potential of human sacrifice, but (unlike Phillipe) he is able to find a substitute 'king'.

This substitute sacrifice is seeker-victim Sergeant Howie (Edward Woodward), a mainland policeman so joylessly puritanical that the film effortlessly sets him up as the shocked audience for explicit maypole songs, school lessons about phallic symbols, fertility dances and a song-of-seduction from landlord's daughter Britt Eckland.[12] Censorious bores are a mainstay of early 1970s sexploitation, too, mischievously exposed to 'obscenity' at every possible opportunity, and this film initially works in a similar way. There is something rather *Health and Efficiency* about most of these rituals (naked girls jumping over bonfires in soft focus), but it is enough to convince Howie that 'degeneracy' and 'corruption of the young' lurk around every corner. Unfortunately for him, there is a rather large Wicker Man lurking around the corner, too. Lured to the island in search of a 'missing' girl, Howie is authority figure (he represents 'the power of a king'), virgin and fool – he is dressed as Mr Punch as they lead him to his fiery death. How far are we supposed to go in accepting Howie as fair game for the flames? The film seems designed to accommodate a range of positions and readings, just as *Eye* blurs Christian and pagan 'faith' – the result of Howie's sacrifice (Christian resurrection, renewal of the crops) will occur outside of the film's narrative and is up for interpretative grabs. But I am not sure that, as Danny Peary (1983: 166) argues, 'both Christianity and paganism are shown to be impotent' – the latter is offered as much more of a spectacle and experience than the former, and Summerisle is a much more eloquent figure than the blustering Howie.

*The Wicker Man* – with its refusal of Judaeo-Christian dualism and its ethnographic approach to magical practices – seems to mark a crisis point for the traditional supernatural film, except for two important considerations. First, the film had no influence whatsoever on what was left of the British horror film and stands outside of any of its dominant traditions. Second, a much more influential (and commercially successful) film made across the Atlantic, namely *The Exorcist*, confirmed that 'popular culture needs and uses the medieval rendition of the supernatural to spice up the banality of the daily grind' (Krzywinska 2000: 31) But it was to take more than pentagrams, kinky ritual sex and horned demons to do the spicing up – the barnstorming Pazuzu, with his/her creative bad language, projectile vomiting and penchant for blasphemous self-abuse seemed also to be rooted *in* the daily grind, in contrast to Dennis Wheatley's drawing rooms and Hammer and Tigon's historical no-time-in-particular. British sex films were well established by the early 1970s and the occult was no longer necessary to justify nudity and sex. *The Wicker Man* suggested that the horror genre was a limited arena for exploring magic-as-counterculture; and the dispassionate tone of *To the Devil a Daughter* confirmed that British horror could no longer summon up the Manichean fervour of its major studio rivals. Recession-hit 1970s Britain was looking so small that surely the Antichrist would have more important places to visit (give or take a brief sojourn in *The Omen*). By the mid-1970s, British horror in general was struggling commercially and scarcely able to compete with the apocalyptic grandeur of Hollywood demons and their offspring. But topicality isn't everything, and perhaps it is appropriate that British occult films should be confined to cult appeal, like arcane and slightly dusty grimoires that insist on being opened.

*I would like to thank Tanya Krzywinska for her advice and expertise while I was researching and writing this essay.*

## Notes

1 These scenes are from *Night of the Demon*, *The Devil Rides Out* and *Blood on Satan's Claw*, respectively.
2 Lewton produced 'B' movies at RKO in the 1940s – his best-known films include *Cat People* (Jacques Tourneur, 1942) and *I Walked with a Zombie* (Tourneur, 1943).
3 There had been cinematic 'Crowleys' elsewhere, of which the most memorable is Boris Karloff's Hjalmar Poelzig in *The Black Cat* (Edgar Ulmer, US 1935).
4 1976 saw the release of *Satan's Slave* and the final Hammer film, *To the Devil a Daughter*. There are a couple of strays. *Terror* (Norman J. Warren, 1978) includes a vengeful witch as part of its messy attempt to be a British *Suspiria* (Dario Argento, Italy 1977), and *Hellraiser*, with its Cenobites and magic(k)al box, belongs to a different time in the genre's history.
5 The books encompassed astrology and fortune-telling alongside Arthur Lyons's *Satan Wants You* and Pauwel and Berger's *The Morning of the Magicians*, exploring such themes as 'man's evolution towards some kind of mutant superman'.
6 As Tanya Krzywinska (2000) explains, the revival of paganism as an alternative to Christianity began in the nineteenth century with the formation of several magic(k)al societies, but it is not until the 1960s that this had a wider popular impact.
7 The Connolly and *I.T.* quotes are both from the inside cover blurb of Symonds's *The Great Beast*.
8 Count Sinistre (Hubert Noel) in *Devils of Darkness* (Lance Comfort, 1965) combines both figures – aristocratic vampire-seducer and necromantic cult leader.
9 Oscar Wilde, that is. Harry Benshoff notes the equation between homosexuality and 'Demonic Possession' in a 1930s *Scribners Magazine* article (1997: 103).

10  Karswell, Mocata, Father Michael (*To the Devil a Daughter*) and Frank (*Hellraiser*) are all destroyed by the deities they invoke rather than by the forces of 'good'.

11  In *Devils of Darkness*, Count Sinistre recruits his coven mainly from the beatnik women who hang out at the bohemian Odd Spot.

12  Structurally, his investigative role parallels Catherine's in *Eye of the Devil*.

## References

Benshoff, H.M. (1997) *Monsters in the Closet: Homosexuality and the Horror Film*, Manchester and New York: Manchester University Press.

Boot, A. (1996) *Fragments of Fear*, London and San Francisco: Creation.

Bourne, S. (1996) *Brief Encounters: Lesbians and Gays in British Cinema 1930–1971*, London: Cassell.

Creed, B. (1993) *The Monstrous-Feminine: Film, Feminism, Psychoanalysis*, London and New York: Routledge.

Crowley, A. (1929/1974) *Moonchild*, London: Sphere.

Dyson, J. (1997) *Bright Darkness: The Lost Art of the Supernatural Horror Film*, London and Washington: Cassell.

Everson, W.K. (1974) *Classics of the Horror Film*, Secaucus, NJ: Citadel.

Hughes, P. (1952/1965) *Witchcraft*, Harmondsworth: Penguin.

Hunt, L. (1996) '*Witchfinder General*' in Black, A. (ed.) *Necronomicon: Book One*, London: Creation, 123–130.

Hunt, L. (1998) *British Low Culture: From Safari Suits to Sexploitation*, London and New York: Routledge.

Hutchings, P. (1993) *Hammer and Beyond: The British Horror Film*, Manchester and New York: Manchester University Press.

Krzywinska, T. (2000) *A Skin for Dancing In: Possession, Witchcraft and Voodoo in Film*, London: Flicks Books.

Newman, K. (ed.) (1996) *The BFI Companion to Horror*, London: British Film Institute/Cassell.

Parry, M. (ed.) (1974) *The 1st Mayflower Book of Black Magic Stories*, London: Mayflower.

Peary, D. (1983) *Cult Movies 2*, London: Vermilion.

Prothero, D. (1997) 'O for Occult', *Sight and Sound* 7, 8: 24–6.

Purkiss, D. (1996) *The Witch in History: Early Modern and Twentieth Century Representations*, London and New York: Routledge.

Russell, S. (1984) 'The witch in film: myth and reality' in Grant, B.K. (ed.) *Planks of Reason: Essays on the Horror Film*, Metuchen, NJ, and London: Scarecrow Press, 113–25.

Symonds, J. (1951/1973) *The Great Beast: The Life of Aleister Crowley*, London: Rider and Co. 1973 edition, London: Mayflower.

Taylor, D. (1996) 'Don't overact with your fingers! The making of *Blood on Satan's Claw*' in Jaworzyn, S. (ed.) *Shock: The Essential Guide to Exploitation Cinema*, London: Titan.

Wheatley, D. (1934/1986) *The Devil Rides Out*, London: Arrow.

Wollen, P. (1995) 'Possession', *Sight and Sound* 5, 9: 20–3.

# 8   The old dark house: the architecture of ambiguity in *The Turn of the Screw* and *The Innocents*

*John C. Tibbetts*

No sooner has she moved into her rooms at Bly House in the opening pages of Henry James's *The Turn of the Screw*, than the new governess immediately notices 'a sound or two, less natural and not without but within'. At first she dismisses these slight disturbances. '[I]t is only in the light, or the gloom, I should rather say, of other and subsequent matters that they now come back to me' (James, 1948: 445).[1]

Ever since the ghost of Hamlet's father stalked the battlements of Elsinore castle, the stock in trade of horror romanticism has consisted of the inhabitants, properties and atmosphere of the haunted house. Without the haunted house, says Eino Railo (1927: 7), 'the whole fabric of romance would be bereft of its foundation and would lose its predominant atmosphere'. These literary 'old dark houses' include such archetypal edifices as Prince Manfred's castle in Horace Walpole's *Castle of Otranto* (1764); the strange country house in Clara Reeve's *The Old English Baron* (1778); Montoni's mountain fortress in Ann Radcliffe's *The Mysteries of Udolpho* (1794); Ambrosio's Capuchin monastery in Matthew Lewis's *The Monk* (1796); the Mettingen estate in Charles Brockden Brown's *Wieland* (1798); Mr Vileny's family home in Jane Austen's *Northanger Abbey* (1818); Roderick Usher's bog-engulfed mansion in Edgar Allan Poe's in *The Fall of the House of Usher* (1839); the infernally possessed house in Edward Bulwer-Lytton's short story 'The Haunted and the Haunters' (1859); the legend-haunted ancestral Pyncheon estate in Nathaniel Hawthorne's *House of the Seven Gables* (1851); the vampire-infested Carfax Abbey in Bram Stoker's *Dracula* (1897); the *Doppelganger*-inhabited New York town house in Henry James's *The Jolly Corner* (1908); the house that serves as a gateway to the cosmos in William Hope Hodgson's *The House on the Borderland* (1908); the deranged Hill House in Shirley Jackson's *The Haunting of Hill House* (1959); and the isolated, malevolent Overlook Hotel in Stephen King's *The Shining* (1977).

Usually there is a specific room, or area, that is the source of the most intense ghosting. It might be the attic from which unholy shrieks emanate in Brönte's *Jane Eyre* (1847); or the locked and bolted upstairs room in J.B. Priestley's *Benighted* (1927); or the secret crypt in Richard Matheson's *Hell House* (1971). And what spectral doings enliven these dreadful places! Thin-sheeted phantoms slip noiselessly through the corridors, half-seen forms shamble down the stairs, a gigantic armoured man stalks the galleries, a wall portrait drips real blood, eldritch hands slip the latch. . . . Add the natural elements to this conspiracy of dread – sudden gusts of wind that extinguish the fleeing heroine's candle, streaks of lightning that fitfully illuminate the horrors emerging from under the bed, and cracks of thunder that punctuate the wails of lost souls – and the recipe for terror is complete.

Dramatists and then film-makers quickly adopted the 'old dark house' formula for popular consumption. Just a few of the classic plays include Matthew Lewis's *Castle Spectre* (1797), G.K. Chesterton's *Magic* (1913), George M. Cohan's *Seven Keys to Baldpate* (1913), and Mary Roberts Rinehart's *The Bat* (1920). From Hollywood came a plethora of hauntings, from silent films like D.W. Griffith's *One Exciting Night* (1923) and Paul Leni's *The Cat and the Canary* (1927) to modern classics like Robert Wise's *The Haunting* (1965).

British haunted-house thrillers have come in fits and starts, beginning in the 1930s with a few Hollywood-style Gothics like *The Ghoul* (1933), whose second half features Boris Karloff as an 'undead' creature stalking a house full of heirs to a fortune, and a cycle of Tod Slaughter Guignol pictures. *Dead of Night* (1945), an anthology film with several sequences set in disturbed houses, promised great things, but that potential was not realized until the 1960s and later, with films like Freddie Francis's *Nightmare* (1964), about attempts to drive a woman insane (à la *Gaslight*) in an old mansion; William Castle's *The Old Dark House* (1963), a luridly comic remake of Priestley's *Benighted*; Roger Corman's *The Masque of the Red Death* (1964), based on Poe's short story about Prince Prospero's plague-ravaged castle; David Greene's *The Shuttered Room* (1967), adapted from H.P. Lovecraft's tale of the maniacal horrors in a New England house; John Hough's *The Legend of Hell House* (1973), adapted from Richard Matheson's novel *Hell House* (which was more or less an updating of Bulwer-Lytton's *The Haunted and the Haunters*); and Pete Walker's *House of the Long Shadows* (1982), a satirical remake of *Seven Keys to Baldpate*.[2]

## What was it?

Occupying a special niche in the pantheon of old dark houses is Bly House, in Henry James's novella, *The Turn of the Screw* (1898). It has aroused more controversy and baffled more readers than perhaps any ghostly tale ever written. Each of its incarnations – as novel, stage play (William Archibald's dramatization, *The Innocents*, 1950), and film (Jack Clayton's *The Innocents*, 1961) – succeeds on its own terms in creating a measure of ambiguity regarding the nature and reality of the haunters and the haunted.[3]

From their Gothic beginnings, the spooks that haunted old dark houses played a game with their readers. Did they vanish in mid-air? Or did they just use a secret trap door? Were they a supernatural manifestation, or a cheap stage trick? They were the Penns and Tellers of their day, magicians simultaneously revealing and concealing their repertory of effects. The plots of the Gothic novels straddled the line between horror and hoax. 'To attain this end,' asserted Clara Reeve, 'there is required a sufficient degree of the marvellous to excite the attention; enough of the manners of real life, to give an air of probability to the work; and enough of the pathetic, to engage the heart in its behalf' (quoted in Varma, 1957: 78). Thus in Brown's *Wieland*, the spectral voices that drive Theodore Wieland to slaughter his family are apparently not a ghostly possession at all, but the vocal suggestions of a diabolical ventriloquist, Carwin. On the other hand, the possibility of supernatural agency is not entirely ruled out.

No one was more notorious for dashing the cold water of reason on ghostly thrills than Ann Radcliffe. After hundreds of pages, *The Mysteries of Udolpho* reveals that the unearthly music in the haunted castle issues not from a ghost but from a conscience-stricken nun with a lurid past; the mysterious voices and the gliding phantom figure belong to an escaped prisoner; and the horror behind the Black Veil is not a decaying corpse but a wax effigy. As ludicrous a 'cheat' as this may seem, there was no denying that Radcliffe had succeeded in overturning our rational defences, if only for a moment. As Edith Birkhead (1963: 51) puts it, '[Radcliffe] deliberately excites trembling apprehensions in order that she may show how absurd they are.'[4] The strange manifestations in Bulwer-Lytton's 'The Haunted and the Haunters' reveal the author's preoccupation with psychic phenomena such as telekinesis, and his speculations that abnormal psychological states might induce – or be stimulated by – preternatural conditions. Bulwer-Lytton's theory that what is labelled 'super-natural' may simply be something in the laws of nature of which we have been hitherto ignorant is echoed in G.K. Chesterton's play, *Magic*. A magician known only as 'the Stranger' produces an illusion – the transformation of a light from red to blue, then back again to red – so inexplicable that, of course, everyone demands a 'natural' explanation. At first he confesses it is indeed an act of magic. But, in the face of his auditors' incredulity, he finally offers a rational solution. 'You cannot think how that trick could be done naturally,' he says. 'I alone found out how it could be done – after I had done it by magic' (Chesterton, 1914: 71–2). Cruelly, Chesterton never discloses what this 'natural' explanation is; he leaves us suspended between rational causes and supernatural possibilities.

Modern 'old dark house' novels, like Jackson's *The Haunting of Hill House* and King's *The Shining*, are sophisticated updates of their predecessors. They fix most – but not all – of the blame for their catalogues of horrors on the psychologically unstable characters of Eleanor Vance and Jack Torrance respectively, who serve as energy sources for the houses' engines of malevolence and dread. Jack's visions cannot be dismissed entirely as hallucinations, because his young son, Danny, who possesses the psychic gift of 'the shining', also perceives them. Similarly, Eleanor is indeed a disturbed and damaged character because of her loneliness, frustration and hidden hate; yet it is not she alone who is affected by the house. Clearly, all these writers are leaving the door to the dungeon open, as it were. They know that too much haste to 'cover up' the supernatural with science and logic and, conversely, to dismiss science and logic entirely for the sake of the supernatural is too simplistic and too dangerous. Jack's wife and son survive their ordeal because they never lose their capacity for logic while still accepting the possibility of the ghostly. As John Montague, the psychic investigator in *The Haunting of Hill House*, sums it up: 'The menace of the supernatural is that it attacks where modern minds are weakest, where we have abandoned our protective armour of superstition and have no substitute defence' (Jackson, 1959: 139–40).

## Henry James's *The Turn of the Screw* (1898)

No novel – and its subsequent play and film versions – has had more ink spilled over the precise nature of its terrors than Henry James's *The Turn of the Screw*. James himself was a monument to personal and professional ambiguity and ambivalence. His citizenship, either American or British, his sexual identity, his densely textured prose – all resist strict categorization. In short, he was born to write this story.

While visiting Edward White Benson, archbishop of Canterbury, in Addington Park on the evening of 8 January 1895, James lamented that all the good ghost stories seemed to have been told. The archbishop then remembered a story about some dead servants and the children they haunted. 'The servants, wicked and depraved, corrupt and deprave the children,' James wrote in his notebook four days later, '. . . so that the children may destroy themselves, lose themselves, by responding, by getting into their power' (Edel, 1948: 425–6). Two years later, James dictated his 'fantastic fiction', *The Turn of the Screw*, to his amanuensis, W. McAlpine.

The unnamed governess's first-person narrative begins with her arrival on a beautiful June day in the 1850s at the country estate of Bly. Two children, Flora and her older brother, ten-year-old Miles (who at that point is away at school) are assigned to her care. After a few days, the first disturbing note in an otherwise peaceful scene is struck when a letter arrives revealing that Miles has been dismissed from school. The governess immediately wonders if Miles has 'contaminated', or 'corrupted' the other children, but on meeting the boy she finds in him 'something divine', responding with a sort of 'passion of tenderness for him' (James 1948: 452). However, one afternoon, a disturbing incident breaks the summer serenity. She suffers a 'bewilderment of vision', seeing the figure of a man atop the tower of the house. Shortly afterward she encounters two more unexpected apparitions – the same stranger peering at her through the window, and the form of a woman in black standing in the garden. Although the children refuse to admit it, the governess is convinced that they too see the apparitions. After hearing the governess's descriptions of the two figures, the housekeeper, Mrs Grose, reveals that they resemble the former valet, Peter Quint, and the previous governess, Miss Jessel, who had both died a year before. Jessel had been of a good family, but she had been somehow corrupted by Quint, a drunken villain. Her misadventure had forced her into committing suicide.

As the summer wears into autumn, the children continue to be models of exemplary behaviour. The governess, though, is increasingly distraught. More appearances by Jessel (seen across the pond, in the stairwell, at a writing desk) and Quint (peering through the window again) have convinced her that they are pursuing some sort of unholy communion with Miles and Flora. The governess grows obsessively protective and presses the children more and more to admit their complicity and appreciate their danger. Realizing that she has lost control over them, she feels that she has no other recourse but to draft a letter explaining the situation to the children's uncle. The letter disappears, and the governess decides she has no choice but to send Flora and Mrs Grose away to the uncle, while she will remain behind in an attempt to talk things out with Miles. Resentful of the governess's obsessive control, Flora denounces her. That night, Miles, under pressure, admits that he had been dismissed from school for 'saying things' and that he had stolen the letter intended for his uncle. When she once again sees Peter Quint's face at the window, the governess tries to shield Miles from the sight. 'It was like fighting with a demon for a human soul,' she states. Terrified at her hysteria, Miles finally asks, 'It's *he*?' And an instant later he shouts, 'Peter Quint – you devil!' (James, 1948: 549–50). He sinks back, dead, into the governess's arms.

What, exactly, *has* happened? What transpired in the past between Quint and Jessel? Were the children involved? If so, were they the 'innocents' they first seemed to the governess, or willing go-betweens? Worse, were they sexually abused by Quint and Jessel, and are they now somehow re-enacting those activities? Is the governess protecting them from real evil, or is she subjecting them to her own obsessive agendas? Is she sexually repressed, and transferring her fantasies onto Miles? And finally, the central question which arises from all this – are the ghosts real or just figments of her imagination?

Particularly striking about James's novella is the contrast between the governess's increasingly possessive, even hysterical behaviour, and the consistent, placid sweetness of the children. At first, obviously enamoured of her employer, whom she is bent on pleasing, she is the very model of gentility and decorum at Bly. She even displays a moment of wry humour when she wonders if Bly contains a 'secret' – 'a mystery of Udolpho or an insane, an unmentionable relative kept in unsuspected confinement (ibid.: 457). But as time wears on she loses her equilibrium and grows increasingly possessive of the children. Just what threat she thinks they face is never made clear. All she can say is that the spirits want 'to get hold' of the children to 'ply them with that evil' (ibid.: 498). Accordingly, she regards the liveliness and secretiveness of the children not as natural behaviour, but as sinister and provocative collusions with Jessel and Quint. She construes Miles's declaration that he is a boy who does not want to be cooped up with females as an act of defiance. Further defied by Flora, who stoutly denies that she sees the apparitions, the governess falls into a hysterical faint. Eventually, she begins to doubt the children's innocence and insists to Mrs Grose that they have seen 'things terrible and unguessable' (ibid.: 504). Her attitude frightens the children, and they plead to be taken away from her. Certainly a root cause of the governess's emotional turmoil is her transfer onto Miles of her hopeless infatuation with her employer. She repeatedly expresses her pleasure when he calls her 'my dear', and there are numerous descriptions of hugs and kisses. In one startling scene, after mockingly telling her to think of him as 'bad', Miles kisses her. 'I met his kiss,' she says to herself, 'and I had to make, while I folded him for a minute in my arms, the most stupendous effort not to cry' (ibid.: 496). By contrast, because she perceives Flora as her rival for Miles's attention, she can now see only hideousness in the little girl: 'Her incomparable childish beauty had suddenly failed, had quite vanished . . . she was hideously hard; she had turned common and almost ugly' (ibid.: 529).

By now, we may well wonder, as have countless commentators and biographers since the book was published, whether there is any real ghosting here at all; perhaps all this turmoil is merely the result of the governess's own psychological and sexual hallucinations.[5] As James's biographer Leon Edel points out, the author himself expressed seemingly contradictory views on the matter. Originally, he had envisioned a tale of a haunting, pure and simple, whereas later, in the 1908 New York Edition revision, he altered the text so as to depict a ghostly possession *alleged* to have occurred, the credibility of which must be determined by the reader. 'The evidence left by James himself,' concludes Edel, 'is that he intended to make the story the record of the young governess' mind, as he did with other of his characters in his ghostly tales' (Edel, 1948: 429). Bly 'is filled not so much with the evil of the ghosts as with the terror of the governess, her wild suppositions and soothing self-consoling explanations' (ibid.: 204). They are, in the words of Howard Kerr (1972: 210), 'occult personifications of the metaphorical illuminations through which those characters . . . sometimes perceived reality'. Other commentators, particularly Edmund Wilson and Elizabeth MacAndrew, have pursued this interpretation at considerable length. According to this reading, the governess seems to be a good character, even a heroine, but is actually an evil, or at least destructive, woman. Quint and Jessel may be real for the governess, MacAndrew suggests, but problematical for everyone else, including the reader. The existence of evil and the ghostly is ultimately a matter of perception. 'It is [the governess] who is the intruder into the children's world,' argues MacAndrew (1979: 238), 'and the supernatural beings who enter it with her are projections of her guilty feelings.' In the end, however, we may simply have to accept that the essence of *The Turn of the Screw* is its very ambiguity on these matters. After all, as James himself put it: 'so long as the events are veiled the imagination will run riot and depict all sorts of horrors.' 'But as soon as the veil is lifted, all mystery disappears and with it the sense of terror' (quoted in Edel, 1969: 214).[6]

# Jack Clayton's *The Innocents* (1961)

Jack Clayton had directed only one major feature film, *Room at the Top* (1958), before taking on *The Turn of the Screw* in 1961. In subsequent films, such as *Our Mother's House* (1967), a strange drama about children who bury their dead mother on their property and try to continue their lives while communicating with her spirit, and *Something Wicked This Way Comes* (1983), an adaptation of Ray Bradbury's Gothic fantasy about an infernal carnival which invades a small Illinois town, he would further confirm his sensitivity to this sort of material.[7] For the screenplay, Clayton called upon William Archibald to adapt his own two-act play based on James's novella. This had premiered in New York at the Playhouse Theater on 1 February 1950. After consulting Harold Pinter and Nigel Kneale, two acknowledged masters of subtle terrors, Clayton turned to John Mortimer and Truman Capote for the final rewrites, although few of Mortimer's contributions seem to have survived to the final cut.

It is apparent from the detailed notes which Clayton kept during his preparations that he was primarily concerned that the film, like the novel and Archibald's play, should have a 'dual life' – on the one hand, the ghosts could be interpreted as projections on the part of the governess (here, as in the stage version, named Miss Giddens), and, on the other, 'there are the ghosts and they are after the children'.[8] Following James's own example, Clayton was careful not to box himself in on the issue of supernatural events versus psychological projections. On the one hand, he went on record as blaming Giddens's repressed sexual desire for the children's uncle – and perhaps, by extension, for Miles – for the disaster at Bly. 'She just sees him once, and he is like a god to her,' Clayton said in an interview. 'She would have left the house long before unless it was her love for him that held her there. Therefore anything that is repeated by the children, or any suggestions about what might have happened in the house before she arrived, would then be magnified, as was common for Victorian people to do' (Gow, 1974: 14). On the other hand, Clayton insisted that Giddens did indeed see ghosts – or at least was convinced she did. 'This is what I love about the story,' he said in an interview for *Show Magazine* (January 1962: 30).

> There is nothing black and white about it; it's full of question marks and possibilities. I don't want, you know, to say absolutely what the picture means. There should be an area of uncertainty; that's what I think James intended. I want the audience to exercise its intelligence.

Clayton hit upon an unusual method of scene dissolves to enhance this ambiguity. A telling example of this technique occurs when Giddens asks the housekeeper if the children have intimated anything about a ghost in the house. At that moment, Flora pokes her head out from behind the sofa and says, 'Know what, Miss Giddens?'

The image then dissolves into the next scene, a conversation between the governess and the housekeeper. But lingering right in the middle of the screen is the persistent image of the child's face. At other times, images of clouds, trees or rain appear in the brief seconds before one shot has entirely yielded to its successor. Clayton explains in the *Show Magazine* interview:

> *The Innocents* is completely mood-oriented and it gave me opportunities to explore this field, which I had never done before; to create, in those multiple dissolves, images which hang there, and have a meaning which applies both to the end of the last scene and the beginning of the next.

The inclusion of one scene, a contribution from screenwriter Truman Capote, might seem on the face of it to tilt the scales towards the definite conclusion that real ghosts inhabit Bly House. After seeing Jessel seated at the schoolroom desk, Giddens advances toward her. The figure vanishes, but a teardrop is left upon the desk. Giddens touches it: it is real. Capote later thought this a mistake: 'Up until then it wasn't clear whether the ghosts were real or in the governess's mind. But the tear was real, and that spoiled everything' (quoted in Svehla and Svehla, 1996: 141).

*Figure 17* Gothic classicism: Deborah Kerr wanders the old dark house in Jack Clayton's *The Innocents* (1961).

Even here, however, interpretations may vary. Events at Bly House are real enough for Giddens at least, and the physical presence of a teardrop merely confirms those perceptions, both visual and tactile. As far as the film viewer is concerned, why is the image of her finger touching the teardrop any more or less credible than the images of Quint and Jessel? For Clayton, the scene has only one purpose: to convey Giddens's growing anxieties about the ghosts:

> What would be the most terrifying thing for me? I might think I was having an hallucination, or that it was some trick of the light. But if I suddenly saw a tear mark on a piece of paper, I think it would really frighten me very much, as well as being very sad.
>
> (Gow, 1974: 14)

As for the second consideration, regarding the process of adaptation, Clayton's notes reveal his reservations about William Archibald's first screenplay attempt. It was too much 'an expanded version of the existing play', which relied on an 'over-abundance' of dialogue regarding the backstory. James's story was itself a 'strange kind of detective story' and 'all the important incidents have in fact occurred before we arrive on the scene'. How to provide this information? Flashbacks might solve the problem. An alternative solution might be to have the governess fill in the information by narrating the story herself. Another problem with Archibald's theatrically oriented adaptation was the paucity of characters and the limiting of all the action to the house. This was fine for the stage, but '[it] does not give us the opportunities that one normally has in a film for constantly varying the tempo, atmosphere and tension by going from one scene to another scene . . . usually with fresh characters'. Clayton suggested expanding the scenic possibilities beyond the house and restoring James's additional locations of a lake and a country church. Perhaps a statuary garden adjoining the house could also be added. Instead of confining Miles's death scene to the house, the action could move outside to the garden.

As for the house itself, its aspect was all important, Clayton stated in his notes. The play had revealed its sinister atmosphere too early; the film must allow the sense of evil to 'slowly grow out of the house, grow out of the scenes, grow out of the atmosphere'. The house must be 'like an enormous old-fashioned rose – but it's too big – it's almost overbloomed . . .'.

Clayton's notes also reveal he was concerned with Archibald's ending. There must be more of a sense that 'evil has been divorced from the earth'. And why not restore some of James's eroticism – entirely lost in Archibald's play – by depicting a last kiss between Miles and the governess? James himself had provided a precedent for such a scene in Miles's bedroom. Why not restore that scene midway through the film and then repeat the kiss at the end? Moreover, the kiss should transpire 'as a grown-up man would kiss her'. But what then? Should Giddens carry Miles's corpse back to the house and repeat the kiss, 'completely on the lips as one would with one's lover'?

Impressed with Archibald's use of music, Clayton suggested that the film should introduce a leitmotif, an 'eerie tune', that could function both diegetically and non-diegetically. It could be sung by the children, and could also reappear in a number of variations in Georges Auric's score. Clayton is unclear how such a tune could be introduced. Perhaps it is something the former governess taught the children and which Giddens finds herself playing on the parlour piano – a metaphor for the ghostly possession in the house . . .

*The Innocents* was the first time Clayton worked in CinemaScope. Freddie Francis photographed the film in Sheffield Park, a Gothic revival estate in Sussex. The shadowy interiors of Bly House, with their decorative antiques, tapestries, staircases and fluttering draperies, were built on the soundstages of Shepperton Studios.

The resulting film, which retains the title of William Archibald's play, reveals that most of Clayton's ideas were incorporated into the final script. It begins with a dark screen and the sounds of a child singing a song. As the credits roll, the face and clasped hands of Deborah Kerr swing into view. 'All I want to do is save the children,' she whispers, 'not destroy them. More than anything I love children. More than anything. They need affection, love . . . someone who will belong to them.' The image fades. The action proper begins as the children's uncle (Michael Redgrave) interviews Miss Giddens (Deborah Kerr) about taking on a job at Bly House. This exchange, missing from the play, was adapted from James's prologue to the novel, in which one of the narrators relates the governess's meeting with her employer, her obvious attraction to him, and the curious instruction that she handle all affairs at Bly herself, without seeking his aid. The screenplay adds certain details to this exchange: the uncle tells her that the former governess, Miss Jessel, has died, leaving Miles at school and Flora in the care of the housekeeper, Mrs Grose. Miss Giddens is clearly impressed by his cosmopolitan charm; as they shake hands, she looks at him with frankly adoring eyes.

Upon her arrival she finds the house occupied only by Flora (Pamela Franklin), two servants and Mrs Grose (Megs Jenkins). Straightaway, like the play, the film loses no time establishing an air of unease. In a detail borrowed from James, as she walks down the broad driveway, Giddens hears the name 'Flora' called out in a high voice – but sees no one in the area. When Flora appears, she immediately seems oddly precocious. In a detail not in the novel but in the play, she twice announces that Miles will be coming home soon, even though the school term is still continuing. In another addition to both novel and play, that night, after prayers, when Giddens assures her that she will go to heaven because she's been a good little girl, Flora wonders aloud: 'And if I weren't, wouldn't the Lord just leave me here to walk around? Isn't that what happens to some people?' She rises from her bed late at night and gazes out upon the grounds. She smiles slightly, but we are not granted a glimpse of what she sees. The next day a note arrives informing them that Miles has been expelled from school and sent home. Unlike novel and play, an additional piece of information is provided concerning the letter, i.e., that Miles 'is an injury to the others'. In a full close-up, Giddens murmurs – in words right out of the novel – that Miles might 'contaminate' and 'corrupt' the other children. Grose laughs and adds, ' – and contaminate *you*?'

After Miles's arrival, more unsettling moments befall Miss Giddens. While gathering roses, she sees a dim figure atop the battlements of the tower (at which point both the music and sound track grow silent for a prolonged moment). During a game of hide-and-seek, she catches a glimpse of a woman in black crossing a hallway; moments later she confronts a man's face staring through the window pane. In an action duplicating both novel and play, she races outside to peer back through the window to a startled Mrs Grose. During an amateur theatrical – a scene derived from the play – Miles wears a kingly robe and recites a spooky poem: 'Enter my lord, Come from thy prison, Come from thy grave! For the moon is arisen!' At an outing by the lake the governess sees the silent, black-clad form of a woman standing in the reeds across the lake. The woman reappears in the schoolroom, sitting at the desk, sobbing (and leaving a very real tear on the slate). Several key dialogue scenes between Giddens and Grose pull all this together and make painfully clear what James had only hinted at – albeit over many pages – namely, that Quint and Jessel had had a physical relationship, carried on openly in 'rooms, used by daylight as though they were dark woods'; that Jessel had been the victim of physical and sexual abuse and had drowned herself in the lake; and that the children had been 'corrupted' and 'contaminated' as a result. Giddens reaches the conclusion that the children are wicked liars who were – and still are – 'playing some monstrous game [that is] secretive, whispery, and indecent'. They are being 'used' by Quint and Jessel as the only way in which they can be reunited in their lust. The children must be watched constantly so as not to succumb to their unholy 'possession'. And they must be forced to acknowledge the haunting as the only way to exorcise 'those devils'.

The famous kiss transpires, as in the novel, after Giddens discovers Miles walking outside in the moonlight, barefoot in his nightshirt. As she tucks him in for the night, he confesses that he and Flora had conspired to be 'bad' so as not to become boring. He then startles her with a very adult-like kiss, held in a prolonged, tight close-up. Another Jamesian scene which survives the translation to film is Flora's hysterical outburst to Giddens after refusing to admit that she sees the figure of Jessel across the lake: 'I think you're cruel. I don't like you!' Flora's screams echo through the house long afterward, and Mrs Grose tells Giddens she is shocked at the 'obscenities' that issued from Flora. Giddens seizes upon this as justification for her conviction that the children are being perverted via ghostly possession. But, in a departure from both James and from the play, Grose angrily turns on Giddens, insisting not only that there was nothing to be seen across the lake but also that Giddens was inducing the girl's hysteria:

*Figure 18* A kiss with a difference: young Miles (Martin Stephens) demonstrates his experience to his governess (Deborah Kerr) in *The Innocents* (American Lobby card).

*Grose*:   All I know, is that Miss Flora was a sweet, innocent child until you came and made her face that – that –
*Giddens*:   – that *woman*!
*Grose*:   No, that *memory*!

Undaunted, Giddens is determined to exorcise the evil by exposing it. She orders Grose to take Flora back to her uncle while she remains behind with Miles to force him to acknowledge the evil. Again, Grose rebukes her, arguing that she is risking damaging the child. But Giddens is firm. 'What am I to tell their uncle,' asks Grose. 'The truth!' answers Giddens. Grose is silent. 'The truth . . .' she breathes, slowly, confusedly.

   Whereas both novel and play had confined the climactic confrontation between Giddens and Miles to the house's interior, the film opens up the scene, beginning in the house, continuing to the pavilion outside, and concluding beyond in the statuary park. After insistent questioning by Giddens, Miles admits that in school he had 'said things'. Not content with this Jamesian hint, however, the screenplay adds to Miles's confession that he had 'frightened the children' and that 'there were screams'. As Giddens begs Miles to say Quint's name, Quint's face appears at the rain-smeared window behind the child. In a sharper rebuke than in either the novel or the play, Miles breaks into hysterical laughter and accuses Giddens of being a 'damned hussey' and a 'dirty-minded hag'. The image is striking: in a tight two-shot Miles screams as he faces the camera while, behind him, Quint's face breaks into silent laughter. They never face each other as they do in the play. Suddenly, Miles breaks away and races into the statuary park, where Quint's form appears among the standing statues. At last, Miles utters the name 'Peter Quint'. In an overhead shot, Quint's gesturing hand hovers over Miles. The child crumples to the ground. Giddens rushes to him and holds him in her arms, murmuring that she 'has him' now. For the second time, their lips meet. After several moments, her head arches backward, and she and the boy fall away from each other, leaving only a dark void in between.

## The architecture of ambiguity

We now turn to a consideration of how the story's central ambiguity – that balancing act between rational and supernatural trappings outlined earlier – is developed and supported on both the page and the screen. For example, the elements of time, place setting and story pacing function in different ways. On the page, James sets most of his action inside Bly House, excepting occasional sequences in the grounds, at church, and at the lake. Events transpire across an approximate six-month span of time, affording him a leisurely pace by which to complicate the story, enhance the suspense, and provoke confusion in the readers' minds. Clayton's film is comparable to the novel in terms of its latitude of time and space. The settings of the house and environs are splendidly picturesque and sumptuously detailed, and key scenes move fluidly from one to the other across an unspecified period of time. However, the film's 99-minute playing time, which is comparable to the stage version's length, shoehorns characterizations and incidents into a rather narrow compass, sacrificing some of the story's subtlety.

Narrative modes differ in each version. In order to distance himself from the story, James utilizes a triple framing device: an unnamed narrator relates the circumstances of an eyewitness tale that is told many years after the fact in the form of a document that is in turn presented at a dinner party by a guest named Douglas. Thus, by the time the story proper begins, the governess is a vaguely defined figure in the middle distance, as it were, and her words provide the only evidence with which the reader can proceed (a questionable presumption, as it turns out). This, of course, is a crucial and necessary ploy in casting doubt on the veracity of ensuing events. 'It involves an epistemological quandary,' writes Jeanne Thomas Allen (1977: 134) in her study of the novel and the film, 'for given the expertly balanced and irresolvable ambiguity, the reader cannot be certain of what has actually happened.' Archibald's play, almost of necessity, maintains an objective, omniscient view. Quint and Jessel are real, corporeal presences. Stage directions indicate that on several occasions they elicit reactions from the children (this is most evident in the final scene when Miles faces Quint and expires after Quint raises his hand in a gesture). The resulting effect damages the story's ambiguity by firmly suggesting that the ghosts are real.

Clayton's film, however, attempts to restore Giddens's specific viewpoint through the employment of particular camera angles and editing techniques. Usually, when the apparitions appear, they are presented either from her foreground point of view in a deep-focus two-shot or via the simple means of eyeline cutting. Either way, the viewer participates in her point of view. When the camera shifts to a more omniscient angle, however, the phantoms vanish. For example, the scene in which she sees Miss Jessel sitting at the school room desk foregrounds Giddens, allowing the viewer to look past her shoulder toward the black-clad woman. However, when the vantage point changes to a reverse angle and the camera dollies with her as she walks toward the desk, the figure vanishes. If Clayton used this strategy entirely consistently throughout, Giddens's subjective inflection of events would be confirmed. However, there are significant variations in this schema. In one scene early in the film, Quint appears at the window *behind* Giddens. Because we see him and she at first does not, his objective presence is implied. This is confirmed during the film's conclusion at the moment of Miles's death. Giddens has raced, breathlessly, after Miles as he flees to the garden. A subjective camera simulates her disorientation with a 360-degree pan, coming to rest momentarily on the figure of Quint, standing atop one of the statue pedestals. So far, so good. But then, in an astonishing departure from Giddens's point of view, an overhead shot reveals her and the boy in the middle distance while in the foreground Quint's gesturing hand dominates the frame (this is the same gesture that Archibald wrote into the last moments of the play). Miles crumples to the ground, lifeless. The effect is extremely discon-certing because, for the first time in the film, the viewer sees the action from Quint's point of view. This apparent inconsistency – or carefully calculated manipulation – disrupts the subjective strategy of much of the rest of the film and suggests the possibility that the ghosts are real. In a counter move, however, the succeeding shot of the kiss – in a prolonged, tight close-up – re-establishes Giddens's 'possession' of Miles. 'Dispossessed by Quint,' writes Jeanne Thomas Allen (1977: 142), 'Jack Clayton's Miles becomes possessed finally and wholly by a new captor.'

Although music and sound effects were, of course, unavailable to James, they are everywhere in evidence in both play and film, and play a key role in this game of ambiguities. Archibald's playscript contains detailed instructions on the use of music. In particular, several songs are introduced that seem to embody, by turns, the sweet innocence of childhood and the darker implications of maturity, while background music inflects key scenes and accompanies transitions from one scene to another, and sounds such as heartbeats and chiming clocks underscore actions with ominous emphases.

Doubtless due to Archibald's influence, the use of music and sounds is extensive in Clayton's film. As in the play, there are two songs, each associated with either

Flora or Miles. Heard against the black screen before the credits is the voice of a child singing 'Willow Waylee':

> We lay, my love and I,
> Beneath the weeping willow
> But now alone I lie . . .
> Oh Willow, I die.
> Oh Willow, I die.

Coming from the lips of a small child, this is especially disturbing. Who has died? Is it just a children's innocent folk song, or does it suggest the death of someone in the film? A leitmotif for the entire film, it reappears in a variety of guises. Flora plays it as a simple tune on the piano, and she hums it softly to herself on several occasions, usually implying the presence of Quint or Jessel – while gazing through her bedroom window, while picking flowers at the moment Giddens sees Quint on the tower, and at the lake just before the appearance of Miss Jessel. (Curiously, at the very moment the that apparitions appear, Flora ceases singing.) It is heard several times from the music box in the attic. And the soundtrack takes it up to underscore many scenes, plaintive and gentle during an outing to the church, violent and dissonant during Giddens's nightmares.

Miles, too, has his own song, 'Enter, my Lord', the same song he declaimed in Archibald's play during the scene in which he and Flora play a 'dress-up' game. The lyrics suggest not only a death, but a return. At the finish of the song, Miles walks to the window. 'Welcome, my Lord,' he repeats.

The sound track is, according to Jeanne Thomas Allen (1977), in many ways more upsetting than the visuals. The use of echoes and electronic effects through-out – which includes distortions of Flora's song – is generally ambiguous and suggestive both of the apparitions and of Miss Giddens's deranged mind. It may be that the echo effects are 'a sign of passing from objectively heard sound into an inner chamber of subjective haunting sound' (ibid.: 141), but, as Allen stresses, the truth is that the viewer simply cannot identify aural shifts in point of view as easily as visual ones.

## The haunted and the haunters

When the mists of ambiguity have cleared, or at least thinned out, it is apparent that all three versions have one very important aspect in common: their suggestion that it is the governess as much as any ghosts who truly 'haunts' Bly House. This is demonstrated in a key scene that appears in all three versions. When the governess sees Quint's face at the window, she races outside in pursuit. Finding nothing, she then turns around to peer back through that same window. Mrs Grose is startled at the apparition – just as if she had seen a ghost, in fact. Bereft of an identity of her own, Giddens is a hollow being searching the corridors and stairs of the old dark house for the very substance and purpose which she lacks.

This is not the only ghost story by James in which the living assume the roles of both the haunted and the haunters. For example, in *The Jolly Corner* (1908) Spencer Brydon's obsessive search for a ghost transforms him into a wraith-like creature stalking the hallways and stairs of his own home: 'People enough, first and last, had been in terror of apparitions, but who had ever before so turned the tables and become himself, in the apparitional world, an incalculable terror?' (Edel, 1948: 742). And in one of James's last ghostly tales, *The Third Person* (1909), two elderly spinsters think they have discovered the ghost of a hanged smuggler in their house. With no other purpose in their life, they are delighted to spend their time in search of an apparition which, if anything, is more real than they are, and which, as James says, 'had converted *them* into wandering ghosts' (Edel, 1948: 651).

What are they all looking for? – Miss Giddens and the rest? Surely not just for spooks and goblins. Whether they realize it or not, they are in fact seeking an identity and a truth about themselves. Their gaze into the spirit world is reversed and thrown back upon themselves, onto the world of the living. As Brydon realizes, 'after confronting the object of his search, what he had come back *to* seemed really the great thing, and as if his prodigious journey had been all for the sake of it' (ibid.: 757).

For the reader of James's novel, the theatre-goer of Archibald's drama, and the viewer of Clayton's film, the great revelation is the degree to which the ghostly actually resides in the living – and, by extension, in *us*. Truly, the old dark house is terrorized by haunters and haunted alike.

## Notes

1   All quotations from *The Turn of the Screw* are taken from the 1908 text in Edel (1948).
2   A partial listing of other representative titles includes *Dark Interval* (1950), a psycho-thriller that anticipates the Hammer cycle of the 1960s; *Someone at the Door* (1950), a creepshow in the manner of James Whale's *The Old Dark House*; Jacques Tourneur's *Night of the Demon* (1957), whose most effective sequences were set in and around the mansion of the evil Dr Karswell; the anthology film *The House that Dripped Blood* (1970), derived from Robert Bloch's stories about the inhabitants of a 'blighted' house; Curtis Harrington's *Whoever Slew Auntie Roo?* (1971), a Grand Guignol catalogue of household horrors loosely patterned after the Hansel and Gretel story; Radley Metzger's *The Cat and the Canary* (1977), yet another remake of the 1922 theatrical 'old dark house' archetype; Neil Jordan's *High Spirits* (1988), about turning a haunted Irish castle into a tourist trap; and Nancy Meckler's *Sister My Sister* (1995), a *Repulsion*-like thriller.
3   There is yet another incarnation of *The Turn of the Screw*. Benjamin Britten, with librettist Myfanwy Piper, brought it to the opera stage in 1954. Despite their avowals that it was not an 'interpretation' but a 'recreation', the staging does include very visible ghosts, who sing some of Britten's most gripping music. One of them even quotes a line from Yeats's poem *The Second Coming* ('The ceremony of innocence is drowned'), which

would seem to suggest that ghosts have indeed corrupted the innocence of the children. A second, very free, movie version of the novel, Michael Winner's *The Nightcomers* (1971), insisted on explaining away all the ambiguities that previous versions had worked so strenuously to promote. Marlon Brando as Quint and Stephanie Beacham as Jessel gleefully induct the children into perverse practices. When they try to leave, the children kill them. At the end, a newly recruited governess arrives, unaware of the dangers awaiting her.

4    Having said that, however, what about the apparitions in the ghost story read by Ludovico during his vigil in the haunted chamber? We never receive a rational explanation of them, which, by now, we have every reason to expect.

5    Freudian interpretations notwithstanding, there is no evidence that Henry James had ever heard of Freud. As early as 1916, speculation arose questioning the sanity of the governess. Edmund Wilson's ground-breaking essay, 'The ambiguity of Henry James', appeared in *Hound and Horn* in 1924 and hypothesized that the governess was a neurotic.

6    An examination of James's other ghostly tales fails to resolve the issue. *Owen Wingrave* (also turned into an opera by Britten) and *The Real Right Thing* have no perceivable ghosts, but many psychological ramifications. *The Ghostly Rental* and *Sir Edmund Orme*, on the other hand, have substantial haunts. Somewhere in between is *The Jolly Corner*, a story that is, if anything, even more baffling than *The Turn of the Screw*. A man confronts a ghost, to be sure, but it is his own *Doppelganger* that appears before him, his alternative self had his life pursued different directions.

7    For an interview with Jack Clayton about his work with children, see Rebello (1983).

8    The author is deeply grateful to Professor Neil Sinyard of the University of Hull for access to Jack Clayton's pre-production notes for *The Innocents*.

# References

Algeo, J. (1983), 'The haunted and the haunters', in Frank N. Magill (ed.), *Survey of Modern Fantasy Literature*, vol. two. Englewood Cliffs, NJ: Salem Press.

Allen, J.T. (1977), '*Turn of the Screw* and *The Innocents*: two types of ambiguity', in Gerald Peary and Roger Shatzkin (eds), *The Classic American Novel and the Movies*, New York: Frederick Ungar.

Birkhead, E. (1963), *The Tale of Terror: A Study of the Gothic Romance*, New York: Russell & Russell.

Chesterton, G.K. (1914), *Magic: A Fantastic Comedy in a Prelude and Three Acts*, London: Martin Secker.

Edel, L. (ed.) (1948), *The Ghostly Tales of Henry James*, New Brunswick: Rutgers University Press.

Edel, L. (1969), *Henry James: The Treacherous Years, 1895–1901*, Philadelphia and New York: J.P. Lippincott Company.

Gow, G. (1974), 'The way things are', *Films and Filming*, April, 11–14.

Jackson, S. (1959), *The Haunting of Hill House*, New York: Viking Press.

James, H. (1922), *The Novels and Tales of Henry James*, vol. XII, New York: Scribners.

James, H. (1948), *The Turn of the Screw*, in Leon Edel (ed.), *The Ghostly Tales of Henry James*, New Brunswick: Rutgers University Press.

Kerr, H. (1972), *Mediums, and Spirit-Rappers, and Roaring Radicals: Spiritualism in American Literature, 1850–1900*, Chicago: University of Illinois Press.

MacAndrew, E. (1979), *The Gothic Tradition in Fiction*, New York: Columbia University Press.

Railo, E. (1927), *The Haunted Castle: A Study of the Elements of English Romanticism*, London: Routledge.

Rebello, S. (1983), '*Something Wicked This Way Comes*', *Cinefantastique*, 13, 5 (June–July): 28–49.

Svehla, G.J. and S. (eds) (1996), *Cinematic Hauntings*, Baltimore, MD: Midnight Marquee Press.

Smith, D.G. (1996), '*The Innocents*', in Svehla and Svehla.

Varma, D.P. (1957), *The Gothic Flame*, London: Arthur Barker.

# 9 Barbara, Julia, Carol, Myra, and Nell: diagnosing female madness in British horror cinema

*Steven Jay Schneider*

At the level of proverb and popular culture, if not in medical science, the connection between madness and England has persisted with remarkable tenacity . . . Most significantly, in England the differences in the perception of madness as it appeared in men and women stand out with particular clarity . . . Even when both men and women had similar symptoms of mental disorder, psychiatry differentiated between an English malady, associated with the intellectual and economic pressures on highly civilized men, and a female malady, associated with the sexuality and essential nature of women. *Women were believed to be more vulnerable to insanity than men, to experience it in specifically feminine ways, and to be differently affected by it in the conduct of their lives.*

(Elaine Showalter 1985: 7, emphasis added)

This essay takes as its focus the depiction of psychologically unstable female protagonists in five critically lauded (if not all commercially successful) British horror films of the 1960s and 1970s: *The Haunting* (Robert Wise, 1963), *Séance on a Wet Afternoon* (Bryan Forbes, 1964), *Repulsion* (Roman Polanski, 1965), *Asylum* (Roy Ward Baker, 1972),[1] and *Full Circle* (US: *The Haunting of Julia* (Richard Loncraine, 1976)). Despite these films' differences with respect to production history, sub-genre and narrative detail, there are a number of complex and highly specific themes relating to female madness which are not only foregrounded in all five pictures, but which constitute what might profitably be viewed as an ongoing intertextual dialogue. In what follows, I shall examine in a preliminary manner the way in which each picture tackles these themes of *Identity*, *Sexuality*, *Domesticity*, *Foreignness* and *Subjectivity*, with an eye towards identifying their Gothic origins, their subtle variations and their complex meanings.

Limitations of space prevent my providing detailed plot synopses of the five films here under investigation. By way of introduction, however, let me just say a few words about the female protagonists at the centre of each of them. Both Julia (Mia Farrow in *Full Circle*) and Myra (Kim Stanley in *Séance*) have lost children, the former to an everyday choking-while-eating incident, the latter during childbirth.

These tragedies seem to have permanently traumatized the women: we learn that both of them have been institutionalized, and both claim to be in contact with their deceased offspring. While Julia winds up committing suicide (or else getting murdered by the ghost of a child who looks just like her dead daughter – the cause of death is left unclear), Myra concocts an elaborate plan to kidnap a little girl, then urges her unwilling husband (at the imagined 'request' of their late son Arthur) to kill the child. Although Myra's murderous desires are left unfulfilled, the same cannot be said for Carol (Catherine Deneuve in *Repulsion*) or Barbara (Charlotte Rampling in *Asylum*). Carol, a beautiful, painfully introverted young woman living in London, progressively loses touch with reality when her sister (who is also her room-mate) leaves town, eventually taking the lives of two men and succumbing to a paralysing psychosis. The only explanation for her condition given in the film is the possibility of sexual abuse by her father or uncle (suggested via a pair of zoom-ins to extended close-ups of a family portrait taken when Carol was an adolescent). Barbara suffers from a different but no less destructive form of psychosis, according to which she falsely believes in the reality of a woman named Lucy (Britt Ekland), who proceeds to murder Barbara's brother and nurse in an effort at liberating her from a highly restrictive living situation. As with Carol, the root of Barbara's malady is left largely undetermined, though evidence suggests that it might stem from (at the very least it gets aggravated by) her continuing addiction to pills. Finally, while Nell (Julie Harris in *The Haunting*) has no urge to kill anyone, in part because of her hyper-sensitive disposition (the result of years of emotional abuse suffered at the hands of an invalid mother, along with a susceptibility to external influence), she becomes the victim of a force which may or may not exist solely in her mind. At *The Haunting*'s conclusion, this force takes control of Nell's car, which promptly crashes into a tree at the foot of the driveway, killing her instantly.

With this admittedly sketchy background in place, we can now proceed with an analysis, both comparative and (to a lesser extent) contrastive, of our disturbed female characters along the thematic lines suggested above.

## Identity

> Each Gothic family . . . is really two families. One is patriarchal, dominated by the all-powerful father figure. He uses the members of the family as extensions and expressions of his power and authority, instruments supporting his masculine identity. The other family is affective or sentimental; its central figure is the loving and caring mother. It defines itself as a circle of love and affection; each member finds identity through submergence into the family as a whole. The patriarchal and maternal families thus reflect on a social level the characteristics of the archetypes of individual identity.
>
> (William Patrick Day 1985: 76)

The traditional Gothic dualism of identity described by William Patrick Day – according to which the opposed social forces of masculinity, rationality and scepticism on the one hand, femininity, sentimentality and sympathy on the other are reconceived as non-exclusive (however difficult they may be to reconcile) personality traits – finds reflection as well as modification in our five British horror films. For while the psychologically unstable women in these films are provided ample opportunity to acquire for themselves 'the characteristics of the archetypes of individual identity', these characteristics are located in particular individuals rather than in families as a whole, thereby adding to the films' interpersonal tensions. Furthermore, the women in question are reluctant or otherwise resistant to change, and ultimately prove incapable of integrating the opposing characteristics within their own personas.

The most dramatic example of this seemingly irresolvable crisis of identity occurs in *Full Circle*, where Julia is positioned between two men of very different natures: Magnus (Tom Conti), the arrogant, domineering ex-husband who will stop at nothing to get her back, and who threatens to have her locked up because of her 'self-destructive' tendencies, and Mark (Keir Dullea), the understanding, effeminate friend (he owns an antique shop, does a Liberace impression, and is described by one woman as 'pretty'), who desires Julia but would never force the issue. By leaving Magnus after her release from hospital a year after their daughter's death, Julia seems well on her way to taking some control over her life, and Magnus's mysterious murder in the basement of her new house can be interpreted as a symbolic or projected denial of the hyper-masculine qualities he represents. But Mark (and the alternative ideal he stands for) fares no better: despite his affection for Julia, she shows practically no interest in pursuing a relationship with him. And he too is killed, getting electrocuted when a radio 'accidentally' falls into his bathtub one evening.

The other films contain further illustrations of the way in which dually presented, archetypal character traits fail to result in a stable, unified identity for our madwomen. In *Asylum* Barbara (through Lucy) stabs to death her over-protective brother in an effort at gaining freedom. But not only does her supposedly sympathetic, ultra-feminine alter ego threaten to abandon her; she effectively pins the crime on Barbara, who winds up incarcerated once again – this time, it would appear, for good.[2] Nell in *The Haunting* rebuffs the not-so-thinly-veiled lesbian advances of fellow Hill House occupant Theodora (Claire Bloom) – who remains a sensitive and compassionate figure despite being shunned – in favour of the dashing, over-confident scientist Dr Markway (Richard Johnson). But, unfortunately, Dr Markway is a married man, and once his wife appears on the scene, Nell is quickly put in her place. This crushing blow is what precipitates the breakdown leading to her death at the film's end. In *Repulsion*, Carol scorns all attempts at joviality and flirtation on the part of her sister's boyfriend Michael (Ian Hendry), but she also expresses anger at and disappointment towards the usually maternal Helen (Yvonne

Furneaux) for leaving her all alone in the flat while she sneaks off for her tryst. Finally, while the parents of the young girl who is kidnapped by Myra and her husband Billy (David Attenborough) in *Séance on a Wet Afternoon* stand as fairly one-dimensional embodiments of feminine sentimentality and patriarchal rationality, Myra herself proves incapable of adopting either of these attributes, much less both of them. When she shows up at the Claytons' home claiming psychic knowledge of what happened to their daughter, Mr Clayton (Mark Eden) rejects her out of hand as an attention-seeking fraud. And Mrs Clayton (Nanette Newman), though convinced (or perhaps just desperate) enough to attend one of her sittings, does not elicit sufficient sympathy from Myra to provoke her to tell the truth or to release little Amanda (Judith Donner). Thus, it would appear that the maladies suffered by the female protagonists in each of our five films receive partial expression in identity crises exacerbated by the women's inability to reconcile opposing archetypal character traits within their own personalities, or by their lack of interest in doing so.

## Sexuality

> The problem of identity is . . . the problem of sexuality. Traditionally, the power of sexuality is the power of reproduction. . . . But the root cause of horror in the genre is the protagonist's inability to control sexuality, to thus define masculine and feminine and create legitimate identity. The identities of the protagonists disintegrate because they cannot control and channel sexuality in a productive way. . . . The question is, then, if the power to reproduce is not beyond the capacity of the Gothic protagonists, why do their attempts end in failure? The answer lies, I think, in the other power of sexuality, the power of pleasure. The protagonists can accept sexuality simply as a means of reproduction, but they repress or reject it insofar as they cannot accept that it is also pleasurable.
>
> (Day 1985: 84–5)

It is a widely recognized and often remarked upon fact that male psychopaths in the horror genre are typically characterized in sexual terms primarily through their ambivalent feelings towards women. At once desiring women enough to engage in illicit acts of voyeurism and hating them for their perceived promiscuity (see for example *Peeping Tom* (1960) and *Halloween* (1978)), these men kill what they desperately wish for but find impossible to possess, or at the very least to contain. In some cases, most notably *Psycho* (1960) and *Dressed To Kill* (1980), the killers over-identify with their victims to such an extent that they commit their crimes while dressing up in women's clothing.

The disturbed female protagonists in our five films, however, do not share these erotic urges expressed violently towards members of the opposite sex. On the contrary, a central feature of these women's neuroses (as conceived of by the male screenwriters and directors of the films) seems to be the near-total lack of sexual interest they take in men. A careful look at these films reveals a troubling set of connections made between asexuality on the one hand, homosexuality on the other, and distinctly feminine forms of madness: no less troubling than – though not at all the same as – the analogous set of connections made in horror films featuring maladjusted males.

Despite being married to Billy, who loves his wife enough to carry out her outrageous plan almost to the very end, *Séance*'s Myra exhibits no signs of being physically attracted to him. *Full Circle*'s Julia rejects the advances of Magnus, Mark and a third (admittedly creepy) man whom she visits in order to learn more about the dead girl who looks just like her daughter. Though Nell in *The Haunting* makes obvious her feelings for Dr Markway, it is more the innocent crush of a teenage schoolgirl than the erotic desires of a mature woman. As for *Asylum*'s Barbara, the only man in her life is her brother George (James Villiers), and while incest between the two stands as a remote possibility, her only concern seems to be with keeping Lucy happy.[3] And Carol's disgust at the very idea of sexual contact with men provides the entire narrative thrust of Polanski's *Repulsion*. Although it may be argued that

*Figure 19* Female 'sittings': Mia Farrow and Mary Morris in *Full Circle* (1976).

the imagined rape sequences suggest another way of understanding her character, the notion that Carol really desires what she appears to find only repulsive is much less plausible than the notion that it is impossible for her to keep what she really does find repulsive from violating her boundaries – spatial, emotional and physical.

But the apparent asexuality of our five madwomen is complemented by a more or less transparently coded *same*-sexuality. This seemingly exclusive combination of attributes is achieved via a presentation of the women's lesbianism as potential (rather than actual), and as social, even political (rather than erotic), for reasons probably having as much to do with Britain's censorship code during the era as anything else.[4] Beautiful, capable Theodora ('just Theo') in *The Haunting* is a woman completely free of male control, sexual and otherwise. It is not the case that Nell finds her unattractive, or what she stands for unappealing – this is obvious from Julie Harris's brilliantly rendered facial expressions and body language; it is just that she is too repressed, or too fearful, to adopt the alternative lifestyle that Theo represents.[5] Then there is Lucy: confident, striking and above all independent, she encourages Barbara to run away with her so that the two can find a place of their own, somewhere outside the sphere of patriarchal authority and domination. Unlike Nell, Barbara accepts the offer after only the slightest hesitation. In *Repulsion*, Carol herself is the one who pushes for an all-female relationship, pleading with Helen to stay home and not take off with Michael. Carol's male suitor neither understands nor accepts her wish that he leave her alone (with fatal consequences), but the fact is, the only person she cares to be around is her sister.

As for Julia, the closest she comes to engaging in an act of sexual intimacy during the course of *Full Circle* occurs one night while she is asleep in her new home; a barely visible hand brushes across her lips, generating a response of unmistakable sensual pleasure. Since this home is haunted by the ghost of a beautiful-but-evil little girl, audiences can draw their own conclusions as to the identity of Julia's nocturnal visitor.[6] The penultimate scene of the film, after Magnus and Mark have both been killed, has Julia hugging the child, whispering: 'It's all settled; everything is right now.' Perhaps in order to heighten our awareness of the significance of this non-traditional living arrangement, director Loncraine has Julia visit the abodes of two other female 'couples' during the picture: a middle-aged psychic who lives with her niece, and the blind mother of a murdered boy who resides with a female companion ('Catherine has been my eyes for a long time', the woman explains to Julia. 'She has many talents.') Even *Séance on a Wet Afternoon*, a film in which expressions of physical desire are notable only for their absence, presents audiences with an alternative, vaguely lesbian, paradigm. Myra's visit to the Clayton estate may not yield the positive response from Amanda's father that she was hoping for, but something about her visitor's gentle manner and soothing words leads Mrs Clayton to break ranks with her husband and to sneak off to Myra's home for an almost exclusively female 'sitting'. Though it would be going too far to conclude that asexuality and lesbianism are pointed to in these films as the sole reasons for their protagonists' respective illnesses, and although the progressive possibilities inherent in such representations should not be discounted, it can hardly be denied that the non-heterosexual characteristics and tendencies figure prominently among the causes, symptoms and/or consequences of specifically female neuroses.

## Domesticity

> Within the home and family, middle-class women throughout the past two-hundred years have been confronted with the problem of increasing leisure time . . . These new situations in male and female roles, these new functions for the family, locate and frame the specific anxieties and fears to which the Gothic fantasy was a response. It was here that the contradictions and tensions between the old myths and new realities took their heaviest toll. The very way in which these people lived posed the questions, What does it mean to be a man or a woman? What does it mean to be part of a family? without providing any clear answer.
>
> (Day 1985: 83)

Although questions such as 'What does it mean to be a man or a woman?', 'What does it mean to be part of a family?' and the like have been given a whole host of troubling, often conflicting, answers in horror movies, it is still striking to note the extent to which the particular institutions of home, parenthood and marriage are interrogated and problematized in the films here under discussion. It is at this domestic level especially that the films transgress generic boundaries, employing psychological realism and 'slice of life' episodes in order to add melodramatic flavour to otherwise fantastic (and phantastic) narratives. Although each one situates differently its female protagonist relative to the space which she inhabits and the people who inhabit it with her, all of them exhibit the same nightmarish inversion of Victorian psychiatric reform, which held that 'the most important feature of the asylum . . . was its "homishness"' (quoted in Showalter 1985: 28).[7] In these films, mental institutions function as past residences, future penitentiaries, or both (as in *Séance*, *Asylum* and *Full Circle*),[8] and are not conceived of as places where 'madness is brought into the circle of the familiar and the everyday, the systems for its treatment restructured in domestic terms'.[9] Rather, it is 'the circle of the familiar and the everyday', with the image of the home at its centre, which gets 'restructured' into a place where female madness germinates, grows and eventually (perhaps inevitably) erupts into violence.

In *Asylum* Barbara's story begins with her return home from an extended stay at a sanatorium; instead of feeling relieved, however, she resents the fact that her brother has arranged for a live-in nurse to watch over her, tell her when she must take naps, and so on. 'But this is my *home*,' she protests. '– *Our* home', George corrects her; 'And I hope that we'll be together here always. You don't want to go back into hospital again, do you?' Though Barbara's lack of domestic freedom may not be the sole reason for the presence of her murderous alter ego, the fact that she must submit to patriarchal authority in her own house (we find out early on that the deed to the property was passed down to Barbara, not to George), certainly stands as a contributing factor.

A similar 'home as prison' theme is present in *The Haunting*. We first meet Nell as she argues with her sister and brother-in-law over whether or not to leave the small room she rents from them to join in Dr Markway's experiment at Hill House. Her sister especially thinks this is a bad idea, and goes so far as to refuse Nell's request to 'borrow' the family car – despite the fact that Nell is part owner! Things were no better for Nell when she was growing up. While her sister moved away and married, she was forced to take care of their sick and demanding mother on her own, never having the opportunity to start a family for herself. As she drives to Hill House after taking the car on the sly, her internal monologue (to which the audience is given access via voice-over narration) reveals her desire that: 'someday, someday, someday I'll have a house of my own.' And near the end of the film, while maniacally climbing Hill House's rickety spiral staircase, she repeats over and over the words: 'I'm home, I'm home, I'm home, I'm home, I'm home.' But if Hill House constitutes home for Nell, it is also the site of her demise. A comparison with *Full Circle* is apt here. Our introduction to Julia comes with her daughter's violent choking incident during an otherwise uneventful breakfast. While Magnus stands around looking helpless and minimizing the extent of the danger, Julia frantically tries to save their child, finally cutting open the girl's throat in a vain attempt at dislodging the obstructing matter. It is not simply the case that *Full Circle* refigures domestic space as a locus of, rather than a refuge from, horror – Kate (Sophie Ward)'s death is nothing less than a tragic-ironic embodiment of the inequality and marital tension existing between her parents. Just like Nell (and Barbara as well), Julia desperately seeks a new home, one where she is not subject to the expectations and demands of a controlling family member (in this case, her husband). And just as in Nell's case, the home she finally decides upon – a Victorian manor in South Kensington – is haunted by the ghosts of previous inhabitants and proves to be a place of death rather than rebirth.

Though Carol's flat may not be 'haunted' in the traditional sense of the term, it too possesses its share of ghosts; ghosts which spring directly from the mind of the protagonist herself. And it too is a place of death – not the protagonist's own (as in *Full Circle* and *The Haunting*) but of two perceived threats, both of whom she murders in cold blood (as in *Asylum*, where Barbara's nurse as well as her brother are victims). Brilliantly combining psychological naturalism with stylistic expressionism, Polanski manages to generate a number of uncanny – which translated from the German 'unheimlich' means 'unhomely' – images and effects.[10] As Ivan Butler (1967/2000: 80) explains,

The flat, shut-off and solitary, reflects Carol's own withdrawn and lonely state, and eventually shares, literally, in her disintegration. By an inspired use of the distortion lens the sitting-room is made to become a vast cavern, the white-tiled bathroom a huge, dim, grey space with a tiny distant washbasin. All sense of proportion is lost. Huge cracks suddenly split the walls of the rooms, and those in the passage grow soft so that her hands sink into them – and later other hands reach through them to grab at her.

Butler continues: 'seldom has an ordinary setting been given such significance. It is, indeed, a central character, and by the end we have lived in it ourselves' (ibid.: 80). Perhaps even more than the technically sophisticated scenes described above, however, it is Carol's pathetic efforts at invoking a semblance of domestic normality – at one point we watch her ironing Michael's soiled vest, with an iron that is not plugged in – which confirm our suspicion that the abuse she suffered as a child (molestation perhaps, even incest) has resulted in her conceiving of 'home' as a place fraught with insecurity and danger. As for Myra in *Séance*, home represents only a place of broken dreams and unfulfilled ambitions. While husband Billy spends most of his time tooling around on a motorbike, following through on Myra's plan to gain respect as a genuine psychic by correctly predicting Amanda's safe return, his wife leaves their depressingly bland North London cottage only once. By transforming the upstairs parlour into a virtual prison, a mock hospital bedroom where the little girl might be kept without realizing the truth of her predicament, Myra in effect places her under house arrest. In this respect, the two females have something in common: Amanda could not leave even if she wanted to, and even if Myra did leave there would be nowhere for her to go.

## Foreignness

> After the 1820s, exotic settings tend to disappear from the genre. . . . The Gothic writers abandon much of their exotic machinery because the internal logic of the genre made this the most reasonable course to follow. The atmosphere of the novels is heightened by a more subtle interpenetration of the exotic and ordinary after 1820.
>
> (Day 1985: 33–4)

It is hardly a coincidence that all of the disturbed females we are examining are associated with foreignness of various sorts, if not quite with exoticism. Carol, who is Belgian, speaks English haltingly and with a thick accent. The difficulty she has expressing herself to the men with whom she comes into contact leads them to misinterpret her lack of interest, even disgust, as mere shyness, or even as a form of flirtation. This stands at once as an indictment of their egotism and, at least for two of them, a fatal error of judgement. Barbara (who has dark hair) may be British upper crust, but the looks and speech of her blonde alter ego suggest that she, at least, hails from somewhere else in Europe.[11] Judging from their accents, both Myra and Julia are American (as are the actresses who play them), the difference being that Julia's husband is *also* American, while Myra's is unmistakably English.[12] As for Nell, her Americanness constitutes a kind of foreignness, despite the fact that Hill House would appear to be located, diagetically speaking, somewhere in the United States. This is because the film's two main characters besides Nell – Theo and Dr Markway – are both British, and because the film's exteriors, including those of the house, were clearly shot on location in England.

Besides the fact that they add to the Gothic dimension of the films as a whole, what are we to make of the fact that our five female protagonists are all, to some extent, outsiders in their own communities? That none of them are native Britons, despite their featured roles in British horror movies? There are of course a great many horror films, encompassing a wide variety of sub-genres, which depict their central monster as foreign 'other', beginning perhaps with Count Dracula (Bela Lugosi in Tod Browning's 1932 version of the film), and including Irena Dubrovna (Simone Simon in *Cat People* (1943)), Mark Lewis (Carl Boehm in *Peeping Tom*) and Peter Neal (Anthony Franciosa in *Tenebrae* (1982)). But in the case of our madwomen, it is precisely that 'subtle interpenetration of the exotic and ordinary' which leads one to wonder whether their foreignness signifies something other than a simple effort on the part of the films' directors and screenwriters at 'alien'-ating them from British audiences (thereby enabling such audiences to pass judgement on them without feeling that they are judging themselves). And, of course, the way we feel about Barbara, Julia, Myra, Carol and Nell is inextricably tied up with, even depends upon, the way they feel about *us* (via our diegetic representatives). Ultimately, these films seem to be saying that it is their central female characters' *own* feelings of being different, not the differences which other people see in them, which play the far more important role in prompting their irrational behaviour.

## Subjectivity

> In the Gothic novel, the sense of a veil of subjectivity hiding the real is an aspect of the Gothic world itself. There time and space are not absolutes through which characters can perceive a common reality and act in more or less secure relationships to the world. Rather, they become, like identity, relative functions of perception. The protagonists find that conventional measures of time and space break down into aspects of their own experiences. . . . The Gothic atmosphere mirrors the collapse of the self, for just as the self is fragmented into a doubled identity, it loses its ability to place itself in relation to an objective world.
>
> (Day 1985: 28)

Finally we come to the theme of 'subjectivity' or, to be somewhat more precise, 'the confusion and occasional conflation of subjective and objective experience'. What this amounts to is the claim that, at various moments in each of our five films, the audience is left more or less in the dark as to whether the strange and troubling phenomena experienced by the female protagonists – phenomena which play a large part in the escalation of their illnesses – are merely subjective in nature (because they are products of their psyche) or whether they are truly objective (rendering them supernatural in origin). It is in order to achieve this epistemologically disorienting effect that the films' directors make use of creative camerawork and a host of special editing techniques. Now, to do full justice to this theme in the five films under discussion would require an essay of its own. Here, a few choice examples of its operation must suffice.

In *Asylum*, a film not known for its complexity at the formal or technical level, director Baker skilfully blurs the boundaries between supernatural and realistic horror. Our first glimpse of Lucy comes via an eyeline match from a shot of Barbara looking up at her room from the car; this match, plus the following facts – neither George nor Nurse Higgins are aware of anyone in the house, and all the evidence points to Barbara as the killer (for example, her fingerprints are found on the murder weapon) – lead us to discount Lucy's existence as a figment of Barbara's imagination. But how do we explain the numerous shots of Lucy which function to validate her existence independently of Barbara's hallucinatory visions? At one point, for example, George checks on Barbara, who is sound asleep in her bedroom; a cross-cut reveals a female hand placing a sedative in George's teacup (Nurse Higgins is not home at the time). In the very next scene, we watch Lucy enter Barbara's room and wake her up from her nap. And another scene begins with a shot taken from behind Lucy's head; in her line of vision is Barbara, who stands in the bathroom facing a mirror. *But Lucy is not reflected in the mirror*, which means that Barbara cannot be returning her stare. All of this is further complicated by the fact that, according to the logic of the framing narrative, Barbara is simply recounting from memory the story of how she wound up institutionalized again. Therefore, the apparent objectivity of Lucy's existence defers (but only somewhat) to the inherent subjectivity of Barbara's recollections.

In *Séance on a Wet Afternoon* we are given no reason to believe that Myra is a legitimate psychic, aside from her own testimony to that effect. That is, until the final scene, when 'Arthur' – speaking through Myra – correctly points out that little Amanda is not dead; this despite the fact that Myra ordered Billy to kill her, and despite Billy's not having revealed that he let the girl go free. How could Arthur have known this, unless Myra's extrasensory powers are real? In *Repulsion* Polanski plays with the collective head of his audience by establishing objective bases for Carol's nightmarish visions early in the narrative, and then by increasing their intensity and impossibility over time. The suddenly appearing fissures, for example, which threaten to destroy Carol's flat near the end of the film, start out as ordinary

*Figure 20*  The real thing? Medium Myra (Kim Stanley) in *Séance on a Wet Afternoon* (1964).

and none too 'subjective' cracks in the walls. And Carol's imagined rapist bears an eerie resemblance to a previously seen construction worker who gave her a lustful stare when she passed him on the street. In *Full Circle* Julia catches glimpses of a young girl whom she falsely believes is her dead daughter. The girl appears without warning, only to disappear just as quickly, and since no one but Julia (and the audience) can see her, we have good reason to doubt the veridicality of her visions. In one scene, however, the girl disappears without the benefit of a cut – at least not one detectable by the audience. Because the shot of the girl is neither an eyeline match nor one taken from Julia's point of view, our confidence in her unreality is shaken.

Last but certainly not least (considering that the film takes as its primary aim the blurring of the boundaries between subjective and objective perception), in *The Haunting* Nell is constantly hearing things, feeling watched and found conversing with apparently inanimate objects. Save for some loud banging on the wall heard by Theo as well as Nell, however, none of the other Hill House residents are provided with any indisputable evidence of the supernatural. So is the house really haunted, or is Eleanor just imagining things? No final answer to this question is given: it is not as if we get to see any ghosts for ourselves.[13] But through his frequent use of canted frames, ultra-wide-angle lenses (which produce unsettling distortion effects), rapid-fire montage sequences, and multi-speed camerawork – including a frenetic swish pan around the girls' room, and a dizzying point-of-view shot down the tower's spiral staircase – director Wise makes a strong case for their existence. So here, just as with each of the other films in this study, we find ourselves unable firmly to differentiate between the objective and the subjective, the supernatural and the psychological, the real and the imaginary; and thus we are forced into an uncomfortably empathetic relationship with the madwomen at the centres of these films.

## Notes

1  *Asylum* is an anthology horror film, consisting of a framing narrative and four completely unrelated 'chapters' or segments. In the discussion to follow, I shall be referring only to the third of these segments.
2  For more on alter egos and various other types of doubles as they appear in the horror film genre, see Schneider (2001).
3  Villiers also has a small part in *Repulsion*.
4  Pete Walker's cult horror film *House of Whipcord* (1974) is notable for making explicit the lesbian desires of a sadistic female prison guard.
5  In Jan De Bont's poorly-realized (to put it mildly) Hollywood remake of *The Haunting* (1999), Theo (Catherine Zeta Jones) admits early on to being a bisexual. Suffice to say, this makes far less radical her symbolic function in the film.
6  Cf. the ravaging of female psychic Florence Tanner (Pamela Franklin) by a disembodied spirit in John Hough's *The Legend of Hell House* (1973).
7  Victorian psychiatric reform was a movement initiated with the opening of the ultramodern Colney Hatch lunatic asylum in Middlesex, England in 1851, and the contemporaneous banning of mechanical restraints as a means of keeping inmates under control.
8  Cf. *Strait-Jacket*, the 1963 Joan Crawford vehicle directed by William Castle and scripted by the *Psycho* author Robert Bloch (who also wrote the screenplay for *Asylum*). Following a pre-credit sequence, this film 'officially' begins with the release of Lucy Harbin (Crawford) from a mental hospital, where she was locked away for twenty years following the axe murders of her husband and his girlfriend. The film ends with Lucy's daughter Carol (Diane Baker) being sent away to a similar institution after committing numerous axe murders of her own. By way of contrast, consider Anatole Litvak's *The*

*Snake Pit* (1948) – the mother of all female insanity movies (pun intended) – which portrays in sympathetic fashion a woman's painstakingly slow recovery from paranoia and psychosis during her stay in an asylum.

9  To paraphrase a remark by Showalter (1985: 28). *The Haunting* stands as an exception to the first part of this claim only because Nell dies at the end of the film. Had she somehow managed to leave Hill House alive, there is good reason to think that institutionalization was in her future.

10  For more on the notion of 'uncanniness' as it relates specifically to the horror genre, see Schneider (1999).

11  Britt Ekland, who plays Lucy, was at the time a well-known Swedish model and actress.

12  Unlike *Séance*, *Full Circle* takes pains to call attention to Julia's Americanness. At one point, a psychic getting ready to conduct a sitting at her house asks for a cup of tea. But Julia doesn't have any tea on hand – only coffee, which the woman kindly but firmly refuses. Later on, Julia remarks to a wholly uninterested neighbour that 'The pound has gone down again.' Nothing equivalent is to be found in *Séance*.

13  Contrast this with De Bont's remake, in which the presence of ghosts in the house is made manifest (to the characters in the film, as well as to the audience) from very early on.

## References

Butler, Ivan (1967), 'The horror film: Polanski and *Repulsion*', reprinted in Alain Silver and James Ursini (eds), *Horror Film Reader*, New York: Limelight Editions, 2000: 80–1.

Day, William Patrick (1985), *In the Circles of Fear and Desire: A Study of Gothic Fantasy*, Chicago: University of Chicago Press.

Schneider, Steven Jay (1999), 'Monsters as (uncanny) metaphors: Freud, Lakoff, and the representation of monstrosity in cinematic horror', reprinted in Alain Silver and James Ursini (eds), *Horror Film Reader*, New York: Limelight Editions, 2000: 167–91.

Schneider, Steven Jay (2001), 'Manifestations of the literary double in modern horror cinema', *Film and Philosophy*, Special Edition.

Showalter, Elaine (1985), *The Female Malady: Women, Madness, and English Culture, 1830–1980*, New York: Pantheon Books.

# 10 The Amicus house of horror

*Peter Hutchings*

There comes a moment in the British horror film *Tales from the Crypt* (1972) when a Christmas carol radio broadcast is broken into by the following words: 'We interrupt this programme for a special announcement. A man described as a homicidal maniac has escaped from the hospital for the criminally insane . . . and may be wearing a Santa Claus costume.' This is not the sort of thing that one expects in a Hammer horror film. It is not just *Tales from the Crypt*'s contemporary settings that separate it out from Hammer's period horror; the announcement's bizarre juxtaposition of elements not usually conjoined – namely, homicidal mania and Santa Claus – also seems alien when placed in the context of Hammer's relatively sober view of the world. By way of a contrast, Amicus, the company actually responsible for *Tales from the Crypt*, was firmly wedded to a sense of the grotesque and the absurd, and the horror films it produced stand as a testament both to the heterogeneity of British horror cinema and to the way in which a range of British horror films differ from and in certain respects offer a challenge to what might be termed the Hammer hegemony.

Of all the British film companies that sought to emulate Hammer's success in the horror genre throughout the 1960s and early 1970s, Amicus was one of the most prolific and distinctive. Between 1964 and 1974 it produced fourteen horror films; these included both portmanteau/anthology films and single-plot dramas. The predominantly British casts and settings of Amicus horrors, the presence within many of them of the British horror stars Peter Cushing and Christopher Lee, and the fact that they were all directed by British directors (notably the horror 'auteurs' Freddie Francis and Roy Ward Baker) working with British crews in British studios, suggest that Amicus should be seen as an integral part of the British horror movement of the 1960s and 1970s.[1]

Despite this, Amicus horror films have not played any significant role in the critical re-evaluation of British horror that was inaugurated by David Pirie's ground-breaking book *A Heritage of Horror* in 1973. In particular, the Amicus films do not sit easily with those critical accounts that have sought to identify British horror as a purely indigenous cultural phenomenon, as – in David Pirie's words – 'the only staple cinematic myth which Britain can properly claim as its own' (Pirie 1973: 9). To put it bluntly, there is something suspiciously 'foreign' about Amicus. For one thing, it tended not to adapt British Gothic tales in the manner of Hammer but turned instead mainly to America for its source material. For another, the company itself was founded and managed by two Americans. Doubts about the extent to which Amicus horror is rooted in British culture have arguably relegated it to the margins of much writing on British horror. A possible response to this marginalization might be to assert the Britishness of the Amicus product, bringing the films into the 'national fold', so to speak, through identifying those thematic or stylistic properties that bind them to other British films or to British culture in general. In this way, any 'foreign' elements could be effaced or contained. This chapter offers a somewhat different approach, however; one that is less concerned to establish the 'purity' of Amicus's Britishness and is more interested instead in the precise nature of its dependence on American-sourced material and the extent to which this material is reworked within a British context of production. Such an approach can potentially highlight aspects of British horror that are obscured by those accounts which have centred on Hammer. A good starting point for this is the Amicus company itself.

Amicus's two founders, the producer Max J. Rosenberg and the producer-writer Milton Subotsky, had first worked together in American television in the 1950s and had subsequently co-produced a number of low-budget American feature films.[2] In 1960 Subotsky came to Britain to be executive producer of, and provide the screen story for, the horror film *City of the Dead* (John Llewellyn Moxey). Remaining in Britain, Subotsky teamed up again with Max J. Rosenberg (who had done some uncredited work on *City of the Dead*) and together they formed Amicus. Its first productions were two youth-orientated musicals of the kind for which Subotsky and Rosenberg had been responsible in the United States: *It's Trad Dad* (1962) – the directorial feature debut of American director Richard Lester, later responsible for such 1960s 'classics' as *A Hard Day's Night* (1964) and *The Knack* (1965) – and *Just for Fun* (Gordon Flemyng, 1963).[3] Then, in 1964, the company switched to horror production with *Dr Terror's House of Horrors* (Freddie Francis). Thirteen more horrors were to follow – *The Skull* (Francis, 1965), *The Deadly Bees* (Francis, 1966), *The Psychopath* (Francis, 1966), *Torture Garden* (Francis, 1967), *The House that Dripped Blood* (Peter Duffell, 1970), *I, Monster* (Stephen Weeks, 1971), *Asylum* (Roy Ward Baker, 1972), *Tales from the Crypt* (Francis, 1972), *Vault of Horror* (Baker, 1973), *From Beyond the Grave* (Kevin Connor, 1973), *And Now the Screaming Starts!* (Baker, 1973), *Madhouse* (Jim Clark, 1974) and *The Beast Must Die* (Paul Annett, 1974).

The American input apparent in Amicus from its inception was maintained throughout its horror productions. Ten of these had screenplays either by Subotsky himself or by the distinguished American horror writer Robert Bloch, and many drew either upon EC horror comics (*Tales from the Crypt* and *Vault of Horror*) or Bloch's own short stories (*The Skull*, *Torture Garden*, *The House that Dripped Blood* and *Asylum*).

As if to underline Amicus's distance from British culture, its main writer, Bloch, rarely visited Britain, preferring instead to post his scripts over from Hollywood. The fact that Amicus specialized in horror films with contemporary settings – it made only two period horrors, *And Now the Screaming Starts!* and *I, Monster* – distanced it yet further from the British genre mainstream, represented at the time by Hammer's period costume horrors, and again appeared to align it more with 1950s American horror fiction. Given this, it is ironic that even as its American sources militate against it being seen as properly British, the very trappings of Britishness apparent in Amicus horror – in the form of actors, directors, settings – seem to have worked against it being thought of in relation to American cinema and American culture. Indeed, when Amicus is mentioned at all in critical histories of the horror genre, it is usually as a minor addendum to Hammer.

Too American to be properly British and too British to pass for American, Amicus hovers uneasily between the two national cinemas. However, what might be termed here the alien or foreign nature of Amicus horror can arguably be related to, and perhaps even typifies, a broader hybridity within the British horror cycle. It is certainly the case that those critics concerned to establish the 'Britishness' of horror have often failed to take into account, not just the input of American individuals such as Subotsky, the screenwriters Robert Bloch and Richard Matheson, the director Jacques Tourneur and the producer Louis 'Deke' Heyward, but also a more general reliance both on American finance and on ideas first developed within American horror. For example, Hammer, ostensibly the most British of British horror companies, was heavily dependent on American financing throughout the 1950s and most of the 1960s, and the Hammer film-makers took as much inspiration from 1930s and 1940s American horror as they did from more obviously British sources. Understanding the way in which American and British influences inter-mingle within Amicus horror can, arguably, aid an appreciation of the way in which British horror in general does not exist as a discrete national object but is instead caught up in a generic history that involves a constant crossing of national borders as both ideas and personnel circulate between countries.

Bearing this in mind, it seems appropriate that the initial idea for making a new 1950s version of the Frankenstein story did not come from Hammer but, instead, from an American who approached Hammer with his own screenplay. This was rejected by Hammer, who subsequently commissioned Jimmy Sangster to come up with another script for what would eventually become *The Curse of Frankenstein* (Terence Fisher, 1957), the first of Hammer's Gothic horrors. It is worth mentioning this here because the American in question was none other than Milton Subotsky, co-founder of Amicus. While Subotsky had no creative input into *The Curse of Frankenstein*, this American can, in a limited but nonetheless significant sense, be seen as the man who started the British horror boom.

Amicus's horror output can readily be divided into two same-sized groups – the single-plot films and the portmanteau films. So far as the former are concerned, there is something to be said for the claim that 'Amicus's talents do not lie in the production of single-plot features' (Hardy 1985: 275). None of the company's seven single-plot horror films are wholly successful in what they set out to do; nor do they cohere, thematically or stylistically. Their achievements, such as they are, turn out to be fragmented and isolated. The most interesting are the first two, *The Skull* and *The Psychopath*. Both benefit from superb scores by Elizabeth Lutyens and both contain highly effective moments in which the resources of cinema are deployed to genuinely unsettling effect.[4] In the case of *The Skull* one thinks of a disturbing, stylized dream sequence and what was, for the time, an unusually open ending, with the skull left free to continue its evil work. *The Psychopath* also boasts an unnerving concluding scene in which John Standing, paralysed because of a broken back and with his face made up to look like that of a doll, is shown helplessly repeating the word 'Mamma'. However, none of these unsettling moments is successfully integrated into the films' overall narratives, and one is left with the impression that the film-makers are uncertain about what to do with some of the more intriguing features of the scenarios with which they are working. This is particularly the case with *The Psychopath*. Written by Robert Bloch, author of *Psycho* (1960), and featuring a case of severe mother fixation, the film was clearly intended to evoke memories of Hitchcock's film. Yet its fascination with the quirkily inventive staging of various murders at the expense of narrative coherence points to another type of horror, one most associated with the Italian film-makers Mario Bava and Dario Argento.[5] However, while Bava and Argento at their best can conjure up a delirious *mise en scène* within which scenes of spectacular violence make an expressive sense, a more prosaic Freddie Francis seems hard pressed to incorporate the moments of spectacular violence that punctuate his film into a cohesive view of the characters and their desires.[6]

Of the remaining Amicus films, *The Deadly Bees* and *I, Monster* (the latter an ill-advised version of *Dr Jekyll and Mr Hyde*) are dreadfully dull. *And Now the Screaming Starts!* is better, but in its treatment of a family curse weighing heavily upon the young, it is indistinguishable from, and less bold in its execution than, similarly themed Hammer films that had been appearing since the late 1960s – notably *Taste the Blood of Dracula* (Peter Sasdy, 1970), *Demons of the Mind* (Peter Sykes, 1971) and *Hands of the Ripper* (Sasdy, 1971). *Madhouse* affords Vincent Price an opportunity to camp it up as a horror film star but the film ends up covering ground that is more effectively covered by other Price vehicles, particularly *The Abominable Dr Phibes* (Robert Fuest, 1971) and *Theatre of Blood* (Douglas Hickox, 1973). *The Beast Must Die*, a whodunit in which we are invited to guess which of the characters is a werewolf, is rather silly, although, intriguingly, its having a black man (the American actor Calvin Lockhart) as its hero suggests, uniquely for British cinema, an attempted alignment with the American blaxploitation horror cinema of the early 1970s which included films such as *Blacula* (William Crain, 1972) and *Abby* (William Girdler, 1974).[7]

Amicus horror's claims for distinctiveness reside largely in its portmanteau/ anthology films – *Dr Terror's House of Horrors*, *Torture Garden*, *The House that Dripped Blood*, *Asylum*, *Tales from the Crypt*, *Vault of Horror* and *From Beyond the Grave*.[8] The idea that several separate and distinct stories can be joined together in one film has been circulating in cinema for a long time (D.W. Griffith's 1916 classic *Intolerance* being an early example). What Amicus did was to use this as a showcase for a range of horror stories, four or five in each film, featuring a mixture of traditional horror themes – vampires, werewolves, re-animated corpses, black magic, voodoo, and so on – along with tales of crime and revenge.

Broadly speaking, there are two types of portmanteau, both of which have had a part to play in British cinema. In the first group are those films in which the separate stories are not related directly to each other but are instead connected via the authorship of the original material upon which the stories are based. So, to give some British examples, the stories that make up *Quartet* (Ralph Smart, Harold French, Arthur Crabtree, Ken Annakin, 1948), *Trio* (Annakin, French, 1950) and *Encore* (French, Pat Jackson, Anthony Pelissier, 1951) are all connected through their being based on Somerset Maugham's work.[9]

The second type of portmanteau – to which Amicus films belong – connects its story segments via a link-narrative. This is usually done by creating an event or setting to which all the stories in some way relate, with this often involving an encounter between the protagonists from the various story segments. Within British cinema, one thinks of a cluster of films that appeared in the late 1940s, a boom period for the British portmanteau; these included *Bond Street* (Gordon Parry, 1948), where all the stories relate to a woman's preparations for her marriage; *Marry Me!* (Terence Fisher, 1949), in which a marriage bureau provides the link; and *Train of Events* (Sidney Cole, Charles Crichton and Basil Dearden, 1949), where the protagonists are linked via their involvement in a train accident.

Perhaps the best-known example of this second type of portmanteau, and one very pertinent to an understanding of Amicus, is Ealing Studios' *Dead of Night* (Alberto Cavalcanti, Crichton, Dearden, Robert Hamer, 1945). In this, a group of individuals meet at a house in the country and proceed to tell each other about their own encounters with the supernatural, with each encounter generating a story segment. Given *Dead of Night*'s considerable status within the British horror genre, it is unsurprising that it is often invoked in critical responses to the Amicus portmanteau, with the Amicus product usually seen as somewhat plodding in the face of *Dead of Night*'s virtuosity. For instance, David Pirie (1974: 72) argues of Amicus's *From Beyond the Grave* that:

> (I)n general the stale repetition of trite supernatural themes demonstrates the limitations of Amicus' basic approach, and the reason why – despite so many attempts – they have yet to come up with anything as good as Ealing's *Dead of Night*. A uniquely feeble link-story hinges together a script in which no attention

at all is paid to character, exposition or dialogue, with the result that everything is dependent on the limited visual suspense of the material.

Putting aside judgements about the film in question (I personally would rate it as one of Amicus's best), it does seem that Pirie, in using *Dead of Night* as a yardstick of quality, does not take sufficient account of the ways in which Amicus portmanteau films are different from their glorious predecessor. Ultimately, thinking of Amicus in terms of *Dead of Night* obscures as much as it reveals.[10]

It is true, as Pirie suggests, that while *Dead of Night* shows us in some detail its characters interacting with each other within its link-narrative, Amicus generally spends as little time as possible on its link-stories. Milton Subotsky, who once described *Dead of Night* as 'the greatest horror film ever', spoke rather dismissively of these parts of his films: 'we always find that we cut those sections shorter and shorter because we find them boring when we get them to the cutting stage' (quoted in Brosnan 1976: 239–40). In line with this, there is an arbitrariness to the encounters of those characters whose individual stories are going to form the Amicus portmanteau's segments. Barely sketched characters just happen to find themselves in the same location – a train carriage (*Dr Terror*), a fairground show (*Torture Garden*), a subterranean room (*Vault of Horror*), and catacombs (*Tales from the Crypt*) – with these settings usually abstracted from any social context. There – in a manner akin to *Dead of Night* – they either recount their own experiences or have visions of what is going to happen to them or what might already have happened to them. This is accomplished in a series of 15–20 minute scenarios, usually with a twist ending to each. *The House that Dripped Blood*, *Asylum* and *From Beyond the Grave* offer a different version in which the key protagonists never meet each other; in *House* and *From Beyond the Grave* they are, respectively, successive inhabitants of a house and customers at a sinister antiques shop. *Asylum* is the main exception in that its link-story – in which a psychiatrist has to identify which of four mental patients is the now-insane asylum director – is lengthier and more elaborate, and, to all intents and purposes, operates as a distinct segment in its own right to be placed alongside those other segments generated by the patients' own stories. (Significantly, this is the only Amicus link itself based on a pre-existing short story, Robert Bloch's 'Mannikins of Horror'.)

In a twist that became increasingly predictable as the Amicus portmanteau cycle progressed, the majority of the characters in each film eventually discover that either they are already dead (*Dr Terror*, *Tales from the Crypt*, *Vault of Horror*) or are probably going to suffer some horrible fate soon (*Torture Garden*), or else they die or go mad in the course of the film (the remainder). These 'gimmick' conclusions clearly owe something to *Dead of Night*'s famous ending in which it is revealed that all that has happened in the film is part of someone's dream. Even so, it is hard to think of many other films which cheerfully kill off so many of their main characters.

The feature which most clearly distinguishes the Amicus portmanteau from *Dead of Night*, and one which sets the general tone of these films, is the presence in many

*Figure 21* Chamber of Horrors: Peter Cushing loses his head in the 'waxworks' segment of *The House that Dripped Blood* (1970).

of them of a character who acts as a kind of horror host or master of ceremonies. The horror host – a sinister but also humorous figure who introduces a tale of horror – was often used on 1950s American television as a way of presenting horror films: examples included Vampira and Roland (a.k.a Zacherly), the latter 'a vampire television host who moved about in a set designed to resemble a subterranean crypt, appearing for commercial breaks, and signing off with the line, "Good night, whatever you are!"' (Erb 1998: 127). The horror host was also a significant feature of the American EC horror comics which Amicus itself would adapt for the cinema in the early 1970s. In comics such as *Tales from the Crypt*, *Vault of Horror* and *Haunt of Fear* the crypt keeper, the vault keeper and the old witch provided ghoulish, lip-smacking prefaces to, and commentaries on, various horror stories (Newman 1996: 160–1). To a certain extent, this was the model adopted by Amicus in its portmanteau films even before its EC adaptations, although it tended to rein in the ghoulishness of these figures and to integrate them more fully into the narrative, permitting them a limited degree of interaction with other characters. It also 'neutralized' their American-ness via casting, the very British Peter Cushing (even when sporting a German accent as he does in *Dr Terror*) and Ralph Richardson doing duty as hosts, and the only recognizably American host being the one played by Burgess Meredith in *Torture Garden*.[11]

In *Doctor Terror* the horror host is Doctor Schreck (played by Peter Cushing; 'Schreck' is, of course, German for terror), in *Torture Garden* the fairground stall holder Doctor Diabolo (Burgess Meredith), in *Tales from the Crypt* the crypt keeper (played, rather improbably, by Ralph Richardson) and in *From Beyond the Grave* the proprietor of the antiques shop (played by Cushing again). In all these cases the host initiates the various stories that comprise the portmanteau – Doctor Schreck through his tarot predictions, Diabolo with his fairground exhibit, the crypt keeper by his sinister questions, and the shopkeeper by selling objects to his customers which will lead them to their doom. This figure is ultimately revealed as a supernatural entity: Doctor Schreck turns out to be Death, Diabolo is the Devil himself (Amicus was never particularly subtle when it came to character names), while the crypt keeper is obviously a denizen of Hell, albeit of unspecified rank. *From Beyond the Grave* is not quite as explicit as this, but even here we are led to believe that the shopkeeper is not entirely human. (For one thing, he seems unaffected by being shot point blank.)

This horror host also has a special relationship with the camera and the audience, showing an awareness of both that is not available to the films' 'normal' characters. At the end of *Torture Garden*, *Tales from the Crypt* and *From Beyond the Grave* the hosts speak directly to the camera (and, by implication, directly to us, the audience). In each case they intimate that we are equally liable to the fate suffered by those within the films. In *Torture Garden* Diabolo explains why he warns his potential victims of their likely fate – 'It's only fair, you know, to give them a chance to escape my domain' – before turning to the camera and asking 'But will you?' The crypt keeper is equally blunt. Having consigned his victims to Hell, he demands 'Who's next?' Then he looks at the camera: 'Perhaps you?' At the end of *From Beyond the Grave* the shopkeeper looks up at the camera as it enters, addressing it (and us) as a new customer. 'Come in,' he says, 'I'm sure I have the very thing to tempt you. Lots of bargains. All tastes catered for. Oh – and a big novelty surprise goes with every purchase. Do come in. Anytime. I'm always open.' Doctor Schreck also looks into the camera, although this time he is seen via the point of view of another character who, near the end of the film, asks him who he really is. 'Have you not guessed?'

replies Schreck as he stares unnervingly out at us, the question as much for our benefit as for that of any of the characters in the film.

This concluding direct address to the camera/audience is also a feature of those Amicus portmanteau films which do not contain a horror host. Here this role is assigned temporarily – and somewhat arbitrarily – to a character who, in every other way, is dissimilar to the likes of Schreck and Diabolo. So in *The House that Dripped Blood* an estate agent invites us to consider applying for the house's tenancy; in *Vault of Horror* one of the dead narrators explains to the audience how they are all compelled to repeat their stories 'night after night for all eternity'; and in *Asylum* the mad Doctor Starr, closing the door on his next victim, looks out at us and says, 'Better keep the door closed and keep out the draughts – as Doctor Starr used to say.'

The effect, in all cases, is to put the audience at a distance from the drama. This goes hand in hand with in-jokes and moments of mild self-reflexivity – so, in *Vault of Horror* a writer wearily remarks that 'There's no money in horror' and reads the novelization of *Tales from the Crypt*, Amicus's previous portmanteau, while in *The House that Dripped Blood* an entire episode is given over to the antics of a horror film star (played in high camp style by Jon Pertwee), providing an opportunity for some

*Figure 22* The axeman cometh: Sylvia Syms is his victim in Roy Ward Baker's *Asylum* (1972).

none-too-subtle digs at Hammer. In a different way *Torture Garden* reminds us of our status as audience through an opening sequence in which the camera is used subjectively to give us a sense that we are approaching Diabolo's show and buying a ticket for the entertainment which it offers.

The reason for this distancing becomes all too clear when we look at the films' protagonists and realize that there are very few individuals with whom one would want to identify. Venality and greed are the order of the day, and there is also a comprehensive lack of regard for the family unit. In the Amicus world wives kill husbands (*Tales from the Crypt*, *Vault of Horror*), husbands kill wives (*Dr Terror's House of Horrors*, *Vault of Horror*), brothers kill sisters (*Vault of Horror*), sisters kill brothers (*Asylum*), nephews kill uncles (*Torture Garden*) and children kill parents (*The House that Dripped Blood*) or arrange to have their parents killed (*From Beyond the Grave*). Even by the standards of 1970s US horror – where the family unit is often figured as monstrous – there is something remarkable going on here.

While 1970s American horror frequently used the broken or corrupt family to symbolize a wider social breakdown, Amicus horror preferred instead to isolate its families from any discernible social context. A good example is the 'And All Through the House' segment from *Tales from the Crypt*. This opens with a loving husband placing a present – labelled 'To Joanne, the best wife in the world' – by the Christmas tree in the family home. He then sits down and reads the newspaper until the beloved wife sneaks up behind him and smashes in his head with a poker. 'Merry Christmas,' she says to the corpse. (We quickly learn that she has done this so that she can claim on her husband's life insurance.) A radio announcement informs us that a homicidal maniac 'disguised' as Santa Claus is on the loose; meanwhile Joanne, the wife, seeks to calm her young daughter who, unaware of her father's death, is looking forward to Santa Claus's arrival. Predictably enough, Joanne soon realizes that the killer (or rather, the other killer) is outside the house trying to get in. However, she cannot call the police until she has made her husband's death look like an accident. This she achieves by pitching him down the cellar stairs. She then cleans up all signs of the murder only to find that her daughter has let Santa Claus into the house. Santa Claus proceeds to strangle Joanne.

This segment could well be used to illustrate David Pirie's dismissal – quoted above – of this type of film. Characterization is minimal, the exposition basic and the dialogue functional. However, it can be argued that the depth of characterization sought by Pirie (and which he finds in *Dead of Night*) would be inappropriate for what this segment is actually trying to do. We are not meant to identify or empathize with any of these characters; instead we view from a distance what is essentially a parody of the traditional family Christmas, one in which both the wife and Santa Claus turn out to be murderers. The incongruity of this particular Christmas scene is further underlined by the carols we hear on the soundtrack – 'Away in a Manger' for the arrival of the homicidal Santa Claus, 'God Rest You, Merry Gentlemen' as the wife pushes her husband's body down the stairs. There is no sense of any critique of the family unit; instead, what one finds is an overturning of a conventional, normative understanding of both Christmas and familial relationships in order to produce a series of shocks. These shocks are not necessarily 'scares' – although the segment does contain some of these – but, rather, relate to a disruption of expectations that is both violent and witty.

A comparable disregard for and violation of a particular sense of propriety is also apparent in these films' treatment of their ostensibly moralistic message – namely that those individuals who do bad things suffer because of them. In most cases, a sense of justice being done is undermined by the sheer excessiveness and cruelty of the punishment handed out. For example, the shop customers in *From Beyond the Grave* might well be greedy, but, by any reasonable moral code, they do not deserve to die. The key line in *From Beyond the Grave* in this respect is not the homily delivered by the shopkeeper near the end of the film: 'The love of money is the root of all evil.' Instead it occurs earlier, in a comment made to a customer who, through an act of minor deception, has purchased an expensive snuff box at a cheap price. 'I hope you enjoy snuffing it,' the shopkeeper says cheerfully to the customer who, unsuspecting, is on his way to certain doom. The joke is on the customer, of course; he won't enjoy snuffing it at all – but we will enjoy watching him snuffing it. This is not because he is morally culpable nor because we feel morally superior to him (we are certainly not being positioned as judges here, and the film offers constant reminders that any one of us could be the next victim). If there is cruelty in this joke, it is not the audience's cruelty nor even that of the shopkeeper. Rather, it derives from a situation in which the punishment for sin is so ridiculously excessive that the moral message – honesty is good – becomes meaningless, and our pleasure has to do with an enjoyment of this meaninglessness. In this sense, the joke is on us and on our own values.

A phrase used by Martin Barker in his discussion of an EC horror comic story (both *Tales of the Crypt* and *Vault of Horror* were based on EC horror comics) is apposite here: 'It shocks us into a momentary awareness, without in any way telling us what in particular to think' (Barker 1984: 115). It is clear that these films – much like those EC horror tales which conclude with moralizing messages – do not expect us to take them seriously as 'morality plays'. If they shock us into a momentary awareness of anything (and I think they do), it is of the contingency and arbitrariness of everyday life. In the Amicus portmanteau, the family unit is simply a series of relationships (parent/child, brother/sister, wife/husband, etc.) which do not appear to carry any inherent emotional charge. There is no such thing as family unity or solidarity here; the family is just a social structure and nothing else. Similarly, morality comprises a set of laws or rules. These might be broken, and punishment may subsequently ensue, but these rules do not connect with or express trans- cendent notions of good and evil. They are just rules, nothing more, and as arbitrary and fundamentally meaningless as the family unit. (This makes for an interesting comparison with 1970s US horror which, for all its criticisms, still tended to view the family unit as a fundamental source of social meaning.) In this respect, what all the distancing devices and techniques deployed in the Amicus portmanteau do is to lead the audience to a position both of scepticism about society's ostensible value system and of an amused indifference in the face of this. While Hammer, for all its iconoclastic sensationalism, always exhibited a sentimental attachment to a moralistic way of seeing, the Amicus portmanteau offered a different view – cynical, sardonic, cruel, modern.

It might well be said that Amicus's debts to American horror are such that it could be seen as an outpost of American film production that just happened to be located within Britain. At the same time, however – and at the risk of being impressionistic – these films feel very British, not just in terms of their casts and settings but also in their attention to and familiarity with the minutiae of British life. In particular, many of the portmanteau tales depend for their effectiveness upon a clear awareness of British class divisions – both in the British-sourced stories such as the Ian Bannen/ Donald Pleasence episode in *From Beyond the Grave* (adapted from the work of the British writer Ronald Chetwynd-Hayes and described by Pirie as 'superbly Pinterish') and in the EC adaptations. For example, note the class tension apparent in the 'Poetic Justice' episode from *Tales from the Crypt*, in which a middle-class householder terrorizes a working-class man who, he feels, is lowering the tone of the neighbourhood. There is also an undeniably British sense of humour at work here: after all, how could a film which offers a pun on the term 'snuffing it' not be seen as British on some level? The changes wrought by Amicus upon the EC horror stories, Bloch's work and other US influences stand, in this respect, as more than just a superficial Anglicization, a simple replacement of American accents with British ones. In their attempts to appeal to what was in the 1960s and early 1970s a substantial market (both nationally and internationally) for British horror, the Amicus film-makers had necessarily to offer a more fundamental re-working of non-British material than this, albeit one in which American influences still remain visible. Seen in this way, as a kind of hybrid enterprise operating within British cinema, Amicus horror as expressed in the portmanteau format provides a salutary reminder not only that there is more to British horror than Hammer but also that there is considerably more to British horror than indigenous British cultural traditions.

In the 'Neat Job' segment from *Vault of Horror* a woman murders her obsessively tidy husband, dissects his body and neatly puts the remains away in labelled jars. At the end of the segment, the camera moves past jars marked 'Hands', 'Brain', 'Nose' and 'Eyes' before alighting on a jar containing some unrecognizable body parts. The jar label reads 'Odds and Ends'. Obviously we are being invited to speculate that these 'bits' are the husband's genitalia, 'bits' which, in the film's terms, cannot be named or easily classified, and which, for 1970s British cinema at least, have to remain 'unmentionable'. So far as classifying Amicus horror is concerned, one cannot help but feel that it, too, belongs in the 'Odds and Ends' jar. In all sorts of ways it does not easily fit in – in the stories it tells and in the way it tells them – and yet, at the same time, it is undoubtedly an important part of the British horror scene. In particular, a consideration of Amicus necessarily problematizes the relation between British cinema and the horror genre – the first by definition nationally specific, the second international, a visible presence in a range of national centres of production. As noted above, definitions and evaluations of British horror have often been based on its relation to British cultural traditions. It does seem that so far as horror is concerned, a stronger sense of the international dimension of the genre is required, of the ways in which ideas, influences and creative personnel (as well as the films themselves) move in and out of national contexts of production. The resulting view of British horror is one more attuned to its place in both national and international histories and contexts. Amicus provides a useful starting point for this in that its non-British influences are especially visible. To locate it within British horror requires a certain rethinking of British horror in general. The 'Amicus House of Horror' might well be smaller than and stand in the shadow of the better-known Hammer House of Horror but it exists in the same neighbourhood, and thinking of Amicus in these terms suggests that the neighbourhood itself might be a somewhat less parochial area than was previously supposed.

## Notes

1  In addition to its horror films, Amicus also produced science-fiction films – *The Terrornauts* (Montgomery Tully, 1967), *They Came from Beyond Space* (Freddie Francis, 1967), *Scream and Scream Again* (Gordon Hessler, 1969 – a co-production with American International Pictures), and *The Mind of Mr Soames* (Alan Cooke, 1969) as well as an adaptation of Margaret Drabble's *The Millstone* entitled *A Touch of Love* (Waris Hussein, 1969). In 1974 the company abandoned horror production and embarked on what would turn out to be its final projects, a series of Edgar Rice Burroughs' adaptations – *The Land that Time Forgot* (Kevin Connors, 1974), *At the Earth's Core* (Connors, 1976) and *The People that Time Forgot* (Connors, 1977). Amicus founders Max J. Rosenberg and Milton Subotsky also produced films away from Amicus – notably two Doctor Who adaptations that featured Peter Cushing as the doctor – *Dr Who and the Daleks* (Gordon Flemyng, 1965) and *Daleks: Invasion Earth 2150 AD* (Flemyng, 1966).
2  These included the youth musicals *Rock, Rock, Rock* (Will Price, 1956) and *Jamboree* (Roy Lockwood, 1957).
3  If nothing else, these films help to explain the otherwise inexplicable presence of British disc-jockey Alan 'Fluff' Freeman in the cast of *Dr Terror's House of Horrors*. He had previously appeared in both *It's Trad Dad* and *Just for Fun*.
4  Lutyens also composed the score for *Dr Terror's House of Horrors*; her sinister, quietly haunting music stands worlds apart from the more brash scores frequently provided for Hammer by James Bernard.
5  Subotsky has claimed that the identity of the murderer in *The Psychopath* was changed during post-production in order to make the mystery harder to solve. This might explain why it is that, at a certain point, the narrative simply ceases to make any sense.
6  For an interesting contrast, see a later Italian horror film, *Profondo Rosso* (Dario Argento, 1975), which contains some *Psychopath*-like elements such as a killer associated with

dolls and an 'unhealthy' mother–son relationship, but which responds much more imaginatively to the fetishistic possibilities of such a scenario.

7  As if to underline this appeal to the market for black horror, *The Beast Must Die* was apparently released on video with the title *Black Werewolf*. (I am indebted to Steve Chibnall for drawing my attention to the blaxploitation connection.)

8  Another portmanteau, *Tales that Witness Madness* (Freddie Francis, 1973), is mistakenly attributed to Amicus on occasion.

9  Other films of this type use the authorial presence of the director to bind together the various story segments. The French film *Le Plaisir* (1952) – which combines its adaptation of Maupassant stories with the formidable authorial presence of the director Max Ophuls – is a good example. Two American horror portmanteau films of this type – *Tales of Terror* (Roger Corman, 1962), based on Edgar Allan Poe stories, and *Twice Told Tales* (Sidney Salkow, 1963), based on stories by Nathaniel Hawthorne – might well have alerted Amicus to there being a market for the anthology horror film.

10  One might well concede that the Amicus portmanteau films are uneven in quality, and that some films and some segments within films are more effective than others. However, it could be argued that it is anyway in the nature of the portmanteau (and not just the ones made by Amicus) to be uneven and inconsistent. Even those critics who see *Dead of Night* as the apotheosis of the portmanteau tend to focus on the 'haunted mirror' and 'ventriloquist's dummy' segments and leave the rest of the film well alone.

11  It is also worth mentioning that Britain had its own horror host, albeit on radio, in the series *Appointment with Fear* (1943–55), in which each episode was introduced by the sepulchral Man in Black. While there is no evidence that Subotsky, the writer of the first Amicus portmanteau, knew of the Man in Black, the actor who played the part – Valentine Dyall – had in fact appeared in the Subotsky-produced *City of the Dead*.

# References

Barker, M. (1984) *A Haunt of Fears*, London: Pluto Press.

Brosnan, J. (1976) *The Horror People*, London: MacDonald & Janes.

Erb, C. (1998) *Tracking King Kong: A Hollywood Icon in World Culture*, Detroit, Ill.: Wayne State University Press.

Hardy, P. (ed.) (1985) *The Aurum Film Encyclopedia: Horror*, London: Aurum.

Newman, K. (ed.) (1996) *The BFI Companion to Horror*, London: British Film Institute.

Pirie, D. (1973) *A Heritage of Horror: The English Gothic Cinema 1946–1972*, London: Gordon Fraser.

Pirie, D. (1974) review of *From Beyond the Grave* in *Monthly Film Bulletin*, 41, 483: 72.

# 11 A descent into the underworld: *Death Line*

*Marcelle Perks*

There are certain films which remain mostly obscure to mainstream audiences but which supply a litmus test for informed good taste among *real* horror fans. The British film *Death Line* (US: *Raw Meat*, 1972) is one of those films. Over the years it has attained a cult following, particularly in the United States, and was the inspiration for Guillermo Del Toro's *Cronos* (1993). Once described (admiringly) by the film critic Robin Wood as 'one of the most horrible horror films ever', this seminal cannibal film, with its postmodern blurring of the boundaries between monster and victim, is the British equivalent of the acknowledged American classic, *The Texas Chainsaw Massacre* (Tobe Hooper, 1974). The fact that it is the American film – released two years later – which has become a household name is a testimony to the fate that inevitably befalls British genre product. Critics, press and distributors have so mishandled our Gothic heritage that the reception of British horror films in their own country is almost as interesting as the films themselves. There is more at stake here, then, than simply making the case for a 'forgotten gem': the example of *Death Line* reveals how the reaction of critics affects the process of distribution, exhibition and, ultimately, production.

In 1968, the American films *Night of the Living Dead* (George Romero) and *Rosemary's Baby* (Roman Polanski) were critically acclaimed as the first 'modern' horror films. By contrast, in the same year Britain's now highly regarded *Witchfinder General* (Michael Reeves) was badly publicized and also vilified by the press. Similarly, another classic, *The Wicker Man* (Robin Hardy, 1973), was initially mishandled by its distributors, British Lion. Released as a supporting feature (to Nicholas Roeg's *Don't Look Now* (1973)), *The Wicker Man* was never even shown to the British press and thus received scant publicity. Even a film-maker of Michael Powell's stature found his career irreparably damaged by the critical backlash to *Peeping Tom* (1960). Horror films simply did not fit into the valorized tradition of social realism in British cinema.

Typically the British critical response to *Death Line* was overwhelmingly negative. Cecil Watson's comment in the *Daily Mail* of 16 November 1972 was typical: 'We spend an inordinate time in the madman's dark, dank and bloody lair peering through the murk at the most revolting sights imaginable and wondering how such a sick and sick-making film came to be made.' Derek Malcolm felt the need to dissociate the film from its British heritage and disliked both *Death Line* and the film with which it was double billed, *Night Hair Child* (James Kelly, 1972): 'if these two films are an example of what British studios have to offer, the sooner they close down the better.'[1] The negative reaction of a handful of British critics (with the exception of the expatriate Robin Wood) embarrassed its distributors, Rank, into restricting the release of *Death Line*.

Ironically, those elements of *Death Line* that outraged the British press were the very qualities that sold horror films in the United States. The publicity campaigns for films like Wes Craven's *The Last House on the Left* (1972) and *The Hills Have Eyes* (1977) played on the films' notoriety in order to market them successfully, and John Pym, in his initial review of Hooper's *The Texas Chainsaw Massacre*, pointed out that its extraordinary success could be partly attributed to its aggressive advertising campaign. The success of low-budget American horror product enabled directors like Craven, Hooper and Romero to become internationally acclaimed. It is unlikely that this would have been the case had they been working in Britain.

In fact, *Death Line* was the directorial debut of an American film-maker, Gary Sherman. After winning several awards for his documentary *The Legend of Bo Diddley*, and working as an art director and cinematographer, he decided that he wanted to direct features. He wrote the script for *Death Line* in between shooting a commercial for Proctor & Gamble on the South Downs. He was assisted by the veteran genre producer Paul Maslansky, who had worked on *Jason and the Argonauts* (Don Chaffey, 1963), and alongside Michael Reeves on *The Long Ships* (Jack Cardiff, 1963) before producing *Castle of the Living Dead* (Luciano Ricci, 1964). *Death Line* is particularly interesting when considered as a British genre film, because it utilizes specifically British myths and iconography as a basis for its horror. Its American director was inspired by the British legend of Sawney Bean. The Bean clan, comprising of three generations, lived in a remote cave in Scotland in the 1780s and survived by slaughtering travellers. When a potential victim escaped, an investigation of their caves revealed that 'legs, arms, thighs, hands and feet of men, women and children, were hung up in rows, like dried beef; a great many limbs laid out in pickle' (Farson 1977: 143).

This scenario is replicated in *Death Line*. When we first descend into the underground world, a long, darkly lit tracking shot pans from a rat chewing a piece of meat to various incongruous human body parts strung up with corpses. Most cannibal films pay homage to an American legend, the real-life cannibal Ed Gein, and assist in what Robin Wood (1984: 187) calls 'the homogenisation of the horror film into something we recognise as American and familial'. The first film version to do this was *Psycho* (Alfred Hitchcock, 1960), and films with which *Death Line* has been compared, such as *The Texas Chainsaw Massacre* and *The Hills Have Eyes*, essentially rework this theme. Even the British cannibal film *Frightmare* (Pete Walker, 1974) is

American in orientation, as its emphasis on the flesh-eating mother pays a literal homage to the devouring mother in Hitchcock's *Psycho*.[2]

Shot entirely on location, *Death Line* also utilizes another specifically British landmark, the London Underground. The use of the closed-down station, British Museum, as a lair for the cannibals recalls the comedy *Bulldog Jack* (Walter Forde, 1935) which spoofed 1933 press reports that the station was haunted by an Egyptian ghost.[3] The television documentary *Underground London*, broadcast in autumn 1971, which depicted the old City and South London line's disused tunnels may also have been an influence. Sherman makes the Underground and the exploitation of its original builders symbolic of Britain's industrial past. Repeated shots of the crumbling masonry emphasize that if this historic Underground was originally built because Britain was a first world power, the country is now, like its transport system, in decline. *Death Line*, then, like *The Wicker Man* and *Witchfinder General*, can be identified as quintessentially British genre fare which engages with a sense of national identity for its meaning. Had it been properly promoted and distributed it might have changed the face of British post-Hammer horror. David Pirie (1973: 22), in his contemporaneous survey of British horror cinema, saw a potential for the genre to develop into a significant national idiom, but this was not realized and promising directors like Stephen Weeks, Peter Sasdy and Peter Sykes were unable to flourish for long within the genre.

What makes *Death Line* so memorable is its iconography (particularly in its underground scenes), the contrast between the overworld and underworld scenes and its knowing satire of the British comedy film. This eclectic mix has earned it a cult status. The film begins with a 'red herring': a psychedelic montage of Soho's neon sex shop signs, which loom in and out of focus to a 'striptease' music sound-track. The generic connotations suggested by the horrific sounding title, *Death Line*, are thus immediately subverted. The glaring colours and seedy shots of London suggest that the film will be more like the soft core British sex films of the 'swinging sixties'. A bowler-hatted, middle-aged man (who will shortly be identified as James Manfred) is comically shown surveying various shop signs advertising 'girls' and 'sex'. The stereotypical moustache, bowler hat and umbrella encourage us to identify him as an eccentric Englishman, but his public perusal of the sex signs also sends up the famous British reserve. As an American, Gary Sherman stuffs his narrative full of jokes about and obvious references to aspects of 'Britishness'.

Manfred is shown only in profile or long shot, and his journey to Russell Square is lit so darkly that we can barely see him. This somewhat peculiar cinematography will only later reveal its full dramatic significance. At Russell Square, he accosts a prostitute, who, unusually for a literal sexual object, is surveyed only briefly by the camera; initially she also has her back to us. Manfred strikes up a deal with the woman, but she snatches the money out of his hand and kicks him in the groin, leaving him alone and in pain on the platform. Manfred's eroticized journey to the tube station makes the unexpected presence of the monstrous, signalled by heavy breathing on the soundtrack, all the more arresting. Manfred is seen attempting to cower away from an unseen assailant, and it is from the monster's point of view that we look at the victim. This scene is intercut by shots of people on a moving tube train, including Alex Campbell and Patricia Wilson, two of the film's main protagonists. Alex and Patricia see Manfred lying unconscious on the stairs. Alex, the American student, is represented as callous and unfeeling – 'In New York, we walk over these people' – but Pat insists that 'We can't just leave him.' The contrast between American and English culture is thus set up as a binary opposition, which gains momentum throughout the film. They look in his wallet to see if he's a diabetic and discover that he is James Manfred, OBE.

Their attempts to obtain help from the guard are delayed when he gives them a complicated reason to explain why he can't ring for help until the lift stops. The hyperbole of his sentences and the general inefficiency poke fun at the British working man at a time when industrial unrest was at its highest point since the general strike of 1926. When Alex eventually returns with a policeman, both men are filmed in extreme long shot and lit very darkly. Again, this appears to signify the monster's point of view. No body is found, and only Manfred's wallet is visible on the stairs. The film's first enigma is thus established.

This first encounter with Manfred, and, through him, with the monster, has disrupted the equilibrium of Pat's relationship with Alex and she is unable to sleep. As this couple will be frequently contrasted with the underground couple, known only as Man and Woman, it is significant that the 'civilized' couple are shown throughout the film doing mostly what the 'monstrous' couple would have done, namely sleeping and eating. The next shot introduces us to Inspector Calqhoun (Donald Pleasence) and Rogers (David Rossington) who together make up the third pair of couples in the film. Much of the contemporary appeal of the film would have depended on its use of these actors who had established a reputation for appearing in both genre and mainstream films. Pleasence's extra-diegetic image as a British character actor is satirized by his almost caricatural role as a working-class policeman in the film. From his first scene, he signals his interest in tea, darts and football, all supposedly typical British working-class traits; he is also sexist and racist. As a cockney who has risen to the level of inspector in the police, he always displays ambiguity towards authority; for example, on hearing of Manfred's disappearance he says 'He's some big shit – er – shot in the Ministry.' In a comic reversal of class relations he is contrasted with the less senior but more refined and knowledgeable Sergeant Rogers.

The narrative, then, interacts between the two overground couples as Inspector Calqhoun attempts to investigate the disappearance of the missing Manfred. These interactions revolve mainly around the antagonism between Alex and Inspector Calqhoun, which is established via a series of binary oppositions: educated/ uneducated, American/British, young/old. For example, Calqhoun exhibits his contempt for education when Alex complains about his wasted time and he tells him 'Why don't you hurry back to school. There might be a protest march worth fighting.'[4]

Rogers is surprised that Calqhoun is bothering with the Manfred case as MI5 will anyway be investigating his disappearance. The search for this VIP becomes crucial to the film's theme of social injustice, in that it suggests that the class-biased attitudes that in 1892 dictated that the tunnellers were 'only' workers who weren't worth digging out, are still in place. Even the working-class Calqhoun distinguishes between Manfred, – 'an important geezer with a lot of top secret information in his head' – and greengrocers and dentists as missing people whose disappearance can simply be filed. Calqhoun then calls in an expert from London Transport CID to throw light on how people could simply disappear on Russell Square station. Richardson tells them about the accident in which eight men and four women were trapped in a collapsed tunnel during its construction, and then abandoned because the company involved went bankrupt. He also mentions the rumours that the tunnel workers survived: 'there was plenty of water, and I would imagine that as each one died, the others would have eaten him.' This not only introduces a possible explanation for the disappearances but also helps to cast those perhaps responsible for them in a relatively sympathetic light.

Calqhoun is surprised at Richardson's proposition and a medium close-up of his shocked face is shown just before he throws his tea bag in the bin. The next shot amplifies the soft, plopping sound of the discarded tea bag to introduce us to the wet and foetid walls of the underworld. At this point, the narrative style of the film completely changes. A long tracking shot depicts an abandoned underground tunnel, a dark and undefined enclosure. The soundtrack utilizes the noises of dripping water and of an amplified heart beat to signal that we are in a 'terrible place'. We see maggots eating a piece of flesh, but, unlike in most cannibal/zombie films, the corpses are not depicted in a realist mode. We can barely make out what we are seeing, which, combined with the considerable amount of time (nine minutes) spent initially in the underworld, increases our sense of dread.[5] The camera completes an almost 360-degree pan of the underworld and then a series of roving shots focuses on the two cannibals. 'The Man' is shot with his back to us and could be mistaken for a woman. His partner, 'The Woman', is heavily pregnant and looks to be near death.

The camera then depicts the boundaries of this underground world through a series of roving shots. The soundtrack changes to more cheerful music, setting up an ambiguous relationship with the 'terrible place'. Unusually, the film then narrativizes Richardson's verbal account of the tunnelling disaster, using only the sound track. A series of dark tracking shots depicts the unfinished work and cave-like *mise en scène* of the underground. This is accompanied by a flash-back account of 'what actually happened', relayed purely through the sound track. The sound of people working and talking is followed by the noise of a roof falling in and screams; seemingly endless shots of tunnels are then shown in the ensuing silence, which emphasizes the terrible predicament of being buried alive.

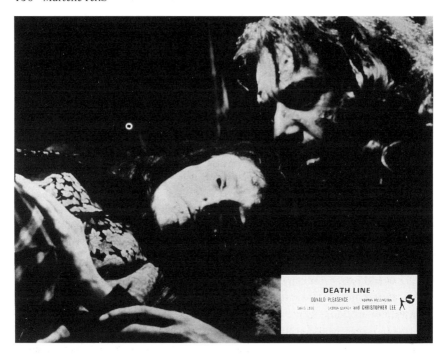

*Figure 23*  Family life in the 1970s horror film: deep underground, the 'Man' (Hugh
Armstrong) tends his dying pregnant 'Woman' (June Turner) in *Death Line*
(1972).

The two survivors of this disaster appear more as victims than monsters. *Death
Line* thus subverts generic conventions by 'making the plight of the monster
sympathetic, even moving, while speaking about it in its own terms' (del Torro
1995). In particular they come across less as cannibals than as victims of social
neglect. The film's use of an engineering marvel such as the London Underground
as a breeding ground for a severely regressed form of humanity clearly suggests the
darker side of civilization, and one that belies its myth of progress. In this respect
Robin Wood (1979: 45) suggests that *Death Line* is a powerful embodiment of the
'Descent myth' which is fundamental to all civilizations and 'shows characters
existing in a state of innocence who, by a process of (often literal) descent, are led
to discover a terrible underlying reality of whose existence they had scarcely
dreamed'.

At this point, the film's exposition has been established, concluding with a jarring
change in narrative style to depict the underworld. The narrative then becomes
schizophrenic, and the differences between overworld/underworld are represented
cinematographically by the alternation between different modes of narration.

The narrative is also divided almost equally between the three couples, Alex/Pat,
the Man/the Woman and the two police officers. Thus there is no obvious main

protagonist with whom we can identify. Horror film narratives often revolve around a protagonist placed in a seeker role who uncovers the mystery of a hideous monster, which is revealed as abject. Initially, the Inspector seems to be set up in this stereotypical role so beloved by Dario Argento. Conventionally, this kind of figure is supposed to work out the enigma, but at the crucial moment when Pat is kidnapped, the Inspector is found wanting (drunk and hung over), thus leaving it to Alex to rescue Pat.

The film also links thematically the two heterosexual couples. After the 'Woman' has died, the 'Man's' literal losing of his loved one is metaphorically replicated when Patricia leaves Alex. When the 'Man' makes a futile attempt to revive his dead mate, by the ritual blood-letting of Manfred's throat, it's significant that Patricia brings Alex a bottle of *red* wine in order to try to rekindle their relationship. The couples are also linked through the idea of woman, signalled as a lack. Both Colqhoun and the 'Man' lose their partners through death (Colqhoun at one point states that 'it reminds me of the night poor Maisie died'); Sergeant Rogers has no woman, and Alex loses his grip on his relationship with Pat. This places the focus of attention firmly on the film's female protagonist, Pat, who becomes a mediator between the overground and underground worlds. She is shown as being innately closer to the underground world by being interested in the notion of the 'other': she buys a book on poltergeists, and is curious about and disturbed by Manfred's disappearance. She is also contrasted positively with Alex (whose violent actions taint him at the end) by her dislike of violence. Her descent into the underworld prompts the interaction between the two worlds.

Pat's disappearance prompts Alex and the police to investigate the possibilities of the underground world. After she recovers consciousness underground, she, like us, is repulsed by the 'Man', but her symbolic exchange of language with him is a breakthrough. She abandons the power of normal speech and adopts her captor's primitive language, expressed in cries and moans. In exchange, the 'Man' articulates the only phrase he knows, 'Mind the doors', to express every nuance of human feeling. The way in which the characters are lit underground also encourages sympathy for the 'monster'. When Alex enters the underground with a torch to find Pat, instead of the standard shot from *his* point of view of the tunnels, we see him from the 'monster's' point of view. The light is focused harshly on him, so that rather than cutting an heroic figure, he seems like an intruder into the underground world. At this point, the three characters are trying to find each other in the dark, and it is noticeable that, when the 'Man' is shown, the *mise en scène* is noticeably lighter, signalling that he is at home here. In contrast, the shots of Alex are dark, thus symbolically vilifying him. Furthermore, the supposedly 'civilized' Alex seems to revert to a form of primitive savagery when he encounters the 'Man', brutally kicking him (possibly to death) in the head.

Equally disturbingly, the film also avoids a 'classic' narrative resolution. At the end, in the time-honoured way, the monster dies. However, normally one would also expect a reconciliation between the remaining protagonists, but Pat and Alex are simply left dumbstruck and shivering by the Inspector, who knows that he has failed. Calqhoun leaves the scene visibly shaken, hands over the case to Rogers, and arranges for others to 'clean up'. The intervention of the 'normal' world, then, has been unable to spoil completely the magic and mystery of the underworld. As the end credits roll, we hear the 'monster's' voice one more time: 'Mind the doors.'

The most horrific aspect of *Death Line* lies in the power and originality of its 'underground' scenes. In this respect, a psychoanalytic reading of the film is revealing. Barbara Creed (1993: 10), drawing on Julia Kristeva's theory of the 'abject', argues that woman's special relation to polluting objects such as excreta and menstrual blood ensures that many of the icongraphic features of horror films are signalled as inherently female. *Death Line* is a particularly rich repository of these abject images: the cannibals' lair is littered with corpses and pieces of mutilated flesh, and Manfred's throat is cut over the body of the 'Woman'. In addition, and as noted earlier, the narrative emphasizes the grisly *mise en scène*, by adopting different narrative strategies to depict the 'underworld'. The overground world is narrativized in a 'classic' realist style, but, once underground, the narrative changes pace and becomes more 'art cinema'-like, lingering over the *mise en scène*, with long,

*Figure 24* Survival tactics: the American advertising for the re-titled *Death Line* emphasizes the idea of humanity stripped to its lowest common denominator.

darkened, tracking shots. The threat, then, does not really emanate from the cannibals, who are represented as overgrown, frightened children, nor from their grisly 'larder' of bodies.

The source of the monstrous depends on the representation of the underworld as a living thing, which is emphasized by the use of an amplified heart beat as a soundtrack to accompany these images. It is shot as womb-like, with an emphasis on the darkened, curved enclosure of the cannibal's cave-like lair which can be reached only through a vagina-like smaller tunnel. Our initial introduction to the underground world is via a long tracking shot which stops on a close-up of a sick, pregnant woman's full stomach, which points literally to the monstrous nature of the woman/womb. Freud linked the womb to the uncanny and suggested that it was something which ought to remain hidden but which comes to light, and, throughout the film, the revelation of the underworld and its denizens is presented in this light. The film also resists conventional narrative resolution: even if the last of the 'monstrous' offspring is apparently dead by the end, the threat of the underground world has not been countered. The nature of the monstrous emanates from the personification of the underground in terms of what Creed calls a 'generative archaic mother', one of most feared images in patriarchal societies. *Death Line*'s insistence that the very ground of the underworld is a living, breathing thing which spreads contamination – the cannibals have plague – signifies this. Creed (1993: 43) argues that in the horror film the ancient connection between woman, womb and the monstrous is frequently invoked. *Death Line*, with its seemingly interminably long tracking shots depicting womb-like images, provides the most sustained example of this type of representation of which I am aware.

*Death Line*'s story of how a group of tunnellers came to be buried alive, and survived by incestuous inbreeding and cannibalism, can also be likened to Freud's account, in *Totem and Taboo*, of how primitive societies reverted from patriarchy to matriarchy and then back to patriarchy again. Kristeva points out that Freud's analysis concentrates on the taboo of murder committed by the sons and ignores the taboo of incest, yet 'the woman – or mother – image haunts a large part of that book and keeps shaping its background.'[6] *Death Line* is significant in that it seems to represent the matriarchal stage of primitive societies. The film's iconographical dependency on womb-like imagery, and its focusing on the cannibal man's attempts to revive his 'woman', make matriarchal concerns central to the narrative. The last remaining male also seems to represent a filial rather than father figure, and the fact that the group has survived by cannibalism can be linked to the devouring of the powerful father figure that Freud described in *Totem and Taboo*.

The 'Man' seems to be a feminized or child-like figure, and, contrary to most Lacanian representations of sexual difference, demonstrates his lack compared to his mate. When we first encounter the 'Man', he could actually be mistaken for a woman. He is shot with his back to us, crying over the prostrate body of his mate, and his long hair and display of tears are more typical of a female demeanour. He is frequently shown hugging himself in a foetal position, which is signified as a feminine movement, and is mirrored by Patricia when she finds herself in his lair. The only time that he behaves in an aggressive 'masculine' way is after his mate dies in childbirth. Psychoanalytic critics have stressed the primacy of the male subject and the male gaze, and the 'Man's' weakness is signalled by his passive gaze. He never actually looks directly into the camera, instead the spectator is placed in a position of dominant specularity through repeated shots of the 'Man's' unfocused eyes, which express his condition of ignorance. Thus the degenerative society that *Death Line* depicts, with its literal enactment of cannibalism and incest, seems an example, *par excellence*, of the primitive matriarchal society which Freud described.

However, the narrative mocks the myth of the mother as sole parent by denying her regenerative powers. Her offspring are monstrous and finally unable to reproduce. The final extinction of the descendants signifies that the archaic mother as womb is also, literally, a tomb. Creed (1993: 47) suggests that woman's maternal function is constructed as abject and links her directly to the cycle of birth, decay and death, and the film's most horrifying image – of the 'Man' crying over his dead pregnant mate – brings all these elements together. The dead female's maternal function is depicted as death-in-life and she is signified as triply abject: as a corpse, complete with a hideously swollen pregnancy, and her face smeared with the abject properties of blood and dirt. The film, then, denies the viability of a parthogenic mother and renders such a possibility an aberration.

*Death Line* also literally links the theme of cannibalism and incest, which are essential (but normally repressed) components of the primal scene (when children fantasize about their parents having sex). *Death Line* was one of the first films to feature cannibalism; this is often an *implied* theme in horror, especially in werewolf and vampire films, but here it is both made explicit and linked with incest. It is not used for mere titillation (we never see the cannibals actually eat any flesh) but is presented as a natural development of the cannibals' predicament in being entombed underground. *Death Line*'s possibly unique explication, then, of the linked themes of cannibalism and incest, coupled with its recurrent womb imagery, posits it as one of the cinema's most potent versions of the *primal scene*, and this helps to explain why its presentation of the underground is so powerful and lingers in the mind for so long.

With its pioneering depiction of cannibalism and visceral horror, *Death Line* anticipated much European and American work in the genre. It is conceivable that if *Death Line* had been handled differently by Rank, and/or the critics had been more receptive to its new spin on our Gothic heritage, the story of post-Hammer British horror cinema would have been very different. As it was, the overwhelmingly negative response to *Death Line* hardly helped the development of British horror cinema after 1972, making it even more difficult for British directors to explore the generic spaces which Gary Sherman's film had so effectively opened up.

# Notes

1 Quoted in del Toro (1995: 41).
2 *Death Line*'s cannibal theme was timely as 1972 turned out to be the 'year of the cannibal' with three other disparate cannibal titles in circulation: *Terror at Red Wolf Inn* (Bud Townsend), *The Mad Butcher* (John Zurli) and *Cannibal Girls* (Ivan Reitman).
3 Most of the underground scenes were shot in an East End storage facility belonging to British Rail. The actual tube station used for filming was Aldwych. Sherman obtained clearance to use it by submitting a non-horror script to London Transport. This information, and much subsequent material, is derived from an interview with Gary Sherman conducted by the author in 1999.
4 Donald Pleasence contributed additional dialogue to Sherman's script.
5 Sherman recalls that the underground scenes were much clearer on the 'dailies'. The tunnel was 'dressed' so that it looked as if it had hundred-year-old debris: 'Dennis did such a great job on the set but it's so dark you can't see all the details, there's skeletons in there . . . there's several skulls.'
6 Quoted in Creed 1993: 132.

# References

Creed, B. (1993), *The Monstrous Feminine: Film, Feminism, Psychoanalysis*, London: Routledge.

Farson, D. (1977), *The Beaver Book of Horror*, London: Hamlyn.

Pirie, D. (1973), *A Heritage of Horror: The English Gothic Cinema 1946–1972*, London: Gordon Fraser.

del Toro, G. (1995), 'Notes from the Underground', *Sight and Sound*, January: 41.

Wood, R. (1979), 'The dark mirror', in R. Lippe, A. Britton, T. Williams and R. Wood (eds), *The American Nightmare*, Toronto: Festival of Festivals, 45.

Wood, R. (1984), 'An introduction to the American horror film', in B. Grant (ed.) *Planks of Reason*, New York: Scarecrow Press.

# 12 A heritage of evil: Pete Walker and the politics of Gothic revisionism

*Steve Chibnall*

> The British horror film perished because of its inability to adapt to a 1970s world beyond Home Counties Transylvania.
>
> Kim Newman (1988: 25)

> I wanted to make contemporary terror pictures that had some kind of statement to make. Now that sounds like I'm being very pretentious. When I say 'statement' I really mean a film with a little more mischief about it.
>
> Pete Walker interviewed in *Fangoria* 27, 1983

David Pirie's seminal *A Heritage of Horror* is rightly revered as a watershed in the study of British genre cinema. Its acknowledged achievement is to have made a convincing case for the importance of 'commercial English films' (Pirie 1973: 8) by showing how the myths, themes and iconography of a specifically English tradition of Gothic fiction found expression in the critically derided genre of horror. The interpretation of the book's role as a retrospective on, and an epitaph for, a golden age of British horror cinema is well established. Its publication in 1973, coinciding as it did with the terminal decline of Hammer studios as a creative force in genre film-making, seems to mark the end of an era. It would be easy to see Pirie as the undertaker of British horror, and his words as the writing on its tombstone. But Pirie came not to bury the Gothic tradition, but to praise its persistence and to celebrate its potential as a vital stream in the imagination of future film-makers in the land of Radcliffe, Lewis, Shelley and Stoker.[1]

Pirie realized that he was writing during a moment of transition when the Gothic strain in English genre cinema was being challenged both by cultural upheavals in Western capitalist society and by new styles of horror cinema developing in America and continental Europe. In the midst of what was in the early 1970s the greatest horror boom the national cinema had experienced, however, he was hopeful that the new wave of young British film-makers would stay true to 'the essential historical virtues of their own tradition' (Pirie 1973: 165), adapting Gothic themes to suit changing times:

Of course even if it *were* possible, I am not advocating a slavish attempt to reproduce the components of Hammer's work in the 1950s. The native emotions and repressions on which these films were based no longer exist and it would be futile to reconstruct them. In any case, it is obvious that, like any other art, the cinema must progress in line with the society to which it relates. [. . .] The most hopeful signs are those which [. . .] combine the best and most traditional elements of the old approach with more complex ideas and emphases.

(166–7)

Unfortunately, his only examples of films that managed to merge horror themes '*overtly* yet inextricably with subversive and complex social/psychological/political ideas' without 'sacrificing the resonance and power of the basic English myths' (166) were American (*Invasion of the Body Snatchers* (1956) and *Night of the Living Dead* (1968) to be precise). At the moment Pirie was expressing these thoughts, however, a director who was capable of adapting the mood and thematics of English Gothic to a changing psycho-social landscape was emerging from the undergrowth of British exploitation cinema. His name was Pete Walker, and for a brief period at the end of Albion's horror boom he took the Gothic tradition and showed that it was not only capable of sustaining new mutated forms, but that it was the ideal host for the darkest of political and social allegories.

After a difficult childhood spent in orphanages, foster homes and Catholic schools in the south of England, Walker came to film directing via unsatisfactory careers in acting and stand-up comedy, a technical apprenticeship at Brighton Studios and a youth spent enthralled by film noir. Returning from a working visit to the United States, he set up a successful business making and distributing 8mm 'glamour' films for home projection before ploughing the profits into a series low-budget sex comedies and thrillers which took advantage of the permissive moral climate of the late 1960s and early 1970s (Chibnall 1998: 33–97). In 1972, however, Walker's cinema took a change of direction when he commissioned the patrician director and screenwriter Alfred Shaughnessy to write a whodunnit about serial murder in an isolated theatrical setting. Even as the scenarist set to work, Pirie (1973: 47) was lamenting the fact that the director of the 1957 *Cat Girl* (Shaughnessy), a film which he hailed as marking 'a crucially liberating moment in British cinema', had never made another horror film.[2] The narrative structure of Shaughnessy's script for Walker may have had more than a whiff of Agatha Christie, but there all similarities with genteel English crime fiction ended. The luridly titled *The Flesh and Blood Show* (1972), with its gloomy *mise en scène* and gruesome Grand Guignol flourishes, became a psychiatric couch for the obsessions of its creators. In the process, it sardonically laid bare the philosophy and mechanics of exploitation film-making, and tapped the vein of youthful discontent with the established order (Chibnall 1997, and 1998: 98–110). 'I love that theme that Freddy Shaughnessy liked, and had in his films, of the past coming back to haunt you', Walker told me in an interview in 1997, 'that's what I liked about *The Flesh and Blood Show*: dark secrets, people disappearing and coming back incognito, bodies buried under the stage that have been there thirty years – all that kind of stuff I find absolutely fascinating.' Clearly, here was a director imbued with the spirit of English Gothicism. He went on to make six more horror films over the next decade before, disillusioned with the parlous state of the film business in the early 1980s, he baulked at the prospect of making straight-to-video movies for 'people with six packs' and turned to property dealing and the exhibition side of cinema. But it is on the three Gothic chillers that Walker made immediately after *The Flesh and Blood Show* in 1973–5 that his reputation as a significant figure in British horror cinema rests. These films – *House of Whipcord* (1974), *Frightmare* (1974) and *House of Mortal Sin* (1975) – build on the legacy of literary and cinematic fiction which Pirie analyses, rather than merely pastiching past texts. They come as close as any British genre offerings released since the publication of Pirie's book to fulfilling his criteria that horror cinema should be 'meaningful' and 'significant in content' as well as 'entertaining and enjoyable' (Pirie 1973: 167–8).

We need to insert a qualification or two here, lest it be thought that what is being claimed for Walker is something far too grand for his modest and unpretentious movies to bear. Walker is no Godard or Buñuel. He has no aspirations to deconstruct bourgeois ideology or the codes of cinema. He is neither a great visual stylist nor an innovator of cinematic form. He is a pragmatist rather than a visionary, and thinks of himself as a conservative rather than a radical. But he is nevertheless proof that mischief and transgression are not the sole preserves of an avant-garde. Like Roger Corman, Walker is a director who is able to combine a feeling for past cinema ('a heritage of horror', if you like) with a keen sense of current controversy. This enabled the best of his 1970s output to capture an essence of the period and, almost unconsciously, to encode key cultural issues and attitudes together with the residues of his own biography into the mythic structures of the Gothic. His skill is not so much in thesis but in synthesis – the drawing together of the diverse strands linking cinema to society at a passing historical moment. To appreciate this, we must first identify those trajectories which, by the end of the 1960s, were impacting on the paradigms of British cinema and creating stress in its generic patterns.

## Generational conflict: political ideology and sexual morality

By and large, British film culture never really got to grips with the 'youthquake' that swept through advanced industrial society in the late 1960s. With perhaps the honourable exception of Lindsay Anderson's *If* (1968), one searches the archives in vain for a full-blown drama of the counter-culture to rival American pictures such as *Easy Rider* (1969) or *Zabriskie Point* (1970), or even the slew of biker and hippie films made by AIP and its competitors. Revolutionary passion in British products tended to be displaced into the domain of allegory where it found its most expressive outlet in genre cinema. Thus one of the more marginal genres in British cinema, the horror film, became the most important site for the allegorical exploration of the struggle between the emergent discourses of radical change associated with youth culture and the beleaguered discourses of reaction associated with its parent culture. If British cinema lacks an *Easy Rider*, it has any number of *Night of the Living Deads*, in which the tensions and contradictions of the age are cloaked in the dark disguise of Gothic conventions.

Leon Hunt (1996a) identifies *The Sorcerers* (1967) as the moment when a new preoccupation with 'generation gap horror' transformed the genre in Britain, producing 'a narrative in which the old, metaphorically cannibalistic generation preys on "Youth" at what should be the moment of its liberation' (164).[3] In the decade that followed, the 'monstrous anachronism' became as significant a generic component as the 'monstrous feminine', its puritan discourses of social order and responsibility transmuted into psychopathic preoccupations with violent repression.[4] At the same time, the pagan iconography and wild hedonism of 'the old religion', a staple of the horror text, became subject to appropriation as signs for counter-cultural ideas and lifestyles. The established narratives of persecution that characterized films like *Witchfinder General* (1968) and *The Devils* (1971) took on a deeper, and very specific, resonance for young audiences. In revisionist horror, the established order is caricatured as a culture of death, a charnel house for youthful ambitions for change. Perverted by power and the repression of their sexual natures, its representatives turn vindictively on a new generation which challenges their orthodoxies and rejects the suppression of their desires. The demon of the establishment takes many forms, but all are projections of counter-cultural angst. We might roughly classify them as follows:

- The crazed scientist (*Scream and Scream Again* [1969], *Horror Hospital* [1973]), derived, in part, from the Gothic template provided by Frankenstein, but perhaps more from Nazi eugenicists.
- The control fiend (*Witchfinder General*, *Night, After Night, After Night* [1969], *Twins of Evil* [1971], *The Wicker Man* [1973], *House of Whipcord*), an embodiment of a morally corrupt and oppressive legal apparatus.
- The monstrous patriarch (*The Corpse* [1970], *The Creeping Flesh* [1972], *Demons of the Mind* [1971], *House of Mortal Sin*, *Satan's Slave* [1976]).
- The devouring mother (*The Fiend* [1971], *Frightmare*).
- The establishment ghoul (*Incense for the Damned* [1970], *The Flesh and Blood Show*).

However, it would be simplistic to read British horror films of the late 1960s and early 1970s, the period of 'the collision between Swinging London and the Gothic tradition' (Newman 1988: 14), as parables teaching the virtues of a subordinate but ascendant ideology. The texts are not as crudely schematic as this, and the support they give to oppositional values is usually neither unequivocal nor uncontested. So, while *Witchfinder General* is uncompromising in its condemnation of the inhumanity represented by Matthew Hopkins (Vincent Price), it recognizes the corrosive effects of misogyny and misanthropy on the psyches of the young. Spiritual corruption is not the exclusive property of the establishment. *Witchfinder General*'s moral ambivalence is more strongly marked in Piers Haggard's *Blood on Satan's Claw* (1970), which, in the aftermath of the Manson murders, struggles to find virtue in either its Satanic youth cult or the cult's nemesis, the bigoted and domineering judge (Patrick Wymark). Although a fairly obvious political allegory of 1968 and all that, and incorporating what its writer has described as 'the New Age outlook', the film remains enigmatically uncommitted, and reluctant to prescribe a position for its audience (Taylor 1996).[5] If Haggard's film is enigmatic, Gordon Hessler's *Cry of the Banshee* (1970) is downright confused. Like *Scream and Scream Again*, an earlier collaboration between Hessler and the young scriptwriter Chris Wicking, *Banshee* suffered from conflict between the radical intentions of writer and director and the more conservative requirements of its backers, AIP. Consequently, Wicking's attempts to draw parallels between the cruel persecution of the film's religious cult and the ruthless treatment of protesters at the Democratic Party convention in Chicago in 1968 were blunted by the conventional representation of the cultists as card-carrying devil worshipers (Rigby 2000: 164). Similarly, in *The Wicker Man*, what in most respects is a witty and satisfying revenge fantasy of counter-cultural triumph over puritan hegemony ends up being compromised by sympathy for Edward Woodward's 'virgin fool' policeman.

The ambiguous politics of *The Wicker Man*, in fact, exemplify the central paradox of much British Gothic revisionism: the use of an atavistic, superstitious past to represent a libertarian future. The intention is surely to find some free 'state of nature', predating the repressive regimes of institutional Christianity and industrial capitalism, but this regression in search of progression allows the films to stray dangerously close to the more reactionary wing of Gothic literature represented by Edgar Allan Poe. Without the subtlety of Shaffer's screenplay and the lightness of Hardy's directorial touch, *The Wicker Man*'s tolerance for aristocratic paternalism and cultural stagnation might suggest a close alignment with Poe. Certainly, the more unambiguously progressive variants of Gothic revisionism rejected Poe's favoured retreat into the past as a strategy for coping with contemporary social disruption. Instead, they implied the need to break with the old. For example, I.Q. Hunter (1996) has pointed to the way in which many British horror films of the 1970s undermined the nostalgic cultural connotations of the English country house as a site of 'heritage' and emphasized its Gothic role as a dark and disturbing symbol of ancient repression: 'Country houses, where the repressed past encounters a forgetful, rational present, are transformed into powerfully relevant symbols of contemporary sexual repression, class conflict and patriarchal violence.' These films were working to ensure the fall of the House of Usher, not only in the form of its bricks and mortar, but also in its metaphorical sense as an outmoded familial institution.

## The monstrous family

The ideas of the family curse and the family secret had long been standard conceits of Gothic horror: a legacy of evil passed from one generation to the next and secret knowledge guarded by an aristocratic patriarch. Contained within and symbolized by the ancestral home, the curse was itself a metonym for the force of destiny that mocked the endeavours of Gothic protagonists and antagonists alike, while the secret represented the hidden sources of patriarchal power. As Gothicism developed and religious paradigms were challenged by psychological (and specifically psycho-analytic) theories of familial dysfunction, the afflictions of individual families came increasingly to be explained not as God's punishment for the past sins of their patriarchs but through the operations of understandable psycho-social mechanisms. A parallel process of demystification, driven by feminist agendas, gradually exposed the secrets of women's oppression within the domestic sphere. Eventually, under the impact of post-Freudian theory and second-wave feminism, the institution of the family itself was pathologized as the prime source of mental illness (Hutchings 1993: 166–84). This shift found cinematic expression in the transformation of the family curse into the cursed family and the family secret into the notion of the secret family. The nuclear family, particularly in its bourgeois form, came to be represented as a hidden site of oppression where monsters were created and violence generated.

Andrew Tudor (1989: 194–5) identifies the appearance of *Psycho* and *Peeping Tom* (1960) as the key moment at which the cinema begins to conceptualize insanity as a constant potential in the everyday order of things, something that emerges imperceptibly from the unseen operation of family life. In the same year, Roger Corman began a series of Poe adaptations which gave a more radical spin to the writer's melancholy pessimism. These films, some of which were made in England, anatomize the patriarchal family in various advanced states of decay, infected with malevolence and perverse sexuality (Horgan 1988: 212–18). By the end of the decade Laingian and feminist critiques of the family were finding loud echoes in British horror films such as *The Corpse* with its vengeful women and indestructible patriarch, the satirical *Mumsy, Nanny, Sonny and Girly* (1970) with its infantile but psychopathic 'happy family', *The Creeping Flesh*, and Hammer's explicit exploration of family psychodynamics, *Demons of the Mind*.[6] In films like these, a combustible mix of family emotion exploded into grotesque spectacles of madness and violence.

## Sadean spectacles

Anglo-Amalgamated's notorious trilogy of films in the late 1950s had supplied a decidedly English inflection to the scopophiliac enjoyment of suffering (Pirie 1973:

99–106).[7] The spectacle of pain, so long associated with continental European practices and theorists (Grand Guignol theatre and the Marquis de Sade, for example), was returned to the home of Selwynism and *le vice anglais*. Hammer, on the other hand, tended to locate their offerings on the continent. This went for even their non-period psycho-thrillers, the majority of which were set overseas.[8] By the early 1970s, with slackening censorship codes and the movement of film-makers between Britain and Europe, the continental practice of punctuating thriller narratives with spectacular murder sequences in the manner of *Psycho* was becoming a familiar part of British horror. Sometimes these bloody production numbers were camply eccentric (*Theatre of Blood* [1973]) and sometimes (as in the films of Spanish director José Larraz, for instance) downright visceral.

## Camp excess

In the 1960s many popular genres reached a decadent phase of development in which audience familiarity allowed writers and directors to play ironically with generic conventions, using ideas of excess to comic effect. Film directors like Alfred Hitchcock and James Whale, in fact, had been inflecting their genre productions with a camp sensibility since the 1930s, and the camp celebration of excess was also clearly evident in horror fandom, notably in Forest J. Ackerman's homage to the monstrous, *Famous Monsters of Filmland* magazine. Pre-eminently, however, it was the television series *The Avengers* which demonstrated that a genre (in this case usually the thriller) could be successfully parodied without sacrificing the excitement generated by its characteristic narrative drive. Creative personnel associated with this series made a direct impact on the trajectory taken by British horror cinema in the 1970s. Designer/director Robert Fuest saturated his faux-Deco *Dr Phibes* films with Gothic excess, self-satire and ironic quotation, while writer/director Brian Clemens pushed Hammer studios further towards sardonic genre parody and the construction of knowing and distanciated viewing positions for their audiences. Michael Reeves would not have approved, and, at Hammer, Terence Fisher was probably uneasy, but *The Avengers*' brand of self-reflexive mockery was positively welcomed by the more cynical talents of Jimmy Sangster and Michael Carreras.

## Paranoia

The role played by ironic excess in the British horror boom of the early 1970s may be understood as an analgesic one. The pain to be relieved derived from disturbances within the narrative organization of the horror film and its positioning of its viewers. Andrew Tudor (1989: 211–23) has characterized the resulting generic shift as one from 'secure' to 'paranoid' horror. Secure horror fiction develops within a society with an established and widely-shared moral order which draws clear distinctions between good/evil and right/wrong. Its function is the reassertion of moral co-ordinates by dramatizing the defeat of some threat to the normative order. The threat is clearly external or culturally 'other' (although it may, in some ways, be attractive), and its defeat is accomplished by accredited expertise or legitimate coercion. The audience is expected to suffer fear and uncertainty before being offered the reassurance that the authorities are still capable of vanquishing disorder. 'Paranoid' horror, on the other hand, questions all the assumptions of the secure paradigm. Rather than clarifying the boundaries between moral opposites, 'paranoid' narratives obscure them, clouding the distinctions between the conscious and unconscious mind, normal and abnormal sexuality, sanity and insanity, health and disease. At the same time, faith in the efficacy and legitimacy of established social and intellectual authorities is undermined, leaving an audience, which is already uncertain about the appropriateness of its identifications, in a general state of doubt and unease. By the mid-1970s, Tudor suggests, 'paranoid' horror had become the dominant genre paradigm, indexing a much wider cultural disruption to the lives of its audiences.

The element of synthesis which Walker would bring to these diverse strands was already present in a few films such as Robert Hartford-Davis's *The Fiend* (1971), a tale which, in aesthetics and theme, anticipated much of Walker's cinema.[9] In true exploitation style, *The Fiend* is a story 'ripped from the headlines' (the London 'Jack the Stripper' killings, thought to be the work of a policeman) in which a fanatically religious and over-protective mother turns her outwardly respectable security guard son into a misogynistic and sexually dysfunctional murderer. *House of Mortal Sin* would revisit much the same ground, although with considerably more punch and panache.

Walker emerged from the conflict between a reactionary establishment and libertarian youth as a kind of cultural carpetbagger, taking full advantage of the ensuing disruption of normative expectations and the final breakdown of organized studio production and distribution caused by the withdrawal of American finance. A self-made man with a strong sense of independence and a certain amount of cultural detachment, he turned a cynical eye on the social upheavals of his age. The results were as pessimistic and morally ambivalent as any Michael Reeves movie, but in place of Reeves's artistic passion and despair Walker substituted a facility for camp irony developed through his long association with the theatrical profession. His films of the 1970s reflect a widespread sense of cultural crisis and disunity and dramatize the moral backlash evidenced in the return of the Conservative government and the evangelical puritanism of Britain's Festival of Light movement. They obsessively refer to the threat posed to the young by a vindictive and morally bankrupt older order and their repressive institutions, but they are far from being political tracts advocating free love and the counter-culture. Instead, Walker almost gleefully depicts his age as one of moral dissolution in which hypocrisy is challenged by a hedonism which is only slightly less ethically repellent. He delights in rubbing up both sides the wrong way, creating mischievously shocking entertainments which marry contemporary discourses of liberty and authority with transgressive sequences of visceral violence.[10] Conceived by Shaughnessy and Walker with a script by the young cineaste David McGillivray, *House of Whipcord* has a retired judge and disgraced prison governor setting up their own private correctional institution for wanton women, and unilaterally bringing back flogging and hanging. The film's thematic links to *Witchfinder General* are strong, and as an allegory of the moral backlash against 1960s permissiveness (in both its Festival of Light and Thatcherite forms) it is powerfully suggestive. It is also wonderfully evocative of what Raymond Durgnat (1970: 165) has called the 'punitive streak' in British puritanism, relating sadism to family hypocrisy and dysfunction (Chibnall 1998: 117–34).

Walker remains of the opinion that 'there are very few "happy families"' (Chibnall 1998: 149), and the one depicted in the McGillivray-scripted *Frightmare* is very disturbed indeed. Sardonically dubbed 'an everyday story of countryfolk' in its publicity, *Frightmare* draws on the story of Hansel and Gretel to tell a tale of hereditary madness and cannibalism in rural Surrey. Prematurely released from a mental hospital where she has been confined for fifteen years, monstrous matriarch Dorothy Yates (Sheila Keith) lures young victims to her country cottage where she extracts their brain matter with a power drill. In the film's chilling final scene, Dorothy's ineffectual husband (Rupert Davies) watches in horror as his wife (the ultimate wicked stepmother) and their delinquent daughter turn murderously on his older daughter. The film is both a sly satire on the pretensions and failings of the psychiatric profession ('they said she was well') and a ferocious attack on the beatification of motherhood and our faith in the essential goodness of family life (Chibnall 1998: 135–49; Hunt 1996b). Just as a mother preys on her family in *Frightmare*, another symbol of love and security, a Catholic priest, preys on his flock in Walker and McGillivray's *House of Mortal Sin*. Father Meldrum (Anthony Sharp) is a pillar of the community who has been warped and cracked by maternal control and sexual denial. 'I was put on this earth to combat sin, and I shall use every available means to do so' he declares as he sets about his parishioners, blasphemously turning the paraphernalia and sacraments of his profession into murder weapons. Although its message is obscured by gratuitously offensive Guignol and softened by camp, the film clearly portrays Meldrum as a symbolic representative of a malign institution. Moreover, his freedom to continue his killing spree at the end of the film suggests that the system which produced him remains a threat to individual and social well-being. The threat will apparently endure as long as 'mothers' and 'fathers' (in both their familial and ecclesiastical forms) are allowed to control the minds and bodies of their children. As a deserted child and lapsed Catholic, Walker's cynicism about family and church is both bitter and personal.

In synthesizing the emerging themes of generational conflict, family monstrosity, Sadean spectacle, camp excess and paranoia, Walker was fully aware that he was developing a new direction which would take British horror beyond the Hammer paradigm. Aligning his intentions with those of Alfred Hitchcock, he even called his

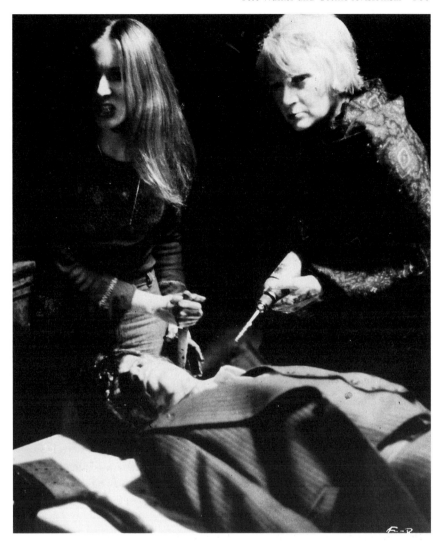

*Figure 25* The devouring mother: Mrs Yates (Sheila Keith) shows her daughter (Kim
        Butcher) how to prepare a meal in *Frightmare* (1974).

films 'terror' pictures in order to distinguish them from the more established form
of Gothic horror, as he explained in *Film Review*, April 1976:

> Really what I'm trying to do is out-Hitchcock Hitchcock by putting a few more
> harder-hitting ingredients into a picture that is rather vintage Hitchcock . . .
> with movies you have to give the public something they don't get on TV. If
> somebody is going to be brutally murdered I think they want to see them
> brutally murdered. . . . There is a niche for a British terror film-maker. I don't

*Figure 26* A pillar of the community? The wicked priest (Anthony Sharp) and his
housekeeper (Sheila Keith) in *House of Mortal Sin* (1975).

think anyone else is actually specialising in them. It seems to be my forte. I
enjoy doing it and it is commercial if you do it properly and effectively.

It is revealing to compare Walker's concept of 'terror' with Hammer's idea of
'horror' because it differs in some important respects from the Gothic orthodoxy
favoured by Hammer's leading director Terence Fisher (Pirie 1973: 50–65; Ringel
1975).

First, whereas Hammer locate their morality plays in a mythic (usually nineteenth-
century) past, Walker's shockers are determinedly contemporary in their settings.
The resulting sense of immediacy helped to give Walker's films their primarily
subjective appeal. Terror is what we feel when we ourselves are in danger, whereas
horror is an emotion we might experience at the plight of others. Horror is terror-
by-proxy. The Hitchcockian school of film-making tries to induce terror among
spectators by using sound, editing and cinematography to produce an illusion of
participation in the action on screen. With Hammer, the period settings, the
costumes and the sober and objective style of filming that Terence Fisher developed
all have the effect of distancing the viewer from the action. Hammer's classical style
creates interested voyeurs, but Walker strives for a greater sense of involvement

and more opportunities for audience members to identify with the protagonists. When he said his films were 'more identifiable' he was following the lead of another of his directorial mentors, Jacques Tourneur, who once remarked:

> If you're going to have horror, the audience must be able to identify with the characters in order to be frightened. Now you can identify with an average guy like me, but how can we identify with a Lower Slobovian or a fellow with a big cape? You laugh at that.
>
> (*Cinefantastique* 2, 4, (1973))

Following the lead of Romero's *Night of the Living Dead*, Walker eschews the exoticism of Hammer and tries to create an illusion of naturalness within the fantastic, of real people in unreal situations.

Second, Walker offers very different objects of identification from those suggested by the classical tradition of Hammer. In Fisher's conventionally bourgeois mythology we are asked to empathize with his demure and naive beauties and to put our trust in a wise and heroic father figure (often Peter Cushing) with a belief in a judicious combination of Christian faith and scientific rationality (Hutchings 1993; Pirie 1973, 1977). In Walker's disturbing tales, this reassuring world is turned upside down. His female protagonists are anything but virginal and his father figures are not to be trusted. He offers, in anticipation of punk, 'no more heroes anymore'. His male protagonists are generally ineffectual and possess no more special qualities than the average viewer. Unlike Fisher's, Walker's world may be free of supernatural threat, but it is a world without reassurance.

Third, Fisher and Walker are at odds again in their attitudes towards physicality and sexual morality. For Fisher the body is a site of danger, subject to libidinous desires which open the soul to evil. Desire must not be over-indulged, but kept in check by abstinence and self-control until it can find safe and legitimate outlets. While Fisher's villains are rampantly sexual, and corrupt others by the exercise of that sexuality, his patriarchal heroes remain celibate as part of their defence against the power of evil. His rigid puritanism could not withstand the onslaught of 1960s sexual libertarianism (if it feels good, do it) any more than his strict dualistic vision of good and evil could cope with the moral relativism of the Aquarian Age's exhortations to 'do your own thing' and 'choose your own gods'. Hammer tried vainly to adjust with its explorations of lesbian vampirism, Victorian hypocrisy and sexual ambiguity, and with attempts at self-parody and modernization in the early 1970s, but it was Walker's brand of wryly humorous and sex-positive nihilism that really filled the vacuum left by the collapse of Terence Fisher's universe.

In Walker's films, danger lies not in the free expression of sexual desire, but in its repression, and Fisher's most cherished institutions – the family, the church, the medical profession, the legal system and the hierarchical ordering of society – become agents of that repression and the generators of violence. The threat in his movies is not from some external and supernatural force of evil, but instead results from the way in which social life is organized and regulated. This makes these films 'progressive' in Robin Wood's terms (Wood 1979), in spite of their director's self-proclaimed reactionary disposition in an interview in *Fangoria* 27, 1983:

> I like the idea of taking people who are in a position of authority and showing that they have either murderous or peculiar quirks about them. Older people always seem to carry more authority. The idea of the young psychopathic killer is an area that I haven't really worked in. I think it's much more upsetting to have old, more mature killers.

The notion that a film-maker would want to leave his audience upset would have been quite unpalatable to the more didactic Terence Fisher. But where Fisher offered moral lessons, Walker left unease, disquiet and a sardonic commentary on a legacy of corruption that not only continues to recommend him to cynical audiences today, but also related his work to Robert D. Hume's contemporary formulation of the Gothic as a genre which 'offers no conclusions' and offers only 'a tangle of moral ambiguity' (Hume 1969: 287, 288).

Fourth and finally, while Hammer's horrors are firmly situated within the tradition of English Gothic drama, Walker's terrors are revisionist in their meanings and representations.[11] His films draw heavily on Gothic elements – the persecuted and the fatal woman, and the sense of menace, isolation and despair – but inflect and reconstitute them in imaginative and contemporary ways. The dark and brooding atmospheres of menace, isolation and despair which often characterize Walker's films are pure Gothic, as are the ways in which they employ cruel and violent spectacles to horrify their audiences. Terence Fisher uses similar devices in his more romantic melodramas for Hammer, but Walker's pieces are more clearly influenced by Grand Guignol in both their explicitness and their undertones of conscious theatricality.

Walker's use of the Gothic tradition's 'persecuted woman' is particularly evident in *House of Whipcord* and *House of Mortal Sin* (although his tragic heroines are significantly less passive than most of their literary and cinematic antecedents), but the way in which he presents his 'fatal woman' differs strikingly from Terence Fisher's treatment. Fisher's femmes fatales are eroticized women who corrupt through their sexuality in the same way that film noir's 'spider woman' operates. In contrast, Walker's dangerous dames are more likely to be de-eroticized crones. They relate to an even older literary source, the folk tale, with its witches, bad mothers and evil queens. Similarly, his villains derive their destructive power not from their sexual seductiveness and alluring cruelty, like Dracula, but from their repressed desires and their social positions of trust and respect. In Walker's modern Gothic they are privileged professional men who replace the decadent aristocrats of the classical tradition.

This contemporizing of the traditional is again evident in the way in which the key setting of Gothic drama and its most potent signifier, the castle, is re-configured more modestly as 'the house'. Its central place in Walker's cinema is confirmed by its presence in the titles of three of his terror pictures, and its prominence in different institutional guises (school, theatre, prison) throughout his cinema. Just as in classical Gothic literature, Walker's antagonists are creatures of a building with a malevolent aura, the 'Terrible House', which Robin Wood (1979) suggests signifies 'the dead weight of the past crushing the life of the younger generation, the future'. All Walker's houses are sites of authority, but the stability of their bricks and mortar stands in stark contrast to the unstable personalities who inhabit them. As symbols they represent a continuity with the past, existing now as they did then. They are the repositories of memory and the conduits through which malign atavistic influences flow, just as they are in classical Gothic stories which are permeated by ideas of fate and destiny. In Walker's films, this concern with the mechanisms of fate is all that remains of the Gothic tradition's fascination with the supernatural. The rest has been lost to the same cynical rationalism which made the romantic hero obsolete in his cinema.

All the elements of Walker's terror films came into prime alignment between 1973 and 1975. By the time he came to make *Schizo* (1976), his fifth picture in the genre, he was beginning to struggle to hold them in place. *Schizo* is the story of a young wife and her sinister middle-aged stalker. Its somewhat ill-disguised twist on the conventional stalk-and-slash narrative is that the potential victim (an undiagnosed sufferer from multiple personality disorder) turns out to be the slasher. The killings are as bloody as ever, and there is the same lack of retribution for their perpetrator, but the oppositional politics of earlier films have become muted in a conscious attempt by the director to broaden the appeal of his work, as he explained in an interview in *Starburst* 57, 1983:

> I wanted less incident and outrage. *Schizo* was an attempt to level off the Gothique and make things a little more threatening than over-the-top. It was purposely underwritten, and I see it as an improvement in an area I wanted to move into.

With the appearance of *The Comeback* (1978), the direction which Walker's cinema was taking became clearer. David McGillivray was replaced as scriptwriter by an earlier collaborator, Murray Smith, and a transatlantic market was directly targeted by the casting of the popular American singer Jack Jones as the film's protagonist and David Doyle (*Charlie's Angels*) in a supporting role. *The Comeback* contains Walker's most accomplished exercises in suspense, but the film's tongue is more firmly in its cheek than ever before. Smith's script was conceived as a pastiche of the psycho-chillers which Jimmy Sangster wrote for Hammer in the 1960s, and his dialogue punctures any pretensions to pure terror which the film might have had with sly touches of macabre humour. Twenty years before *Scream* (1997) Walker happily chances his arm at genre parody and even lampoons his own themes when the psychos are revealed as a puritanical old couple whose daughter (a sociology student!) had been driven to suicide by unrequited passion for Jones.

By Walker's final film, *House of the Long Shadows* (1983), camp parody and pastiche have become ends in themselves, thoroughly predominating over all the other themes which his mid-1970s pictures had so artfully integrated. Supplied by Cannon Films with a dream cast of horror genre greats – Vincent Price, Peter Cushing, Christopher Lee and John Carradine – together for the first and only time, Walker realized that a new generation of cinemagoers would struggle to accept them in straight roles and so decided to play for laughs: 'Well we can't go and make a Gothic film that's going to be taken seriously, so what we'll do is a little self-satire.'[12] Out of this realization, Michael Armstrong fashioned a script of wit and substance, playing with ideas about genre, performance and dramatic truth, much as Shaughnessy had done in *The Flesh and Blood Show*. It was a fitting elegy for both a version of Gothic melodrama that faded away in the 1970s and for Walker's own career as an astringent genre revisionist. As Vincent Price gloomily intones in *House of the Long Shadows*, 'the old order is gone forever, and now we too must crumble into dust.'

## Notes

1  'On present reckoning at least (although it is much too early to say with any certainty), the Gothic cinematic revival in England looks like having a more lasting popular success than the original literary movement from which it derives' (Pirie 1973: 165).

2  Pirie presumably did not classify Shaughnessy's creepy thriller, *The Impersonator* (1961), as a horror film.

3  Peter Hutchings's (1993: 140) analysis, however, suggests that this is an incomplete reading of *The Sorcerers*, a film which also offers 'a critique of the lifestyle and values of a consumption-centred youth culture which is seen to encourage a desire for sensation that can never be satisfied'.

4  For an unusual reversal of this process, see *What Became of Jack and Jill?* (1971), a film in which the young prey on the old.

5  Fresh out of Cambridge University, screenwriter Robert Wynne-Simmons had to battle with Tigon, the film's producers, in order to retain the element of moral ambiguity in his script: 'Undoubtedly the cults were not all purity and innocence. . . . [But] evil though this creature might be, it was somehow more alive than the Patrick Wymark character whose viewpoint was essentially a dead one' (Taylor 1996).

6  Jonathan Rigby's insightful and comprehensive account of British horror cinema provides an excellent analysis of all of these films, but particularly of the little-seen *The Corpse* and *Mumsy, Nanny, Sonny and Girly* (2000: 156–9).

7  The films were *Horrors of the Black Museum* (1959), *Peeping Tom*, and *Circus of Horrors* (1960).

8  This changed to some extent after 1965, when, even in its period horrors, Hammer's vision becomes much more ethnocentric. In films such as *The Reptile* (1966) and *Plague*

*of the Zombies* (1966), and in Hammer imitations like *The Ghoul* (1975), the monstrous continues to be something of foreign origin, but increasingly it comes to haunt us in Britain – a post-colonial return of the repressed.

9   *The Fiend* was scripted by one of Walker's early collaborators, Brian Comport.

10   'I deliberately rub people up the wrong way. I want them to come into the cinema and be shocked.' Pete Walker, in the *Sun*, 24 April 1975.

11   For a recent discussion of variations on Gothic themes, see Punter 2000.

12   Pete Walker interviewed by the author, January 1997.

# References

Chibnall, Steve (1997) 'Double exposures: observations on *The Flesh and Blood Show*', in Deborah Cartmell, I.Q. Hunter, Heidi Kaye and Imelda Whelehan (eds) *Trash Aesthetics: Popular Culture and its Audience*, London: Pluto.

Chibnall, Steve (1998) *Making Mischief: The Cult Films of Pete Walker*, Guildford: FAB Press.

Durgnat, Raymond (1970) *A Mirror for England: British Movies from Austerity to Affluence*, London: Faber.

Horgan, David J. (1988) *Dark Romance: Sex and Death in the Horror Film*, Wellingborough: Equation.

Hume, David R. (1969) 'Gothic versus romantic: a revaluation of the Gothic novel', *PMLA* 84 (March): 282–90.

Hunt, Leon (1996a) '*Witchfinder General*', in Andy Black (ed.) *Necronomicon Book One*, London: Creation Books.

Hunt, Leon (1996b) '*Frightmare*: Pete Walker's psycho-delirium classic', in Andy Black (ed.) *Necronomicon Book One*, London: Creation Books.

Hunter, I.Q. (1996) 'Deadly manors: the country house in British exploitation films', in Paul Cooke, David Sadler and Nicholas Zurbrugg (eds) *Locating Identity: Essays on Nation, Community and the Self*, Leicester: De Montfort University: 45–55.

Hutchings, Peter (1993) *Hammer and Beyond: The British Horror Film*, Manchester: Manchester University Press.

Newman, Kim (1988) *Nightmare Movies*, London: Bloomsbury.

Pirie, David (1973) *A Heritage of Horror: The English Gothic Cinema 1946–1972*, London: Gordon Fraser.

Pirie, David (1977) *The Vampire Cinema*, Feltham: Hamlyn.

Punter, David (ed.) (2000) *A Companion to the Gothic*, Oxford: Blackwell.

Rigby, Jonathan (2000) *English Gothic: A Century of Horror Cinema*, London: Reynolds & Hearn.

Ringel, Harry (1975) 'Terence Fisher: the human side', *Cinefantastique*, 4, 3: 5–18.

Taylor, David (1996) 'Don't overact with your fingers! The making of *Blood on Satan's Claw*', in Stefan Jaworzyn (ed.) *Shock! The Essential Guide to Exploitation Cinema*, London: Titan: 85–95.

Tudor, Andrew (1989) *Monsters and Mad Scientists: A Cultural History of the Horror Movie*, Oxford: Blackwell.

Wood, Robin (1979) 'Introduction', in Robin Wood and Richard Lippe (eds) *American Nightmare: Essays on the Horror Film*, Toronto: Festival of Festivals: 7–28.

# 13  On the side of the demons: Clive Barker's pleasures and pains

## Interviews with Clive Barker and Doug Bradley

*Paul Wells*

Clive Barker, novelist, artist, writer and director, has already achieved considerable success in two major aspects of the horror genre. First, he has resurrected a notion of 'British horror'; previously mainly understood as a phenomenon of Hammer Films (see Hutchings 1993), the maverick talent Michael Reeves (see Pirie 1973) or exploitation auteurs like Pete Walker (see Chibnall 1998). Barker, with his self-conscious re-working and re-configuration of the British horror tradition, has simultaneously progressed the tradition but also called attention to its neglected backwaters, and re-engaged with the centrality of 'Englishness' at the core of the genre.

Second, Barker has added a significant myth to the canon of horror monsters with the invention of Pinhead (Doug Bradley) and the Cenobites in the *Hellraiser* series – *Hellraiser* (1987); *Hellbound: Hellraiser II* (1988); *Hellraiser III: Hell on Earth* (1992); *Hellraiser IV: Bloodline* (1995); and in the variety of monsters in *Nightbreed* (1990). In *Hellraiser* Barker uses the theme of sado-masochism not merely to draw together the issues of eroticism and brutality, but to emphasize the protean nature of the body and identity. Barker's sense of the mutability of the flesh, and the combinative sense of organs and tissue, is played out through characters with ambivalent sexual orientations, and the problematics of bodily need. Barker's bodies are concerned with perspectives outside social orthodoxy, and 'horror' comes out of the fear of a perverse yet partially desired experience of a marginalized or unknown 'otherness'. Arguably, this is an insightful address of the quintessentially 'English' attitudes towards the body. On the one hand, the English are perceived as physically inhibited, private, controlled and remote; on the other, they may be viewed as physically (if secretively) indulgent, brutal and impassioned when given an appropriate cause to be so. This is the tension Barker implicitly explores, critically engaging with the complexities of sexuality and gender in relation to particular forms of controlled violence.

Taking up the work of Georges Bataille, Joel Black suggests that:

Killing and coitus are pre-eminently *private* acts, intensely personal experiences
. . . because they impart a wordless kind of knowledge mediated by the body.
The carnal knowledge shared by lovers, of by murderer and his victim or
witness, does not involve the communication of discursive meaning between
two discrete individuals, but a communion at the instant of death between
bodies that are no longer distinct from each other.

(1991: 121)

Barker's work seeks to explore and illustrate the intensity of this 'communion' and
the private discourses that underpin it. Barker thus significantly differs from David
Cronenberg, for example, in not merely seeing the body in its own self-determined
flux, but in addressing issues of restraint, repression and release, and the aesthetic
that may emerge from *excessive* acts of 'change' upon the body. This aestheticization
of bodily violence may range from self-mutilation to unknowable assault.

Sexuality is intrinsically entwined with the pleasures and pains of violent
imposition. As Doug Bradley has noted about the design of his character, Pinhead,
in the interview included later in this chapter, the grid-iron pattern of nails in
Pinhead's skull is an act of controlled brutality that results in an aesthetically pleasing
yet perverse beauty. Barker's work becomes especially important in this respect, in
the sense that he effectively contemporizes the sexuality of the horror film through
this aesthetic. Rather than defining 'pain' as the consequence of punishment or
attack, the aesthetic embraces it as a model which makes the implied discourse of
the Gothic – the attractiveness of the perverse and the transgressive – both a literal
and symbolic set of events. Interestingly, this is also given an intrinsically 'English'
veneer of almost aristocratic superiority by its containment within an apparently
distanciative 'wit' – an image of the villain especially appealing to American
audiences, who likewise engaged with Anthony Hopkins as Hannibal Lector in
Jonathan Demme's *Silence of the Lambs* (1991).

Like many of the key artistic achievements in recent horror texts, however,
*Hellraiser* has been significantly diminished by the rise of the franchised sequel. Clive
Barker's response to this has been to try to participate as much as possible in the
progress of the *Hellraiser* series in an executive producer role, but more importantly,
to continue his work as a novelist and screenwriter in a spirit of continually testing
the parameters of the genre. This has resulted in the emergence of another significant
monster in the genre in the figure of the 'Candyman', an urban legend, in *Candyman*
(1992) and *Candyman2: Farewell to the Flesh* (1995). This black, hook-armed demon,
played by Tony Todd, is an ideologically charged 'monster', clearly playing out
narratives of racial vengeance and redemption in modern America. Summoned by
calling his name in front of a mirror, the Candyman – in Barker's vision, a revisionist
version of the 'noble savage' – effectively reminds contemporary culture of
its collective sins, most particularly in regard to the treatment of non-white
communities and civil liberties. The 'Candyman' in this respect represents the core

problem of American society, and merely enhances the sense of urban brutality, moral decay and social instability already evidenced in the corrupt material world to which he returns. Though Barker did not direct the 'Candyman' films, his vision of the 'horror' at the heart of an increasingly arbitrary and de-historicized social sensibility is clear. *Lord of Illusions* (1996), based on his short story, 'The Last Illusion' from the *Books of Blood*, maintains this theme by addressing once more how the sins of the past will inevitably revisit those who committed them.

The following 'discussion' is compiled from a series of interviews and informal exchanges that have taken place between the author and Clive Barker over ten years (1989–99), and serves to summarize some of the chief ideas, issues and concerns of Barker's highly influential and distinctive work. It is followed by an interview with Doug Bradley, Barker's long-time friend and colleague, who plays Pinhead in the *Hellraiser* series, which offers some invaluable insights in support of Barker's perspective.

WELLS:  When people think of the British horror film, they invariably think of Hammer. What did you think of the Hammer movies?

BARKER:  I didn't really see the Hammer pictures until I was eighteen, but I saw the posters, and the posters were more of a major influence on me than the movies. Somebody told me that, in some cases, they actually designed the posters before they made the movies! I think Corman did the same thing – it's a great marketing and continuity ploy, and the posters certainly attracted my attention. I remember the poster for *Frankenstein Created Woman*, which had this girl in a weird kind of green test tube with these little bands covering her pubic area and breasts. That was a terrible turn-on when I was fourteen! I was a little disappointed when I actually saw some of the movies – I saw them in the wrong order. I didn't see the original *Dracula* or *Curse of Frankenstein*, and only caught the later sequels which were much inferior. Those originals stand up really well. In fact, the original Hammer *Dracula* is certainly one of my top ten horror movies, partly because it works as an adventure as well as a horror movie. It is actually low on the gore factor, even though at the time it caused a major outrage. I saw *Frankenstein Must Be Destroyed* and *Frankenstein Created Woman* before I saw *Curse of Frankenstein*, and I felt sorry for Christopher Lee, because some thirty years after the Universal pictures, he was still following in the steps of Karloff and Lugosi, and it was as if he could be nothing but inferior. I think Lee and Cushing did well though, and their performances were distinctive.

WELLS:  It seems to me that they were central to the ways in which Hammer movies took hold in the public imagination.

BARKER:  Yes, and the colour. Those were classic stories re-told for a new audience. They were very romantic movies. Cushing's Baron Frankenstein is a classic Byronic romantic hero; he's a dashing and attractive character. Christopher Lee's Dracula has a great sexual frisson, which is completely lacking in Lugosi's somewhat lumpen broken English version. I always understood why Karloff was effective, but I never understood why people found Lugosi persuasive. This may be heretical, of course! In Hammer's re-telling, the colour, the slickness, the panache, moves the horror movie on, and I believe they are best viewed as Gothic adventures.

WELLS: How far do you embrace the 'Gothic' in your own fiction, and outlook?

BARKER: I don't think you can ever avoid the long shadow of the Gothic, but I think one of the distressing elements of the influence of the Gothic is that it brings with it a whole theological machinery which in my view is redundant. When the first *Dracula* was made, I wonder how many people who were actually watching the picture believed in the power of the crucifix. I would imagine, even then, comparatively few. The modern audience can only take that kind of narrative machinery if the tongue is reasonably firmly in the cheek. The value system which underpins theological metaphors is deteriorating. But what I believe is still intact – for me anyway – is the kind of imaginative scope of those novels; there was a real sense that they wanted to take in heaven, hell and earth between, and to the extent that that is also my ambition, then they are a key influence. Trying to read *The Castle of Otranto* or *The Monk* was sometimes like scaling Everest with one ice-pick and half a shoe. They are very wordy, and when they get excited, passages turn purple, and the prose goes the same way. I think in a way it was Edgar Allan Poe that really gave me the taste of the Gothic, because they were short, sharp, dark fictions, usually over in twenty pages. They were an intensification of the Gothic impulse. There is something very Gothic too, about *The Fall of the House of Usher*. Poe compressed great Gothic novels into twenty pages and really succeeded in creating burgeoning decadent prose.

WELLS: How does your own work fundamentally differ from the established traditions of British horror fiction and film?

BARKER: The basis of the horror movie is horror fiction, and the major novels of the genre are British. *Frankenstein*, *Dracula*, *Dr Jekyll and Mr Hyde*, *The Hound of the Baskervilles*, and then there is a whole slew of science-fictional horror – H.G. Wells, and so on. So, I can draw from this rich context if I want to. I can draw from the Gothic novels, if I want to, but I want to do something particular. One of the things I don't like about modern fantasy fiction is the fact that it is either so epic in scope that the world described is beyond my power to identify with it – a sub-Tolkeinian invented world, if you like – or else, so small-scale, so domestic – *Poltergeist*, or something like that – that the fantastical elements are reduced by association. I think there is a middle area in there which I find intriguing in which you begin with the domestic and then open out the vistas. Then maybe you expand to take in another cosmos!

WELLS: Is that what you felt that you were doing with the first *Hellraiser* movie?

BARKER: Firstly, I wanted to make a movie that flew in the face of what I viewed as the increasing trivialization of horror movies. I think that there are too many 'ironic' horror movies that don't have any effect. I don't believe the basic function of horror fiction is to give people cheap chuckles. For one thing, it is an easy gag. It is like having a fat opera singer falling flat on his face, because 'opera' is a high cultural form, and that status is undermined. Horror fiction is reaching for high cultural status in the scale of its potential content. You are talking about death, obsession, insanity – the conventional subjects of horror fiction; these are *not* and *should not* be light subjects. It is unfortunately very easy when you are using this rich visual material and very rich sub-text to make a laugh out of it. I'm not terribly interested in going the easy way; I want to create a kind of undertow in a movie that may never leave your mind. *Hellraiser* is basically about a man who does a deal with the forces of darkness in pursuit of the ultimate physical, sensual experience, and gets torn apart for his troubles. The Cenobites are experts in 'pain and pleasure indivisible'! They have made an aesthetic, a kind of lifestyle out of corrupting their own bodies, tearing them apart and putting them back together with hooks and skinning devices. This is difficult material if you consider that there is beauty and elegance in the image at the same time as complete repulsion in the subject matter. I like that tension and paradox.

WELLS:  Those contradictions seem to be at the heart of all your work. I've seen some of your paintings, and of course, I've read the *Books of Blood* and your subsequent novels. There is a very definite sense of authorial distinctiveness, but at the same time, a respect for the broader traditions in 'fantasy' art.

*Figure 27* Embracing the monstrous: Clive Barker on the set of *Hellraiser* (1987).

BARKER: I've painted and done illustrations since I was a kid. I enjoy drawing and painting – it's an immediate release of all those subconscious thoughts and emotions. I try not to inhibit myself. It can be a very physical experience; very different from the stillness of writing, even though I write long-hand. There is such a rich history of 'fantastic art' – Bosch, Goya, Blake – it is complex, and important because it is the tradition which precedes fantasy art makers today. Their work is a reflection of the 'dream-lives' that went before us. It seems to me that this kind of art, or horror fiction, or horror films, is, at its best, giving us material to go into our dreams with. It is going to throw up images which are going to represent the ways in which we contextualize our daily experience. Many of those are going to be confrontations with things that we forbid ourselves – forbidden sexual ideas or fantasies, fears about death, or anxieties that we just cannot, or will not articulate. It's not the kind of thing we're going to talk about over a dinner party. Those fears can only be addressed in the language of the dream. And horror fiction, whether it be on the screen or on the page, gives our conscious minds a vocabulary by which we can confront those fears, and hopefully, shape our world view with the understanding that they are part of us, and have to be embraced. Take someone like Stephen King. He constantly cleanses the house, but you cannot lock all the dark doors and windows. Something is going to get in again!

WELLS: I remember that you once wrote about King's work. What impresses you about his horror fiction?

BARKER: Accessibility. I think if you pick up a King book and get ten pages into it you immediately encounter characters that you recognize, if not as people, then as archetypes. There's a Norman Rockwell accessibility. He spends a lot of time setting those people up, making you feel their reality, and he surrounds them with 'brand' names. People don't drink bourbon; they drink a specific bourbon. You know what his characters eat and drink. He seals the moment. It's like a time-capsule of consumerism. Then he introduces the darkness – a possessed car, a rabid dog, vampires, whatever; in many cases very conventional images of horror, but they become as real as the breakfast that the character ate before he got killed! Horror fiction is basically metaphor. You are creating images and ideas that represent other things. Horror writers represent and illustrate the fears and desires which are actually part and parcel of their characters' lives, and show how individuals can destroy themselves; how families get pulled apart; how a whole social order might be subverted. The interesting thing with King is that in many ways his fiction reinforces the bourgeois status quo and becomes a celebration of the values which are put under threat in the first place. I would align it with Spielberg. But it is not the vision of Edgar Allan Poe – he spends most of his time in the minds of the distressed or the obsessive or the marginalized – or even a lot of contemporary British writers, like Ramsay Campbell, and it is certainly different from my own! I don't want to buy into what I see as 'escapist' fiction and the myth of bourgeois perfection. There is only the 'itch of the irrational' in this kind of horror. That somehow this ordered, reasonably well-off, two-car, multi-television, computer game world is going be spoiled. Suddenly, from somewhere, comes this damn thing to spoil it all! It is simply an anxiety that nothing can quite be 'fixed' or perfect. It is very modern in some ways, but I prefer the celebration of the monstrous, and that can definitely be traced in the British 'Gothic' sensibility. There is a romantic element in those monsters; a moral ambiguity that is very attractive. There are no simple dichotomies between good and evil – that plays too much into the hands of the fundamentalists – there is only contradiction. Our notions of good and evil are very complex, very ambiguous; it is far more interesting to look at minds and bodies that are somehow 'out of kilter'; which for some reason are flying in the face of the moral majority. It is great to try to understand 'monsters' and celebrate their perversities. That is what I enjoy dealing with.

WELLS:   Certainly a great deal of American horror has been directed at that kind of reactionary social model, with all of its seemingly in-built complacencies and assumptions. In many ways, British horror has always been a little more psychotic and brutal, but very few have acknowledged the importance of that, and the ways that it tells us so much about the things the British – though this has always been the English really – have repressed or denied.

BARKER:   The interesting thing is that it's devils and demons and blood-letting, but it is moral; still the issues are about some notion of 'good' somehow triumphing over an increasingly ambiguous notion of 'evil'. But in British horror, it is about control, too. An audience can liberate themselves for the couple of hours of the movie, but they realize if they dabble in some of this stuff, there are going to be terrible consequences. You are dealing with primal imagery from folk-lore, the aural tradition of ghost stories, ancient story-telling devices – fears long held, but you can release them through language, or through the visceral impact on screen – the stuff you cannot do on the page. The sheer physical appearance of the monstrous and its ambiguity. *Hellraiser* tried to achieve images with a visual undertow where things could be beautiful and repulsive simultaneously; images that could fascinate and disgust in equal measure. The best horror does that. There is a strange, and, to my mind, very fascinating glamour associated with the monstrous.

WELLS:   Obviously you have been involved with the *Hellraiser* sequels, as a producer and so forth, but the next film you actually directed was *Nightbreed*. What did you want to achieve in that?

BARKER:   I was trying to take the idea of the glamour in the monstrous to its logical extreme. I had a hero who is a monster, and behaves in some senses like a traditional movie hero, and a heroine who ends up a monster. I had *sixty* other monsters! All had different designs. It was great fun creating each monster – partly referring back to my own paintings, partly back to Bosch, partly to other movie monsters. But the real villains of the piece are the human characters – the cops, the priests, the psychoanalysts. David Cronenberg plays a psychoanalyst who is in fact a serial killer, and I tried to stress that the truly horrific elements resided in the human sensibility. I was trying to invert the conventional morality of horror movies; again making the monstrous persuasive and romantic, while making the forces of law and order, which in a conventional horror narrative, are also the forces for 'good', the subject of unacceptable villainy and troubling morality. All the figures of authority are the bad guys, and it was a challenge to make them so in a plausible way, while retaining the complex ideas which frighten people in the 'monster' figures. In my mid-teens, when I first read ghost stories and fairytales with dark and horrific elements, I found that I was always on the side of the demons. *Nightbreed* is my attempt at making a fairytale which is completely on the side of the demons.

WELLS: One of your many achievements, in many senses, is to have brought the horror genre home. Is that a fair comment?

BARKER: Horror movies have become pretty insular. I think that by merely rejecting the wielded crucifix, the holy water gag, and nowadays, the funny-guy monster, or 'get-the-reference' horror movie – basically, getting rid of redundant iconography – and trying to add to the canon of monsters and their meanings, I hope I have made a contribution. *Lord of Illusions*, the last movie I directed, opens things up a little, makes things a bit more open-ended and spectacular, but no less frightening for being up front. *Chinatown* meets *The Exorcist*, that sort of thing. The dread here is the idea of terrible secrets revealed, something really scary. *Lord of Illusions* looks at magic and illusion, but goes back to theatre and the idea of spectacular tricks, like staging your own death! Basically, the movie is about that feeling that the audience gets when they might be witnessing the trick going wrong – the fear that this lady who has just been sawn in half won't fit back together. She really has been sawn in half! The trick has gone horribly wrong. Actually, the guys who see this in the movie were all horror fans – they were at some convention, and came along dressed up, and had a cool time as extras in a huge shot outside the Pantages Theatre.

WELLS: A lot of contemporary movies are very slick, but don't seem to be addressing any psychological and emotional issues. They are recycled 'boo' movies. They don't seem to strike any chords. *Lord of Illusions* seems to be trying to do something different.

BARKER: There is a psychological depth to the story, which I think is missing from a lot of horror movies, because Swann, the magician, has killed his own mentor, Nix, who has taught him all this genuine magic stuff, and who he fears is not really dead. He is not really an illusionist; he is a guy with real power – Swann gets overtaken by the whole thing. The narrative doesn't cheat on that – it shows the consequences of that supernatural element as the story goes along. The scare stuff, the violence, is part of the psychological structure. Scott Bakula makes it work because he's a regular guy in the middle of this world, a mature guy, not one of the 'slasher movie' kids, who audiences can identify with but don't care about. He says in the movie, 'I've signed on for all the Gods in my time. You cannot have too many saviours.' He's been around, so the horror is much more intense because it is not a teen-scream thing. He's just covering his bases in these atheistic, secular times.

WELLS:  You've been in the horror business a considerable time now. Does it still give you the same sense of engagement and fascination?

BARKER:  All horror comes from lived experience. A lot of what is human is terrifying – the vulnerability of our bodies; the fact that people can be very cruel; stuff about insanity, betrayal – it is all pretty tough. It is obvious that we know how to push our own self-destruct buttons. It is funny, actually, because it is my optimism and my old-fashioned belief in 'love' that makes me see this dark stuff so clearly! I can look at it; in fact, I can't look away.

## Doug Bradley: watching from a place of safety . . .

The interview with Doug Bradley which follows took place in June 1995.

WELLS:  How did you prepare and develop the character of Pinhead?

BRADLEY:  Early on I had the luxury of talking to Clive, who gave me invaluable imaginative insights; then I read the screenplay again and again, making decisions about the character, but the whole thing fell into place for me the first time that I put on the full make-up. It was a very strange experience, and something I had never been through before. It took about six hours and by the end of it I was in a semi-trance. I looked up and there staring back at me from the mirror was Pinhead. For all intents and purposes I could no longer objectively prove that I existed. I remember asking everyone if they would leave the make-up room and for about twenty minutes I sat and got to know this guy. There and then I made lots of decisions about him just picking up sense impressions from looking at him, and being able to animate the image. I had seen sketches, and the make-up done on a life-cast of me, but they were inanimate; now I could make him speak, make him laugh, make him frown, make him sneer. It was overwhelming.

WELLS:  Pinhead seems to me to be a highly introspective character.

BRADLEY:  The most immediate impression I got from him was this terrible sense of melancholy. This seemed against the grain in regard to the kind of sadistic monster he seems to be at first glance. We have a guy here with a lot of nails banged into his head; now if you wanted to you could create that image and it would be a bloody mess. You couldn't look at it, you wouldn't want to look at it. But it struck me that there was an aesthetic to this image; a kind of beauty. Someone had taken the trouble to think about what they were doing in setting out this grid-iron pattern which gives a clarity and a cleanliness to the image that draws the gaze in. I coupled this with the internalized, curiously passive, sense of burden, emptiness and melancholia inside him.

WELLS: There is also a strong sense of 'Englishness' about him, too. How far was that tradition of the monster informing your thinking about Pinhead?

BRADLEY: America is very keen on bad guys with English accents, which is keeping Alan Rickman, Stephen Berkoff and Anthony Hopkins in plenty of work! At first, in *Hellraiser*, New World Productions – the American producers – had a question mark about whether they would overdub my vocal performance, but luckily for me, as the process went on they liked what they were getting, and stayed with my 'Englishness'. It makes much more sense really because Clive had written a character with a literary sophistication; he likes the 'well turned phrase', the epigram – 'No tears please, it's a waste of good suffering.' I thought when I read this for the first time that what we had here in the British horror movie was a cross between Oscar Wilde and Noel Coward. That told me a lot about his poise and bearing, and that he was self-aware enough to comment about himself in an intelligent and witty fashion. Pete Atkins, the screenwriter for *Hellraiser II* and *Hellraiser III*, was careful, though, not to let Pinhead degenerate into another Freddy Krueger. That was unfortunate because Freddy was an interesting character, and Robert Englund's work was excellent, but he did become a stand-up comic. With Pinhead, when 'Punk' collides with this sense of the 'Papal', it is not played for laughs.

WELLS: Were there other 'movie monsters' who influenced your work, or who you think carry with them an interesting perspective?

BRADLEY: The grandfather of them all, of course, is Boris Karloff's monster. *Bride of Frankenstein* remains my favourite horror film. I was never much a fan of Lugosi. Christopher Lee was very affecting. As a teenager I cut my teeth on the Hammer films when Granada went through a period in the late 1960s of showing a Hammer movie every Monday night. Lee and Peter Cushing were a big influence. It is not a horror film in the strictest sense, but I loved Jean Cocteau's beautiful film, *Beauty and the Beast*. Jean Marais's performance as the Beast is exquisite, as was the make-up. All of these monsters have a sense of pathos, and bathos, which I think is the essence of the monster. If a monster is simply monstrous, there is nothing to explore, nothing interesting, no ramifications, no echoes of humanity. The monster is a reflection of ourselves; the monster is within us all, and the horror film merely takes an aspect of that, makes it live, and makes the audience identify with it. We can all empathize with Frankenstein's monster, the Hunchback, the Beast, Dracula, and I hope people can find empathy with Pinhead.

WELLS: The horror film is constantly caught up in 'moral panics' and debates about the influence and effect of violent imagery upon audiences. How do you address these perspectives from your point of view as someone playing Pinhead and being in 'violent' films?

BRADLEY: We all have things that frighten us, whether they be phobias, or fears that arise from watching images that we cannot escape when watching news and current affairs programmes. In regard to the debates about violence in film and television, I have concerns about news items and explicit footage of war, murder and famine in bulletins preceding children's programmes. My son is old enough to understand this, but not old enough to find any context in which to place this information. The moral crusades bore me, and the arguments are circular and unpersuasive. It happened with Nickelodeons, Superman comics, *Clockwork Orange*. Hammer films, which we look back on as 'oh so safe, cute and cuddly', were greeted at the time by howls of protest. I have no problem with the *Hellraiser* series because it is self-evidently fantasy, and self-evidently made for adults, and I cannot believe that the horror film can be blamed for the ills of society. The real site, in my view, for psychological problems, both in real life and the horror film, is the family, and that is why *Hellraiser* is important. It is a domestic tragedy, 'a horror movie written by Ibsen', and it can take you right to the heart of the real pain and complexity of lived experience.

WELLS: What are your recollections of being frightened or being affected by horror films?

BRADLEY: My very first memory, again, is not really a horror film. It was Jack Clayton's *The Innocents*, his adaptation of *The Turn of the Screw*, and it frightened the life out of me. I have childhood memories of television programmes like *Pathfinders to Venus*, the classic serial of my era, *Jane Eyre*, which scared the hell out of me, and any ghost stories. The thing I knew was that I liked the feeling of being frightened. My mother would say, 'Switch it off' when I was terrified, but I would say 'No, I want to watch it, but I want to watch it from a safe place, sitting on your knee.' That is what horror cinema is all about; watching a horror film from the safe place of the stalls is a great experience. The television is a bit different, of course. I remember going to the toilet when those late night Hammer movies were over, and positioning myself with my back to the wall so that unguarded space behind me could be observed, and that 'the thing', whatever it was, wouldn't come and get me!

## References

Black, J. (1991) *The Aesthetics of Murder*, Baltimore and London: Johns Hopkins University Press.

Chibnall, S. (1998) *Making Mischief: The Cult Films of Pete Walker*, Guildford: FAB Press.

Hutchings, P. (1993) *Hammer and Beyond: The British Horror Film*, Manchester and New York: Manchester University Press.

Pirie, D. (1973) *A Heritage of Horror: The English Gothic Cinema 1946–1972*, London: Gordon Fraser.

# 14  Dying light: an obituary for the great British horror movie

*Richard Stanley*

Darkness first. Then a flickering beam splits the gloom.

The shambling beast goes through its motions once more, progressing steadily towards its calvary atop the Empire State building, confused, outflanked and outnumbered, beset by biplanes, the avatars of an uncaring new age which he cannot hope to comprehend. It is May 1993, and a butchered print of *King Kong* (1933), shorn by the British censor of several of its more intense moments, is the last film to run through the gate at the Scala cinema in King's Cross. When the screen goes dark this night it will mark the end of an era, a passing with implications that few people in the smoky auditorium are fully conscious of. Those who are, are either drunk or weeping openly.

Before it was a cinema, the Scala had been London's first Primatarium, a vast ape house, painted jungles crawling across its walls and its sepulchral auditorium filled with astroturf. When I last looked there were still deserted cages in the basement and if you inhaled deeply enough you could just catch the faint hint of musk and dried urine, a safari smell that took me back to my earliest childhood.

*King Kong* was the first film I ever saw, at the tender age of four and was also the first film to play the Scala once the apes were finally shipped out and the bankrupt Primatarium was converted into a repertory cinema in 1981 by the young Stephen Woolley and his partner Nik Powell, who had been one of the prime movers in the foundation of Richard Branson's Virgin empire. Together, the two young entrepreneurs set about using the crumbling venue as a platform for the launch of the distribution business that was to become Palace Pictures.

Several inspired choices in acquiring British distribution rights helped to bankroll Palace's eventual move into production, notably Jean-Jacques Beneix's *Diva* (1982) and a hyper-kinetic ultra low budget American horror film entitled *The Evil Dead* (1983), which was directed by the 21-year-old Sam Raimi. Despite unease at the British Board of Film Censors (BBFC), one of whose examiners said that she felt her 'bodily integrity' had been threatened by the film, it was passed (albeit with cuts) and Palace released it simultaneously on video and theatricallly in order to make the most out of their meagre promotional budget, a decision that outraged the rest of the British film industry which, at that time, was still terrified that video was about to finish off the movie business once and for all. However, the horror genre seemed set to undergo a major revival with the new technology offering the promise of a nightmare in every living room.

As it turned out, the old guard of the film industry weren't the only ones to be outraged. Late in 1983 the moral crusader Mary Whitehouse screened clips from *The Evil Dead* and a number of other so-called 'video nasties' to a large number of MPs at the House of Commons, as a highly effective means of lobbying the Thatcher government to introduce tight state controls on the burgeoning video industry.

The 'video nasty' furore had already been running for some time in the press, and a particularly hysterical campaign in papers such as the *Sun* and *Mail* had helped to create a climate in which the government felt obliged to take action, partly to appease traditional Tory voters but also to deflect attention from the more deep-rooted social, economic and environmental factors underlying the rising crime statistics which were then embarrassing the traditional 'law and order' party.

Empowered by the Director of Public Prosecution's willingness to use the Obscene Publications Act against violent (as opposed to the more usual pornographic) material, the police began a series of raids on video retailers, eating their way steadily back up the supply lines to distributors such as Palace and their headquarters above the Scala cinema.

Acting on a last-minute tip-off, the manager of Palace's marketing, sales and video distribution, Irving Rappaport, the brother of actor David Rappaport, had every copy of *The Evil Dead* removed from the property and hidden in a local church. Enraged when they came up empty handed during the initial raid on the Scala, the forces of law and order then descended on the main warehouse from which they removed the offending film's master tapes and a case against it was prepared by the Director of Public Prosecutions.

After Sam Raimi, Nik Powell and several others testified at Snaresbrook Crown Court a verdict of not guilty was returned on 7 November 1983, and the resulting publicity ensured *The Evil Dead*'s rise to the top of the video charts, breaking all records at that time and putting Palace Pictures well and truly on the map.

It made sense that the company's flagship production would be a borderline horror project, Neil Jordan's dream-like fantasy *The Company of Wolves* (1984). Produced by Steve Woolley and Chris Brown, the film took its inspiration from the work of Angela Carter, offering a very personal vision of the werewolf myth and a darkly Gothic reworking of the Grimms' fairy tales, one infinitely more in keeping with their roots than the dumbed-down pastiches familiar from the Disney stable.

A waif-like Sarah Patterson embodied an adolescent Little Red Riding Hood, lost in a deep and particularly gloomy studio forest haunted by Stephen Rea's sad-eyed lycanthrope and very capably supported by Angela Lansbury as her all-wise grand-mother and David Warner as her concerned father. I must admit to having a particular soft spot for Warner as a result of his role as the gorilla-loving eccentric in Karel Reisz's *Morgan: A Suitable Case for Treatment* (1966), a film which always leaves a warm glow in my heart.

The success of *The Company of Wolves* at the box office set Steve Woolley and Nik Powell on their way to becoming major players in the British film industry, leaving the Scala's programming to be taken over by the young Jo-Anne Sellar, who had started at the cinema as an usherette, literally picking the gum off the seats and affecting a China Blue wig as she patrolled the tenebrous aisles.

Sixteen years old and on the run from the military police, I took refuge in those aisles during my first winter in London, as much for warmth as anything else. It was my good fortune that I stumbled onto the scene just as Jo-Anne's programming scaled new heights promising unbroken all-day-all-nighters of obscure Euro horrors, spaghetti westerns, pop art and mild sexploitation.

On my second night in the capital I experienced something of an epiphany when I found myself sitting through all of Dario Argento's work for the first time in a single continuous screening. Staggering out into the grey light of that mid-1980s dawn, I knew in my heart that my life would never be the same again.

The Scala became my sanctuary, my alma mater, a house of dreams redolent of an opium den with its haze of psychoactive smoke and its delirious, half-glimpsed denizens. I would camp with my bedroll on the front tiers of the red-lit, cat-haunted auditorium in which the first few rows had been so utterly destroyed by various nutters that it had become more expedient to let people lie on the steps, make love, shoot up or just catch a few hours' sleep. If I didn't exactly grow up in the ape house then I certainly came of age there, fumbling in the dark with fellow film junkies while a relentless progression of imagery flowed past and over us, leaving us changed in various complicated ways. Sometimes I would open my eyes at 3 am and have no way of knowing if I was dreaming or not, and, as I slowly learned about the art of light, so the Scala brought me into contact with some of the auteurs who had helped create this formidable body of work.

I met visiting film directors ranging from Sam Raimi and Alejandro Jodorowski (who had more or less invented the midnight movie back in the 1960s with his notorious psychedelic western *El Topo* (1972)) to Dario Argento himself with whom I was eventually to strike up a halting friendship. Palace had picked up Argento's confused and maggot-ridden Jennifer Connolly vehicle *Phenomena* (1985) for a video release (inevitably heavily censored) and followed this through by putting out his brother Claudio's production of Jodorowski's exquisite Mexican serial murder romance *Santa Sangre* (1989).

*The Company of Wolves* had set the stage for a final cinematic flowering of the Gothic tradition, led by bad boy Ken Russell's *Gothic* (1986), a hallucinatory and extremely camp fantasia based around that notorious party at the Villa Deodati at which Mary Shelley was inspired to create the Frankenstein myth and where the ground was paved for Bram Stoker's *Dracula* by the fevered work of Doctor John Polidori, incarnated on screen by Timothy Spall, who proceeded to steal the show and then eat the furniture. Failing to duplicate *The Company of Wolves'* delicate balancing act between art house angst and outright horror, *Gothic* was released to a lukewarm reception, almost single-handedly prompting Virgin to disengage itself from the film industry once and for all.

A second film from Russell in 1988, *The Lair of the White Worm*, continued in the same vein, adapting Bram Stoker's flawed final novel into a lunatic farrago of cheesy, fetishistic imagery featuring Amanda Donohoe as an alluring snake woman slithering around the home counties, poisoning boy scouts and intimidating a very confused-looking Hugh Grant. Perhaps the less said about this the better, although I do have a pleasing memory of a red-faced and suitably daemonic Ken Russell standing propped in the doorway of a Soho preview theatre, staring down the various reviewers as they filed past him, doing their very best to avoid eye contact. I think he must have known that it was all over for him but just wanted to face it out like the ruined, mad-arsed renegade of British cinema that he was. Direct. Looking at it and knowing it for what it was.

The director Bernard Rose fared considerably better with the moody rite-of-passage thriller *Paperhouse* (1989), produced by Tim Bevan, whose themes of childhood nightmares manifesting uncontrollably in waking reality far outshone its other *Elm Street*-inspired contemporaries such as Harley Cokliss's *Dream Demon* (1988).

Continuing their astute distribution policy, Palace picked up *A Nightmare on Elm Street* (1984)and its sequels for the United Kingdom and had put *Dream Demon* into production in the hope of duplicating the success of the Freddy Krueger films with a home-grown product. Unfortunately lightning failed to strike twice, although Timothy Spall did get another chance to chew the scenery, this time as a disintegrating tabloid journalist haunting Jemma Redgrave's dreams, along with his equally moribund partner Jimmy Nail.

A much-needed jolt in the arm came with the release of British horror author Clive Barker's debut feature as a director, *Hellraiser* (1987). Hyped by Stephen King as the 'future of horror', Barker had survived two earlier brushes with the film industry when his stories provided the basis for a pair of highly forgettable features directed by George Pavlou, *Underworld* (1985) and *Rawhead Rex* (1986). The latter is an utterly deranged Irish monster movie in which a stuntman in an unconvincing creature costume (complete with red flashing eyes!) emerges from beneath a standing stone to drag bare-breasted traveller babes from their caravans, and piss on the local priest, none of which is as much fun as it sounds.

Despite its threadbare budget, *Hellraiser* proved to be a quantum improvement on this tepid fare, telling the admirably twisted and good-looking tale of a puzzle box dubbed the 'lament configuration' which opens the doorway to a world inhabited by sado-masochistic demons known as Cenobites, chief among whom is the icon Pinhead, played by Doug Bradley in make-up designed by the talented Chris

Halls, working out of Bob Keen's Image Animation shop at Pinewood. Years later, working under the name of Chris Cunningham, Halls, would direct two seminal music videos for The Aphex Twin, and may well prove to be one of the most important genre figures of the generation to come.

Two sequels were produced in the United States, both scripted by Pete Atkins, who succeeded in screwing up whatever it was that Barker had got right in the first place. Barker's second film as a director followed in 1990, a bizarre Freudian phantasmagoria entitled *Nightbreed*; this starred David Cronenberg as a psychopathic psychiatrist, apparently modelled on Hannibal Lecter, who tries to pin his crimes on one of his patients who in fact turns out to be a genuine monster. Let down by unusually ragged plotting and unconvincing make-up, *Nightbreed* seemed to disappoint everyone save Alejandro Jodorowski, who rightly proclaimed it to be the first truly gay horror fantasy epic, preoccupied, as it is, with the unconsummated relationship between doctor and patient. However, such subtleties escaped most audiences and *Nightbreed* failed to work any wonders at the box office.

Spurred on by *Hellraiser*'s success, Steve Woolley remained determined to come up with his own horror hit, a British equivalent of *The Evil Dead*, the film that had kickstarted Palace's fortunes in the first place. To this end he optioned my first professional screenplay, *Hardware* (1990), a Gothic cyberpunk fantasy with strong lashings of gore, a project that grew out of the music video and album cover work in which I'd been engaged for the then flourishing Goth scene.

In point of fact, *Hardware* went into pre-production at a time when I thought I had put the movie business behind me for good. Having become embroiled with a Muslim guerrilla organization, I was about as far away from the Scala as I could possibly be, doing my bit to help the mujahedin to fight the communists in Afghanistan. I had just crossed the border back into Pakistan in order to get medical attention for one of my companions who had been wounded in the battle for Jallalabad when I found myself collared by the anxious producers and returned to England to start shooting my first feature as a director. Most people undergo a few years of counselling after living through similar experiences but I found myself acting out my combat psychosis on a movie set instead, with a tantalizing array of explosives and lethal-looking action props at my disposal.

Jo-Anne Sellar was chosen as *Hardware*'s producer, reinforcing the link with the Scala, whose programming had by then been taken over by Jane Giles. Jo-Anne was determined to strut her stuff and although the material was eventually much softened by the understandably nervous backers, the completed feature still managed to get an X-rating in the United States, a classification that made it effectively impossible to distribute commercially without further cuts.

In keeping with an honourable Scala tradition, Jo-Anne and I hit the daytime chat show circuit, campaigning for changes in the Motion Picture Association of America (MPAA)'s rating systems and generally doing our best to get up the establishment's collective nose. *Hardware* premiered at Cannes to glowing notices and the Scala crew and I partied the night away on the decks of a Russian research vessel anchored just offshore, berthed between Polanski's galleon from *Pirates* (1986) and an American aircraft carrier.

Abandoning ship just before dawn I tried to go for a spin on a power boat with one of the producers of *Hellraiser* and two young actresses from *Letter to Brezhnev* (1985), only to run out of gas and find ourselves drifting slowly but steadily out to sea. The 1980s were over, the Berlin Wall had come down and the wave we'd been cresting was just about to dry up.

Although never quite the hit that Steve had wanted, *Hardware* still performed extraordinarily well for its budget of well under £1m, grossing enough to keep Palace afloat through a particularly lean season, the year of David Leland's *The Big Man*, Neil Jordan's *The Miracle*, *The Pope Must Die* and two Lenny Henry comedies. Initially I had expected other production companies to follow *Hardware*'s lead, thus opening the way for a new generation of British genre directors and proving once and for all that horror material could be profitably produced in the United Kingdom. The signs, however, weren't particularly encouraging, especially if *I Bought a Vampire Motorcycle* (1990), a would-be black comedy starring a lost-looking Michael Elphick, and *Beyond Bedlam* (1992), a strident and unconvincing serial killer fantasy, were anything to go by. The two films that tried to imitate *Hardware* most directly were, if anything, even worse. *Split Second* (1992) was a flabby Rutger Hauer vehicle which shared *Hardware*'s locations but whose incoherent script, indifferent production design and gaping plot holes betrayed the lack of a strong hand at the tiller, the project having apparently had its directors fired and replaced several times in mid-flow by disgruntled producers. *Death Machine* (1995), the debut feature from Steve Norrington, who had cut his teeth on the *Hardware* FX crew, was little better. Its plot, creature design and casting choices were virtually a carbon copy of *Hardware*'s raw components, despite the fact that *Hardware* was itself born of 1980s trends started by *Alien* (1979), *Terminator* (1984) and the continuing cycle of women-in-jeopardy slasher flicks. Its thin blood depleted by inbreeding, *Death Machine* remains a somewhat blunt and unrewarding experience, going direct to video and effectively bringing the mini-cycle to an end.

My second feature, *Dust Devil* (1993), had been put into production in the rush of euphoria that followed *Hardware*'s release, but, by the time we reached post-production, the writing was already on the wall.

Palace Pictures was experiencing grave cashflow problems that exerted a heavy toll on the production and although Nik and Steve continued to choose their projects wisely, lining up *The Player* (1992), *Reservoir Dogs* (1992) and *Howard's End* (1991) for distribution, they found themselves hard hit by the recession, increasingly forced into a corner by Polygram and the new corporate culture which was taking control of the industry.

When Polygram reneged on a deal to buy the Palace group outright, they were left with little choice but to file for administration in May 1992, winding up the

*Figure 28* African horror: Richard Stanley (right) directs Robert Burke on the set of *Dust Devil* (1993).

*Figure 29* The last picture show: Richard Stanley surveys the dust-covered cinema in *Dust Devil*.

company and leaving debts outstanding all over Soho. Polygram promptly took over the entire back catalogue, as well as all the films which remained unreleased, trapped along with *Dust Devil* in the distribution pipeline. I never saw the second half of my fee for the production and was forced to pour my own funds into its completion, costing me my home and bringing me to the verge of bankruptcy; indeed, I was still trying to finish the edit while already on the run from the bailiffs.

By winter I found myself back on the streets, spending two nights in a bus shelter in South London before taking refuge in the only sanctuary left to me: the Scala cinema, where Jane Giles allowed me to spread my bedroll in a room above her office.

The Scala had developed some major problems of its own by then. The building's lease had expired and the unscrupulous landlord was doing his best to force out the cinema and the freaks that ran it. Furthermore, the rapidly expanding video market had eaten into the Scala's attendance, reducing audiences to record lows; none of which was helped by the programming inevitably growing a little stale given the increasing absence of good new product.

The all-day-all-nighters had simply dried up as people preferred to abuse themselves in the privacy of their own homes, and the auditorium had fallen into greater disrepair. As the recession began to bite, so the entire area slid into decay, the darkening streets of King's Cross growing so crime-ridden that few people wanted to risk getting beaten up just to catch a creaky old horror movie in a venue that now counted rats and bad plumbing among its many attractions. Times were changing fast and there was nothing any of us could do about it.

At first we believed the video revolution would bring with it a new era in communication, an age of wider public access and unprecedented freedoms, but, instead, it brought new nightmares and old daemons in new forms. The winter of 1993–4 was one of the coldest and loneliest that I can remember, but, in the end, it was a flickering image on a CCTV camera that really brought the house down. The ultimate British horror movie turned out to be a simple thing. Just one static wide-angle shot and one location – a shopping centre on the outskirts of Liverpool – and a cast of three, their backs turned towards the camera: two children leading a toddler by the hand like friendly older brothers, the crowd flowing by obliviously, unwitting extras in an unnoticed drama.

It was February 1994 and two-year-old James Bulger had just been abducted by two older boys from outside a butcher's in a shopping centre in a suburb of Liverpool. The rest of this awful story is by now too well known to need re-telling, but the key point, in this context, is that, once the two boys who were charged with killing James were in custody, it was only a matter of time before talk turned to their viewing habits, a move only encouraged by the police releasing to the press a list of the video titles which their parents had recently rented. This included a low-budget American horror movie entitled *Child's Play III* (1993), a late entry in a franchise spun around a walking, talking killer doll named Chucky.

Although there was no discernible connection between any of the events in this production and the facts of the Bulger case itself, the ominous title alone, along with the reality that an emotionally disturbed ten-year-old might have gained access to an '18' certificate film in the first place, gave the average person in the street, and, in the end, the Conservative government itself, an easy out, a convenient, although in fact entirely risible, 'explanation' for an otherwise unthinkable crime. The appalling abuse that at least one of the two young killers had suffered at the hands of his family was ignored as child psychiatrists crawled out of the woodwork to pontificate at length on television chat shows, making great play of the alleged ill-effects of 'violent media' on children. Needless to say, the tabloids seized on the story with a vengeance, whipping up public hysteria once again over the so-called 'video nasties', their front pages proudly sporting images of bonfires of horror cassettes.

The Liberal Democrat MP and moral guardian David Alton skilfully rode the wave of public opinion, ably furthering his particular cause by using the Bulger case to lobby remorselessly for even tighter state controls over video, threatening to introduce a measure which would have effectively banished most horror videos, and perhaps, indeed, all videos unsuitable for children, from the shelves of British shops.

Under the circumstances I did the only thing I could. Putting on my last surviving suit and borrowing a tie, I sallied forth from the Scala, pulling a few strings to insinuate myself onto a parliamentary sub-committee hastily convened to debate further video censorship, and Alton's proposed measure in particular. I was the only film-maker present, and the only creative person, aside from Martin Amis, to appear before the sub-committee, which was otherwise composed largely of juvenile care workers and the inevitable child psychiatrists.

Knowing in advance that any argument based on the right to freedom of expression would fall on deaf ears, I realized that the only chance I had of getting my message across would be by appealing to their business sense. Although anxious as ever not to be portrayed as 'soft' by the right-wing press, the Conservative government of John Major nonetheless recognized that even tighter controls on film and video would inevitably impact on the lower end of an industry already hard hit by the recession and struggling in a market place dominated almost exclusively by American product. It would thus be my role before this committee to present the case for the British horror film by arguing that the industry needed exploitation product such as the Hammer output and *Carry On* films of the past in order to support the handful of 'quality' productions that it turned out each year and to keep crews in employment while they waited around for the next E.M. Forster adaptation. Under the circumstances I believe I made my case quite eloquently.

When I was done, I noticed Lady Howe of the Broadcasting Standards Commission staring at me a little disdainfully, having no doubt earmarked me for the professional pornographer that I probably was. 'Are you a mother, Mr Stanley?' she asked me, deadpan, as if unaware of the absurdity of the question. Of course I wasn't, and my admission of this rather obvious fact simply paved the way for the inevitable moral tirade she had been waiting all morning to get off her chest, reiterating everything Mary Whitehouse had said ten years earlier. Only this time people seemed more inclined to listen.

At one point, several glossy video catalogues were passed around as examples of the sort of sadistic filth apparently commonly available by mail order from video retailers in the United Kingdom. The various care workers and concerned parents duly shook their heads and tut-tutted as they cast their eyes over the lurid box covers, prompting Lady Howe to remark that this was exactly the sort of thing that Alton's measure was designed to clean up. Recognizing several of the retailers in question I couldn't resist the opportunity to point out that some of the titles in the catalogue were in fact silent movies such as F.W. Murnau's *Nosferatu* (1921), Robert Wiene's *The Cabinet of Doctor Caligari* (1920), Benjamin Christensen's *Häxan* (1921) and Carl Dreyer's *Vampyr* (1931), films which had fallen into the public domain and which were routinely tarted up with saucy S&M-oriented covers by companies such as Nigel Wingrove's Redemption Films. Being good capitalists they were just out to make a fast buck by recycling cheap product and flogging off creaky old warhorses that had already been playing the National Film Theatre and late night television for decades. Some of the material was old enough to have run into trouble once before: in Nazi Germany, where another set of moral authoritarians and right-wing idealists had set out to clean up 'decadent' art once and for all, a campaign that could not exactly be said to have led to a kinder or better society.

Even I realized that I might have gone a little too far in drawing this last analogy. A child psychiatrist instantly shot to his feet, glaring at me as if I were the devil incarnate, the beast walking on its hind legs and come amongst them. 'Are you Jewish, Mr Stanley?' he demanded, which I wasn't. 'Well, I happen to be Jewish,' he continued, 'and I want to tell you that you have no right invoking the spectre of the Holocaust at this table!' At this point there was such a fuss that the committee had to go into recess, and, over tea and chocolate biscuits my sponsor, who had helped get me into this event in the first place, informed me that if I opened my mouth one more time they would have me ejected from the room. I didn't even try to say anything more after that. Like Martin Amis, who failed to utter a single comprehensible word throughout, I contented myself with observing the proceedings as the various care workers had their say and further video censorship looked increasingly inevitable.

Even outside Whitehall, however, I was hard pressed to find anyone who shared my views. The debacle also proved to be the last straw for my then girlfriend who had been around just long enough to know that things weren't about to get any better. Clearing my odds and ends forcefully from her apartment, she singled out a copy of *The Bird with the Crystal Plumage* (1970), Dario Argento's debut feature, for particular condemnation. 'This is exactly the sort of shit I don't need in my life any more!' she spat, flinging the tainted cassette in my general direction, followed a moment later by a VHS copy of Michael Mann's flawed occult thriller *The Keep* (1984).

It was just one more betrayal in a whole series, but it was the one that counted most to me. We might have been mismatched as a couple but we had been together for more than ten years and, loving her as I did with all my heart, her opinion counted. And it was, it seemed, the same opinion as just about everyone else in the country at that time.

It was against this unpropitious backdrop of moral frenzy that *Dust Devil* finally opened, premiering at the Scala to good reviews and underwhelming audiences. It was hardly the Odeon Leicester Square but, under the circumstances, the choice of venue for *Dust Devil*'s London run seemed oddly appropriate. Shot on location in Namibia, with American leads and a storyline that revolved around African magic, *Dust Devil* scarcely qualified as a British horror film at all, and, after a sputtering tour of various regional repertory houses, it found its way swiftly to video, poorly mastered and effectively dumped onto the market by Polygram, who had little interest in promoting the left-over titles which it had inherited from Palace.

Although the limited nature of *Dust Devil*'s release, stretching to just one print paid for out of my own pocket, left me saddened and frustrated, I would have been sadder still had I realized that it was to be the last British horror film to receive any form of theatrical release to date – and almost ten years have gone by at the time of writing.

New titles have sporadically surfaced over the years but crippled by poverty row budgets and Z-grade casting they have, without exception, gone direct to video. Some, like Mariano Baino's *Dark Waters* (1993), offered interesting location work and moody cinematography at the expense of narrative coherence, while others, like Alberto Sciamma's *Killer Tongue* (1996), offered nothing.

*Funny Man* (1994) sported an all-too-brief cameo from an ageing and increasingly under-used Christopher Lee before degenerating into typical teen-oriented old-dark-house slasher antics, while Julian Richards's staggeringly inept occult thriller *Darklands* (1997) attempted to transplant the all too familiar plotline of *The Wicker Man* (1973) to Wales. Although the undeveloped theme of collusion between pagans and right-wing authorities is undeniably a compelling one, the film wastes any potential inherent in the idea through its wooden characterization and mind-blowingly tedious exposition, failing to grasp or in any way appreciate the subtleties of a genuine tradition. Sadly, however, *Darklands* set the pace for the 1990s, a decade whose only genre entries amounted to amateurish efforts, home movies and fan boy fluff too impoverished or basically incompetent to reach a wider audience. In this respect, *White Angel* (1998), *Razorblade Smile* (1999) and *The 13th Sign* (2000) all spring to mind. Although *The 13th Sign*, an old-fashioned diabolists-on-the-loose movie dressed up with modish millennial trappings, does show some promise in comparison to the other horrors unleashed since the collapse of Palace Pictures, it is still a long way below the minimum standard of even the most vilified 1980s product.

Anyone who really knew what they were doing escaped to Hollywood a long time ago. Bernard Rose, the talented director of *Paper House*, came up with a palpable hit in the form of Clive Barker's *Candyman* (1992), while Barker himself fared rather less well with his third directional outing, *Lord of Illusions* (1995), produced by Jo-Anne Sellar, who has since struck gold with P.T. Anderson's *Boogie Nights* (1997) and its follow-up, *Magnolia* (1999).

*The Crying Game* (1992) proved to be a major hit, and Steve Woolley followed Neil Jordan with *Interview with a Vampire* (1994), while Steve Norrington tagged along on the vampire wave with *Blade* (1998), his much improved answer to *Death Machine*. None of these films, alas, could be said in any significant way to be British.

The Scala cinema survived for more than a year after the death of its parent company, just about making ends meet. The last nail in the coffin lid was finally driven home by the Scala's projectionist when he blew the whistle on a long-standing practice of illegally screening Stanley Kubrick's *Clockwork Orange* (1971), usually billed as a 'surprise film' alongside Lindsay Anderson's *If* (1968) and *O Lucky Man!* (1973). The triple bill drew a loyal core of skinheads and wannabee droogs who sometimes brought their pit bulls with them, but, if Jane Giles came to rely on their unsteady revenue, it was against the wishes of MGM and Kubrick himself, who had personally requested that the film be withdrawn from exhibition in Britain. The projectionist in question earned himself a fat pay-off and sheltered employment at the MGM preview theatre in return for testifying against the Scala's management at the resulting trial, and in May 1993 the cinema finally went dark.

The audience catches its breath as the great beast plunges to the street, skyscrapers trembling at its fall. The cinema is literally coming apart around us now. There is the sound of screams and breaking glass from the foyer and more fighting going on in the aisle where Jane is kicking someone twice her size, waiting until she's got him down before jabbing her pointy shoe into his groin.

Sad really. Nothing left that anyone can do.

Carl Denham proclaims his eulogy: 'He's dead. The planes killed him!' 'No. It wasn't the planes. It was beauty that killed the beast.' Max Steiner's score crashes over the decaying sound system, but I am already out in the foyer stealing the posters, not wanting to see the lights go up.

Seven years have passed since that night. *A Clockwork Orange* was re-released to packed houses following the death of Stanley Kubrick and has recently appeared on video just in case someone out there doesn't already own a bootleg.

James Bulger's killers, now dubbed Adult A and Adult B and shielded by new identities, are to be released soon, apparently rehabilitated although, of course, the video legislation which the government passed in order to pacify the Alton lobby, a compromise measure brokered largely by Tony Blair and Jack Straw, then still in the opposition, remains firmly in place.

A night-club now operates in the former ape house and, although I frequently walk past, I have never had the heart to look too closely. That's me now, going down the street, eyes down, looking at the cracks between the paving stones.

# Filmography of British horror films of the sound era

*L.S. Smith*

This is a filmography of British sound films containing a significant horror element. In most cases only films of sixty minutes or longer have been included. However, a few exceptions have been made to allow the inclusion of titles that are discussed in the articles in this collection. The filmography is ordered chronologically by UK release date (or by date of registration as a British film when release was severely delayed) in the first instance, and then alphabetically by the film's UK release title. No distinction has been made between films with a substantial theatrical release and those with very few cinema showings. Genre is difficult to define at the best of times. When one adds to that the complication of determining a country of origin, particularly in the post-1970 period, the problems increase exponentially. What follows is a brief rationale as to what type of film is included, or excluded, and why.

Essentially this filmography has a single broad criterion to define whether a film should be considered 'horror': is one of its primary intentions (I use the word advisedly, as many films listed below quite clearly fail in practice) to evoke fear or horror? Consequently there is no place for *Carry on Screaming* (1966), or any of the other numerous British films which mix comedy and horror, if their main raison d'être is to make the audience laugh. I appreciate that fear and horror themselves can be seen as contested terms, however this, admittedly subjective, criteria for inclusion is the one which was decided upon. That having been said, the filmography errs on the side of inclusivity. No doubt there are titles below that are usually considered thrillers or science fiction, but they have been included because they meet the broad criteria laid down above.

The criteria for classifying a film as British also present problems. This really becomes a serious issue around 1970 when the number of international co-productions increased dramatically. The standard reference works, such as *The Monthly Film Bulletin*, *Sight and Sound*, Denis Gifford's *Catalogue of British Films* and *The Aurum Encyclopaedia of Horror Cinema* have been used as a guide to classification, and co-productions have generally been included. When compiling a document containing as much detailed information as this there is clearly scope for errors and/or omissions. In an attempt to make this as accurate as possible each entry has been at least double sourced, with the vast majority at least triple sourced. The format of the filmography closely follows that devised by I.Q. Hunter (1999) for *British Science Fiction Cinema*. Each film listed in the filmography has certain core pieces of information associated with it. The abbreviations for each are as follows:

**Abbreviations used:**

US    American title/running time
bw    black and white
col    colour
*pc*    production company (distributors are not listed)
*d*    director
*prod*    producer (executive and associate producers are not shown)
*sc*    author of screenplay
*story*    original story by. The author of a source novel, play, TV serial, etc. is identified specifically.
*cast*    four leading players

*Dark Red Roses*
1929 67m bw; *pc* British Sound Film; *d* Sinclair Hall; *prod* Sinclair Hall; *sc* Leslie Howard Gordon, Harcourt Templeman; *story* Stacy Aumonier; *cast* Stewart Rome, Francis Doble, Hugh Eden, Kate Cutler.

*The Bells*
1931 75m bw; *pc* British Sound Film; *d* Harcourt Templeman; *prod* Sergei Nolbandov; *sc* C.H. Dand; *play* Alexandre Chatrian, Emile Erckmann; *cast* Donald Calthrop, Jane Welsh, Edward Sinclair, O.B. Clarence.

*The Hound of the Baskervilles*
1931 75m bw; *pc* Gainsborough Pictures, Gaumont-British; *d* V. Gareth Gundry; *prod* Michael Balcon; *sc* V. Gareth Gundry, Edgar Wallace; *novel* Arthur Conan Doyle; *cast* John Stuart, Reginald Bach, Robert Rendel, Frederick Lloyd.

*Castle Sinister*
1932 50m bw; *pc* Delta, Filmophone; *d* Widgey R. Newman; *prod* Widgey R. Newman; *sc* Widgey R. Newman; *cast* Haddon Mason, Ilsa Kilpatrick, Eric Adney, Wally Patch.

*The Frightened Lady*
1932 87m bw; *pc* Gainsborough, British Lion Film; *d* T. Hayes Hunter; *prod* Michael Balcon; *sc* Angus McPhail, Bryan Edgar Wallace; *play* Edgar Wallace; *cast* Norman McKinnell, Cathleen Nesbitt, Emlyn Williams, Gordon Harker.

*The Lodger (US: The Phantom Fiend)*
1932 84m bw; *pc* Twickenham; *d* Maurice Elvey; *prod* Julius Hagen; *sc* Ivor Novello, Miles Mander, Paul Rotha, H. Fowler Mear; *novel* Marie Belloc Lowndes; *cast* Ivor Novello, Elizabeth Allan, A.W. Baskcomb, Jack Hawkins.

*The Ghoul*
1933 85, 73m bw; *pc* Gaumont-British; *d* T. Hayes Hunter; *sc* Roland Pertwee, Rupert Downing; *cast* Boris Karloff, Cedric Hardwicke, Ernest Thesiger, Dorothy Hyson.

*The Scotland Yard Mystery (US: The Living Dead)*
1934 65m bw; *pc* British International; *d* Thomas Bentley; *prod* Walter C. Mycroft; *sc* Frank Miller; *cast* Gerald du Maurier, George Curzon, Grete Natzler, Belle Chrystal.

*The Tell-Tale Heart (US: Bucket of Blood)*
1934 53m bw; *pc* Clifton-Hurst; *d* Brian Desmond Hurst; *prod* Harry Clifton; *sc* David Plunkett Greene; *story* Edgar Allan Poe; *cast* Norman Dryden, John Kelt, Yolande Terrell, Thomas Shenton.

*The Unholy Quest*
1934 57m bw; *pc* Equity British, Widgey R. Newman Productions; *d* R.W. Lotinga (Newman); *prod* Bert Hopkins, Widgey R. Newman, Reginald Wyer; *sc* Widgey R. Newman; *cast* Claude Bailey, Terence de Marney, Christine Adrian, John Milton.

*Maria Marten, or Murder in the Red Barn*
1935 67m bw; *pc* King, MGM; *d* Milton Rosmer; *prod* George King; *sc* Randall Faye; *cast* Tod Slaughter, Sophie Stewart, D.J. Williams, Eric Portman.

*The Mystery of the Marie Celeste* (US: *The Phantom Ship*)
1935 80m bw; *pc* Hammer; *d* Denison Clift; *prod* Denison Clift, H. Fraser Passmore; *sc* Denison Clift, Charles Larkworthy; *cast* Bela Lugosi, Shirley Grey, Arthur Margaretson, Edmund Willard.

*The Crimes of Stephen Hawke*
1936 69m bw; *pc* Ambassador Film, George King Productions; *d* George King; *prod* George King; *sc* Jack Celestin, H.F. Maltby, Paul White; *cast* Tod Slaughter, Marjorie Taylor, D.J. Williams, Eric Portman.

*The Man Who Changed His Mind*
1936 66m bw; *pc* Gainsborough Pictures; *d* Robert Stevenson; *prod* Michael Balcon; *sc* John L. Balderston, Sidney Gilliat, L. Du Garde Peache; *cast* Boris Karloff, Anna Lee, John Loder, Frank Cellier.

*Sweeney Todd, the Demon Barber of Fleet Street*
1936 65m bw; *pc* George King Productions; *d* George King; *prod* George King;

*sc* Frederick Hayward, H.F. Maltby; *cast* Tod Slaughter, Stella Rho, John Singer, Eva Lister.

*It's Never Too Late To Mend*
1937 70m bw; *pc* George King Productions; *d* David MacDonald; *prod* George King; *sc* H.F. Maltby; *novel* Charles Reade; *cast* Tod Slaughter, Jack Livesey, Marjorie Taylor, Ian Colin.

*Sexton Blake and the Hooded Terror*
1938 70m bw; *pc* Ambassador Film, George King Productions; *d* George King; *prod* George King; *sc* Pierre Quiroule, A.R. Rawlinson; *cast* George Curzon, Tod Slaughter, Greta Gynt, Tony Sympson.

*Dark Eyes of London (US: The Human Monster)*
1939 76m bw; *pc* Argyle, Pathé; *d* Walter Summers; *prod* John Argyle; *sc* John Argyle, Patrick Kirwan, Walter Summers; *cast* Bela Lugosi, Hugh Williams, Greta Gynt, Wilfred Walter.

*The Face at the Window*
1939 70m 65m bw; *pc* British Lion, Pennant; *d* George King; *prod* Randall Faye, George King; *sc* A.R. Rawlinson; *play* F. Brooke Warron *cast* Tod Slaughter, Marjorie Taylor, John Warwick, Leonard Henry.

*Crimes at the Dark House*
1940 69m bw; *pc* George King, Pennant; *d* George King; *prod* Odette King; *sc* Edward Dryhurst, Fredrick Hayward, H.F. Maltby; *novel* Wilkie Collins; *cast* Tod Slaughter, Sylvia Marriott, Hilary Eaves, Geoffrey Wardell.

*The Door with Seven Locks (US: Chamber of Horrors)*
1940 79m bw; *pc* Rialto Film; *d* Norman Lee; *prod* John Argyle; *sc* Gilbert Gunn, Norman Lee; *novel* Edgar Wallace; *cast* Romilly Lunge, Lilli Palmer, Leslie Banks, Richard Bird.

*Gaslight (US: Angel Street)*
1940 88m bw; *pc* British National Films; *d* Thorold Dickinson; *prod* John Corfield; *sc* Bridget Boland, A.R. Rawlinson; *play* Patrick Hamilton; *cast* Anton Walbrook, Diana Wynyard, Robert Newton, Frank Pettingell.

*Tower of Terror*
1941 78m bw; *pc* Associated British Picture Corporation; *d* Lawrence Huntingdon; *prod* John Argyle; *sc* John Argyle, John Reinhart; *cast* Wilfred Lawson, Michael Rennie, Morland Graham, George Woodbridge.

*Dark Tower*
1943 93m bw; *pc* Warner; *d* John Harlow; *prod* Max Milder; *sc* Reginald Purdell, Brock Williams; *cast* Ben Lyon, Herbert Lom, Anne Crawford, David Farrar.

*A Place of One's Own*
1944 89m bw; *pc* GFD; *d* Bernard Knowles; *prod* R.J. Minney, Maurice Ostrer; *sc* Brock Williams; *novel* Osbert Sitwell; *cast* Margaret Lockwood, James Mason, Barbara Mullen, Dennis Price.

*Dead of Night*
1945 102m (US 77m) bw; *pc* Ealing Studios; *d* Alberto Cavalcanti, Charles Crichton, Basil Dearden, Robert Hamer; *prod* Sidney Cole, John Croydon; *sc* John V. Barnes, Angus MacPhail, T.E.B. Clarke; *cast* Mervyn Johns, Frederic Valk, Michael Redgrave, Googie Withers.

*Latin Quarter (US: Frenzy)*
1945 80m bw; *pc* British National, Four Continents Films; *d* Vernon Sewell; *prod* Louis H. Jackson, Derrick de Marney; *sc* Vernon Sewell; *play* Pierre Mills, Charles de Vylars; *cast* Derrick de Marney, Joan Greenwood, Joan Seton, Beresford Egan.

*The Curse of the Wraydons*
1946 94m bw; *pc* Ambassador Film Productions; *d* Victor M. Gover; *prod* Gilbert Church, J.C. Jones; *sc* Owen George; *play* Maurice Sandoz; *cast* Tod Slaughter, Bruce Seton, Andrew Laurence, Alan Lawrence.

*The Ghosts of Berkley Square*
1947 85m bw; *pc* British National; *d* Vernon Sewell; *prod* Louis H. Jackson; *sc* James Seymour; *novel* Caryl Brahms, S.J. Simon; *cast* Robert Morley, Felix Aylmer, Yvonne Arnaud, Claude Haulbert.

*Things Happen at Night*
1947 79m bw; *pc* Alliance Film Studios, Tudor; *d* Francis Searle; *prod* James Carter, St John Leigh Clowes; *sc* St John Leigh Clowes; *play* Frank Harvey; *cast* Gordon Harker, Alfred Drayton, Garry Marsh, Gwynneth Vaughan.

*Uncle Silas (US: The Inheritance)*
1947 103m bw; *pc* GFD, Two Cities; *d* Charles Frank; *prod* Laurence Irving, Joseph Somlo; *sc* Ben Travers; *story* Sheridan Le Fanu; *cast* Jean Simmons, Derrick de Marney, Katina Paxinou, Derek Bond.

*The Greed of William Hart (US: Horror Maniacs)*
1948 80 75m bw; *pc* Ambassador Film; *d* Oswald Mitchell; *prod* Gilbert Church; *sc* John Gilling; *cast* Tod Slaughter, Henry Oscar, Ann Trego, Jenny Lynn.

*The Queen of Spades*
1948 96m bw; *pc* ABPC; *d* Thorold Dickinson; *prod* Jack Clayton, Anatole de Grunwald; *sc* Rodney Ackland, Arthur Boys; *story* Alexander Pushkin; *cast* Anton Walbrook, Edith Evans, Yvonne Mitchell, Ronald Howard.

*The Man in Black*
1949 80m bw; *pc* Hammer; *d* Francis Searle; *prod* Anthony Hinds; *sc* John Dickinson Carr, John Gilling, Francis Searle; *cast* Betty Ann Davies, Sheila Burrell, Sid James, Anthony Forwood.

*Dark Interval*
1950 60m bw; *pc* Present Day; *d* Charles Saunders; *prod* Charles Reynolds; *sc* John Gilling; *cast* Zena Marshall, Andrew Osborn, John Barry, John Le Mesurier.

*The Fall of the House of Usher*
1950 (certificated 1948) 70m bw; *pc* GLB, Vigilant; *d* Ivan Barnett; *prod* Ivan Barnett; *sc* Dorothy Catt, Kenneth Thompson; *story* Edgar Allan Poe; *cast* Gwen Watford, Kay Tendeter, Irving Steen, Vernon Charles.

*Room to Let*
1950 68m bw; *pc* Hammer; *d* Godfrey Greyson; *prod* Anthony Hinds; *sc* John Gilling, Godfrey Greyson; *novel* Mary Belloc Lowndes; *cast* Jimmy Hanley, Valentine Dyall, Christine Silver, Merle Tottenham.

*Someone at the Door*
1950 65m bw; *pc* Hammer; *d* Francis Searle; *prod* Anthony Hinds; *sc* A.R. Rawlinson; *cast* Yvonne Owen, Michael Medwin, Hugh Latimer, Danny Green.

*Ghost Ship*
1952 69m bw; *pc* Abtcon Pictures; *d* Vernon Sewell; *prod* Nat Cohen, Stuart Levy; *sc* Vernon Sewell, Philip Thornton; *cast* Dermot Walsh, Hazel Court, Hugh Burden, John Robinson.

*Stolen Face*
1952 72m bw; *pc* Exclusive Pictures; *d* Terence Fisher; *prod* Anthony Hinds; *sc* Richard Landau; *cast* Paul Heinreid, Lizabeth Scott, Andre Morell, Mary MacKenzie.

*Gilbert Harding Speaks of Murder*
1953 76m bw; *pc* Danziger; *d* Paul Dickson; *prod* Edward J. Danziger, Harry Lee Danziger; *sc* Paul Tabori, James Eastwood, Kate Barclay; *cast* Kay Walsh, Betty Ann Davies, Patrick Barr, Hubert Gregg.

*Three's Company*
1953 78m bw; *pc* Douglas Fairbank Jr; *d* Terence Fisher, Charles Saunders; *prod* Douglas Fairbanks Jr; *sc* Richard Alan Simmons, Larry Marcus, John Cresswell; *cast* Basil Sydney, Elizabeth Sellars, George Benson, Douglas Fairbanks Jr.

*The Quatermass Experiment (aka The Quatermass Xperiment; US: The Creeping Unknown)*
1954 82m (US: 78m) bw; *pc* Hammer, United Artists; *d* Val Guest; *prod* Anthony Hinds; *sc* Richard Landau, Val Guest; *TV serial* Nigel Kneale; *cast* Brian Donlevy, Richard Wordsworth, Jack Warner, Margia Dean.

*Three Cases of Murder*
1954 99m bw; *pc* Wessex, London Films; *d* Wendy Toye, George More O'Ferrall, David Eady; *prod* Ian Dalrymple, Hugh Perceval; *sc* Ian Dalrymple, Donald Wilson, Sidney Carroll; *cast* Alan Badel, Hugh Pryse, Leueen MacGrath, Orson Welles.

*Alias John Preston*
1955 66m bw; *pc* Danziger; *d* David McDonald; *prod* Edward J. Danziger, Harvey Lee Danziger, Sidney Stone; *sc* Paul Tabori; *cast* Christopher Lee, Alexander Knox, Betta St John, Peter Grant.

*X the Unknown*
1956 81m (US 79m) bw; *pc* Hammer; *d* Leslie Norman; *prod* Anthony Hinds; *sc* Jimmy Sangster; *cast* Dean Jagger, Edward Chapman, Leo McKern, Anthony Newley.

*The Abominable Snowman (US: The Abominable Snowman of the Himalayas)*
1957 91m (US 85m) bw; *pc* Hammer; *d* Val Guest; *prod* Audrey Baring; *sc* Nigel Kneale; *cast* Forrest Tucker, Peter Cushing, Maureen Connell, Richard Wattis.

*Cat Girl*
1957 75 67m bw; *pc* Insignia Films; *d* Alfred Shaughnessy; *prod* Herbert Smith; *sc* Lou Rusoff, Peter Hennessey; *cast* Barbara Shelley, Robert Ayres, Kay Callard, Paddy Webster.

*The Curse of Frankenstein*
1957 82m col; *pc* Hammer; *d* Terence Fisher; *prod* Anthony Hinds; *sc* Jimmy Sangster; *cast* Peter Cushing, Christopher Lee, Hazel Court, Robert Urquhart.

*Escapement (US: The Electronic Monster)*
1957 72m bw; *pc* Amalgamated; *d* Montgomery Tully; *prod* Alec Snowden; *sc* Charles Eric Maine; *novel* Charles Eric Maine; *cast* Rod Cameron; Mary Murphy, Meredith Edwards, Peter Illing.

*The Man Without a Body*
1957 80m bw; *pc* Filmplays; *d* Charles Saunders, W. Lee Wilder; *prod* Guido Coen; *sc* William Groter; *cast* George Coulouris, Robert Hutton, Julia Arnall, Nadja Regin.

*Night of the Demon*
1957 95m (US 82m) bw; *pc* Sabre; *d* Jacques Tourneur; *prod* Frank Beviss; *sc* Charles Bennett, Hal E. Chester; *cast* Dana Andrews, Peggy Cummings, Niall MacGinnis, Athene Seyler.

*Quatermass 2 (US: Enemy From Space)*
1957 85m bw; *pc* Hammer; *d* Val Guest; *prod* Anthony Hinds; *sc* Nigel Kneale, Val Guest; *cast* Brian Donleavy, John Longden, Sid James, Bryan Forbes.

*The Blood of the Vampire*
1958 85m col; *pc* Aristes Alliance, Tempean Productions ; *d* Henry Cass; *prod* Robert S. Baker, Monty Berman; *sc* Jimmy Sangster; *cast* Donald Wolfit, Vincent Ball, Barbara Shelley, Victor Maddern.

*Dracula (US: Horror of Dracula)*
1958 82m col; *pc* Hammer; *d* Terence Fisher; *prod* Anthony Hinds; *sc* Jimmy Sangster; *cast* Peter Cushing, Christopher Lee, Michael Gough, Melissa Stribling.

*Fiend Without a Face*
1958 74m bw; *pc* MLC Producers Associates; *d* Arthur Crabtree, Marshall Thompson (uncredited); *prod* John Croydon, Richard Gordon; *sc* Herbert J. Leder; *story* Amelia Reynolds Long; *cast* Marshall Thompson, Terry Kilburn, Michael Balfour, Gil Winfield.

*First Man into Space*
1958 77m bw; *pc* Amalgamated; *d* Robert Day; *prod* John Croydon, Charles Vetter Jr; *sc* John C. Cooper, Lance Z. Hargreaves; *story* Wyatt Ordung; *cast* Marshall Thompson, Marla Landi, Robert Ayres, Billy Nagy.

*Grip of the Strangler (US: The Haunted Strangler)*
1958 81m 78m bw; *pc* Amalgamated, Producers Associates; *d* Robert Day; *prod* John Croydon, Jan Read; *sc* Jan Read, John C. Cooper; *cast* Boris Karloff, Tim Turner, Jean Kent, Vera Day.

*The Revenge of Frankenstein*
1958 89m col; *pc* Hammer; *d* Terence Fisher; *prod* Anthony Hinds; *sc* Jimmy Sangster; *cast* Peter Cushing, Francis Matthews, Eunice Gayson, Michael Gwynn.

*The Spaniard's Curse*
1958 80m bw; *pc* Wentworth Films; *d* Ralph Kemplen; *prod* Roger Proudlock; *sc* Kenneth Hyde; *story* Edith Pargeter; *cast* Tony Wright, Lee Patterson, Michael Hordern, Susan Beaumont.

*The Trollenberg Terror (US: The Crawling Eye)*
1958 84m 82m bw; *pc* Tempean Productions; *d* Quentin Lawrence; *prod* Robert S. Baker, Monty Berman; *sc* Jimmy Sangster; *story* Peter Key; *cast* Forrest Tucker, Laurence Payne, Jennifer Jayne, Janet Munro.

*Womaneater*
1958 71m bw; *pc* Fortress Films; *d* Charles Saunders; *prod* Guido Coen, Richard Gordon; *sc* Brandon Fleming; *cast* George Coulouris, Vera Day, Joy Webster, Peter Wayn.

*Behemoth, the Sea Monster (US: The Giant Behemoth)*
1959 79m bw; *pc* David Diamond, Artistes Alliance; *d* Eugene Lourie; *prod* Ted Lloyd; *sc* Eugene Lourie; *cast* Gene Evans, André Morell, John Turner, Leigh Madison.

*Cover Girl Killer*
1959 61m bw; *pc* Parroch; *d* Terry Bishop; *prod* Jack Parsons; *sc* Terry Bishop; *cast* Harry H. Corbett, Felicity Young, Spencer Teakle, Victor Brooks.

*The Flesh and the Fiends (US: Mania)*
1959 97m bw; *pc* Regal, Triad; *d* John Gilling; *prod* Robert S. Baker, Monty Berman; *sc* John Gilling, Leon Griffiths; *cast* Peter Cushing, June Laverick, Donald Pleasence, George Rose.

*Horrors of the Black Museum*
1959 81m col; *pc* Carmel, Merton Park, Anglo-Amalgamated, Herman Cohen; *d* Arthur Crabtree; *prod* Jack Greenwood; *sc* Aben Kandel, Herman Cohen; *cast* Michael Gough, June Cunningham, Graham Curnow, Shirley Anne Field.

*The Hound of the Baskervilles*
1959 87m 84m col; *pc* Hammer; *d* Terence Fisher; *prod* Anthony Hinds, Michael Carreras, *sc* Peter Bryan; *cast* Peter Cushing, Christopher Lee, Andre Morell, Marla Landi.

*Jack the Ripper*
1959 88m 84m bw; *pc* Midcentury; *d* Robert S. Baker, Monty Berman; *prod* Robert S. Baker, Monty Berman; *sc* Jimmy Sangster; *cast* Lee Patterson, Betty McDowall, Eddie Byrne, Ewen Solon.

*The Man Who Could Cheat Death*
1959 83m col; *pc* Hammer; *d* Terence Fisher; *prod* Michael Carreras, Anthony Nelson Keys; *sc* Jimmy Sangster; *play* Barré Lyndon; *cast* Anton Diffring, Hazel Court, Christopher Lee, Arnold Marle.

*The Mummy*
1959 88m col; *pc* Hammer; *d* Terence Fisher; *prod* Michael Carreras; *sc* Jimmy Sangster; *cast* Peter Cushing, Christopher Lee, Yvonne Furneaux, Eddie Byrne.

*The Stranglers of Bombay*
1959 81m 76m bw; *pc* Hammer; *d* Terence Fisher; *prod* Anthony Hinds; *sc* David S. Goodman; *cast* Guy Rolfe, Allan Cuthbertson, Andrew Cruickshank, George Pastell.

*Bluebeard's Ten Honeymoons*
1960 92m bw; *pc* Allied Artists; *d* W. Lee Wilder; *prod* Roy Parkinson; *sc* Myles Wilder; *cast* George Sanders, Corinne Calvet, Jean Kent, Patricia Roc.

*The Brides of Dracula*
1960 85m col; *pc* Hammer; *d* Terence Fisher; *prod* Anthony Hinds; *sc* Jimmy Sangster, Peter Bryan, Edward Percy; *cast* Peter Cushing, Martita Hunt, Yvonne Monlaur, Freda Jackson.

*Circus of Horrors*
1960 91m col; *pc* Lynx Films, Independent Artists; *d* Sidney Hayers; *prod* Julian Wintle, Leslie Parkyn; *cast* Anton Diffring, Erika Remberg, Yvonne Monlaur, Donald Pleasence.

*City of the Dead (US: Horror Hotel)*
1960 78m bw; *pc* Vulcan; *d* John Moxey; *prod* Donald Taylor; *sc* George Baxt; *cast* Christopher Lee, Patricia Jessel, Betta St John, Dennis Lotis.

*Dr Blood's Coffin*
1960 92m col; *pc* Caralan; *d* Sidney J. Furie; *prod* George Fowler; *sc* Jerry Juran, James Kelly, Peter Miller; *cast* Kieran Moore, Hazel Court, Ian Hunter, Kenneth J. Warren.

*The House in Marsh Road (US: The Invisible Creature)*
1960 70m bw; *pc* Eternal; *d* Montgomery Tully; *prod* Maurice J. Wilson; *sc* Maurice J. Wilson; *cast* Tony Wright, Patricia Dainton, Sandra Dorne, Derek Aylward.

*Never Take Sweets from a Stranger (US: Never Take Candy from a Stranger)*
1960 81m bw; *pc* Hammer; *d* Cyril Frankel; *prod* Anthony Hinds; *sc* John Hunter; *cast* Gwen Watford, Patrick Allen, Felix Aylmer, Niall MacGinnis.

*Peeping Tom*
1960 102m col; *pc* Michael Powell Theatre; *d* Michael Powell; *prod* Michael Powell; *sc* Leo Marks; *cast* Carl Boehm, Anna Massey, Maxine Audley, Moira Shearer.

*The Two Faces of Dr Jekyll (US: House of Fright, Jekyll's Inferno)*
1960 88m (US 80m) col; *pc* Hammer; *d* Terence Fisher; *prod* Michael Carreras; *sc* Wolf Mankowitz; *novel* Robert Louis Stevenson; *cast* Paul Massie, Dawn Addams, Christopher Lee, David Kossoff.

*Village of the Damned*
1960 77m bw; *pc* MGM; *d* Wolf Rilla; *prod* Ronald Kinnock; *sc* Sterling Silliphant, Wolf Rilla, George Barclay; *novel* John Wyndham; *cast* George Sanders, Barbara Shelley, Martin Stephens, Michael Gwynn.

*The Curse of the Werewolf*
1961 88m col; *pc* Hammer; *d* Terence Fisher; *prod* Anthony Hinds; *sc* John Elder; *cast* Clifford Evans, Oliver Reed, Yvonne Romaine, Catherine Feller.

*The Full Treatment (US: Stop Me Before I Kill!)*
1961 109m bw; *pc* Falcon; *d* Val Guest; *prod* Val Guest; *sc* Val Guest, Ronald Scott Thorn; *cast* Claude Dauphin, Diane Cilento, Ronald Lewis, Francois Rosay.

*Gorgo*
1961 78m col; *pc* King Brothers; *d* Eugene Lourie; *sc* John Loring, Daniel Hyatt; *story* Lourie, Hyatt; *cast* Bill Travers, William Sylvester, Vincent Winter, Bruce Setton.

*The Hands of Orlac*
1961 105m bw; *pc* Pendennis Films, Riviera International Film; *d* Edmond T. Greville; *prod* Steven Pallos, Donald Taylor; *sc* John Baines, Edmond T. Greville, Donald Taylor; *novel* Maurice Renard; *cast* Mel Ferrer, Christopher Lee, Dany Carrel, Lucile Saint-Simon.

*The Innocents (US: Suspense)*
1961 99m bw; *pc* 20th Century-Fox, Achilles; *d* Jack Clayton; *prod* Jack Clayton; *sc* William Archibald, Truman Capote; *novel* Henry James; *cast* Deborah Kerr, Peter Wyngarde, Megs Jenkins, Michael Redgrave.

*Konga*
1961 90m col; *pc* Merton Park Studios; *d* John Lemont; *prod* Samuel Z. Arkoff, Nathan Cohen, Stuart Levy; *sc* Herman Cohen, Aben Kandel; *cast* Michael Gough, Margo Johns, Jess Conrad, Claire Gordon.

*The Shadow of the Cat*
1961 79m bw; *pc* BHP Films; *d* John Gilling; *prod* Jon Pennington; *sc* George Baxt; *cast* André Morell, Barbara Shelley, William Lucas, Freda Jackson.

*The Snake Woman*
1961 68m bw; *pc* Caralan; *d* Sidney J. Furie; *prod* George Fowler; *sc* Orville H. Hampton; *cast* Susan Travers, John McCarthy, Geoffrey Denton, Elsie Wagstaff.

*Taste of Fear (US: Scream of Fear)*
1961 81m bw; *pc* Columbia, Hammer; *d* Seth Holt; *prod* Jimmy Sangster; *sc* Jimmy Sangster; *cast* Susan Strasberg, Ronald Lewis, Ann Todd, Christopher Lee.

*The Terror of the Tongs*
1961 79m col; *pc* Hammer, Seven Arts; *d* Anthony Bushell; *prod* Kenneth Hyman; *sc* Jimmy Sangster; *cast* Christopher Lee, Geoffrey Toone, Barbara Brown, Yvonne Monlaur.

*Captain Clegg (US: Night Creatures)*
1962 82m col; *pc* Hammer, Major; *d* Peter Graham Scott; *prod* John Temple-Smith; John Elder; *novel* Russell Thorndike; *cast* Peter Cushing, Yvonne Romaine, Patrick Allen, Oliver Reed.

*Corridors of Blood (or The Doctor from Seven Dials)*
1962 (produced 1958) 86m bw; *pc* Amalgamated, Producers Associates; *d* Robert Day; *prod* John Croydon; *sc* Geoffrey Faithfull; *cast* Boris Karloff, Betta St John, Christopher Lee, Adrienne Corri.

*Night of the Eagle (US: Burn Witch Burn)*
1962 87m bw; *pc* Independent Artists; *d* Sidney Hayers; *prod* Albert Fennell; *sc* Charles Beaumont, Richard Matheson, George Baxt; *story* Fritz Leiber; *cast* Peter Wyngarde, Janet Blair, Margaret Johnston, Anthony Nichols.

*The Phantom of the Opera*
1962 84m col; *pc* Hammer; *d* Terence Fisher; *prod* Anthony Hinds; *sc* John Elder; *story* Gaston Leroux; *cast* Herbert Lom, Heather Sears, Edward De Souza, Thorley Walters.

*The Tell-Tale Heart (US: Hidden Room of 1,000 Horrors)*
1962 78m bw; *pc* Danziger, Brigadier; *d* Ernest Morris; *prod* Edward J. Danziger, Harry Lee Danziger; *sc* Brian Clemens, Eldon Howard; *story* Edgar Allan Poe; *cast* Laurence Payne, Adrienne Corri, Dermot Walsh, Selma Vaz Dias.

*Vengeance (US: The Brain)*
1962 84m bw; *pc* CCC Filmkunst, Stross; *d* Freddie Francis; *prod* Arthur Brauner, Raymond Stross; *sc* Philip Mackie, Robert Stewart; *novel* Curt Siodmak; *cast* Anne Heywood, Peter van Eyck, Cecil Parker, Bernard Lee.

*The Very Edge*
1962 90m bw; *pc* British Lion Film; *d* Cyril Frankel; *prod* Raymond Stross; *sc* Leslie Bricusse, Vivian Cox, E.J. Howard; *cast* Jeremy Brett, Maurice Denham, Verina Greenlaw, Jack Hedley.

*Children of the Damned*
1963 90m bw; *pc* MGM; *d* Anton M. Leader; *prod* Ben Arbeid; *sc* John Briley; *cast* Ian Hendry, Alan Badel, Barbara Ferris, Alfred Burke.

*The Day of the Triffids*
1963 95m col; *pc* Security Pictures; *d* Steve Sekely; *prod* George Pitcher; *sc* Philip Yordan; *novel* John Wyndham; *cast* Howard Keel, Nicole Maurey, Janette Scott, Kieron Moore.

*Devil Doll*
1963 80m bw; *pc* Galaworld, Gordon Films; *d* Lindsay Shonteff; *prod* Lindsay Shonteff; *sc* George Barclay, Lance Z. Hargreaves; *story* Frederick Escreet Smith; *cast* Bryant Haliday, William Silvester, Yvonne Romaine, Sandra Dawn.

*The Eyes of Annie Jones*
1963 71m bw; *pc* Parroch-McCallum, Associated Producers; *d* Reginald LeBorg; *prod* Jack Parsons; *sc* Louis Vittes; *cast* Richard Conte, Francesca Annis, Joyce Carey, Myrtle Reed.

*The Haunting*
1963 112m bw; *pc* Argyll Enterprises; *d* Robert Wise; *prod* Robert Wise; *sc* Nelson Gidding; *novel* Shirley Jackson; *cast* Julie Harris, Claire Bloom, Richard Johnson, Russ Tamblyn.

*The Kiss of the Vampire*
1963 88m col; *pc* Hammer; *d* Don Sharp; *prod* Anthony Hinds; *sc* John Elder (Anthony Hinds); *cast* Clifford Evans, Noel Willman, Edward de Souza, Jennifer Daniel.

*Maniac*
1963 86m bw; *pc* Columbia, Hammer; *d* Michael Carreras; *prod* Jimmy Sangster; *sc* Jimmy Sangster; *cast* Kerwin Mathews, Nadia Gray, Norman Bird, Lilianne Brousse.

*The Black Torment*
1964 85m col; *pc* Compton-Tekli; *d* Robert Hartford-Davis; *prod* Robert Hartford-Davis; *sc* Donald and Derek Ford; *cast* Heather Sears, John Turner, Ann Lynn, Peter Arne.

*The Curse of the Mummy's Tomb*
1964 81m col; *pc* Hammer; *d* Michael Carreras; *prod* Michael Carreras; *sc* Henry Younger; *cast* Terence Morgan, Ronald Howard, Fred Clark, Jeanne Roland.

*The Curse of Simba*
1964 77m bw; *pc* Galaworld, Gordon Films; *d* Linsay Shonteff; *prod* Kenneth Rive; *sc* Tony O'Grady, Leigh Vance; *cast* Bryant Halliday, Dennis Price, Lisa Daniely, Mary Kerridge.

*Dr Terror's House of Horrors*
1964 98m col; *pc* Amicus; *d* Freddie Francis; *prod* Max J. Rosenberg, Milton Subotsky; *sc* Milton Subotsky; *cast* Peter Cushing, Neil McCallum, Alan Freeman, Roy Castle.

*The Earth Dies Screaming*
1964 62m bw; *pc* Lippett Films; *d* Terence Fisher; *prod* Robert Lippett, Jack Parsons; *sc* Henry Cross (Harry Spalding); Willard Parker, Virginia Field, Dennis Price, Thorley Walters.

*The Evil of Frankenstein*
1964 84m col; *pc* Hammer; *d* Freddie Francis; *prod* Anthony Hinds; *sc* John Elder; *cast* Peter Cushing, Peter Woodthorpe, Duncan Lemont, Sandor Eles.

*The Gorgon*
1964 83m col; *pc* Hammer; *d* Terence Fisher; *prod* Anthony Nelson Keys; *sc* John Gilling; *story* J. Llewellyn Devine; *cast* Peter Cushing, Christopher Lee, Richard Pascoe, Barbara Shelley.

*The Masque of the Red Death*
1964 90m col; *pc* Alta Vista, Anglo-Amalgamated; *d* Roger Corman; *prod* Roger Corman; *sc* Charles Beaumont, R. Wright Campbell; *story* Edgar Allan Poe; *cast* Vincent Price, Hazel Court, Jane Asher, David Weston.

*Nightmare*
1963 82m col; *pc* Hammer; *d* Freddie Francis; *prod* Jimmy Sangster; *sc* Jimmy Sangster; *cast* David Knight, Moira Redmond, Jennie Linden, Brenda Bruce.

*Night Must Fall*
1964 99m bw; *pc* MGM; *d* Karel Reisz; *prod* Albert Finney, Karel Reisz; *sc* Clive Exton; *cast* Albert Finney, Mona Washbourne, Susan Hampshire, Sheila Hancock.

*Paranoiac*
1964 80m bw; *pc* Hammer; *d* Freddie Francis; *prod* Anthony Hinds; *sc* Jimmy Sangster; *cast* Janette Scott, Oliver Reed, Sheila Burrell, Maurice Denham.

*Séance on a Wet Afternoon*
1964 115m bw; *pc* Beaver Films, Allied Film Makers; *d* Bryan Forbes; *prod* Richard Attenborough; *sc* Bryan Forbes; *novel* Mark McShane; *cast* Kim Stanley, Richard Attenborough, Mark Eden, Nanette Newman.

*Silent Playground*
1964 75m bw; *d* Stanley Goulder; *prod* George Mills; *sc* Stanley Goulder; *cast* Jean Anderson, Bernard Archard, Basil Beale, Roland Curram.

*Witchcraft*
1964 79m bw; *pc* Lippert Films; *d* Don Sharp; *prod* Robert Lippert, Jack Parsons; *sc* Harry Spalding; *cast* Lon Chaney, Jack Hedley, Jill Dixon, Viola Keats.

*The Collector*
1965 119m col; *pc* Collector, Columbia; *d* William Wyler; *prod* Jud Kinberg, John Kohn; *sc* Stanley Mann, John Kohn; *novel* John Fowles; *cast* Terence Stamp, Samantha Eggar, Mona Washbourne, Maurice Dallimore.

*The Curse of the Fly*
1965 86m bw; *pc* Lippert Films, Shepperton Studios; *d* Don Sharp; *prod* Robert L. Lippert, Jack Parsons; *sc* Harry Spalding; *cast* Carole Gray, George Baker, Brian Donlevy, Jeremy Wilkins.

*Devils of Darkness*
1965 88m col; *pc* Planet Films; *d* Lance Comfort; *prod* Tom Blakeley; *sc* Lyn Fairhurst; *cast* William Sylvester, Hubert Noel, Diana Decker, Carole Gray.

*Fanatic (US: Die! Die! My Darling!)*
1965 97m col; *pc* Hammer; *d* Silvio Narizzano; *prod* Anthony Hinds; *sc* Richard Matheson; *novel* Anne Blaisdell; *cast* Tallulah Bankhead, Stefanie Powers, Peter Vaughan, Maurice Kaufmann.

*Hysteria*
1965 85m bw; *pc* Hammer; *d* Freddie Francis; *prod* Jimmy Sangster; *sc* Jimmy Sangster; *cast* Robert Webber, Anthony Newlands, Jennifer Jayne, Maurice Denham.

*Monster of Terror (US: Die, Monster, Die!)*
1965 78m col; *pc* Alta Vista; *d* Daniel Haller; *prod* Pat Green; *sc* Jerry Sohl; *story* H.P. Lovecraft; *cast* Boris Karloff, Nick Adams, Freda Jackson, Suzan Farmer.

*The Nanny*
1965 93m bw; *pc* Hammer, Seven Arts; *d* Seth Holt; *prod* Jimmy Sangster; *sc* Jimmy Sangster; *novel* Evelyn Piper; *cast* Bette Davis, Wendy Craig, Jill Bennett, James Villiers.

*The Night Caller (US: Blood Beast from Outer Space)*
1965 65m bw; *pc* Armitage; *d* John Gilling; *prod* Ronald Liles; *sc* Jim O'Connolly; *novel The Night Callers* by Frank Crisp; *cast* John Saxon, Maurice Denham, Patricia Haines, Alfred Burke.

*Repulsion*
1965 104m bw; *pc* Compton-Tekli; *d* Roman Polanski; *prod* Gene Gutowski; *sc* Roman Polanski, Gerard Brach; *cast* Catherine Deneuve, Ian Hendry, John Fraser, Yvonne Furneaux.

*The Skull*
1965 83m col; *pc* Amicus; *d* Freddie Francis; *prod* Milton Subotsky, Max J. Rosenberg; *sc* Milton Subotsky; *story* Robert Bloch; *cast* Peter Cushing, Christopher Lee, Patrick Wymark, Jill Bennett.

*A Study in Terror*
1965 95m col; *pc* Compton-Tekli; *d* James Hill; *prod* Henry E. Chester; *sc* Donald Ford, Derek Ford; *cast* John Neville, Donald Houston, John Fraser, Anthony Quayle.

*The Tomb of Ligeia*
1965 81m col; *pc* Alta Vista; *d* Roger Corman; *prod* Pat Green, Roger Corman; *sc* Robert Towne; *story* Edgar Allan Poe; *cast* Vincent Price, Elizabeth Shepherd, John Westbrook, Derek Francis.

*Circus of Fear (US: Psycho-Circus)*
1966 89m col; *pc* Circus Film; *d* Werner Jacobs, John Llewellyn Moxey; *prod* Samual Z. Arkoff, Peter Welbeck; *sc* Harry Alan Toers; *novel* Edgar Wallace; *cast* Christopher Lee, Leo Genn, Anthony Newlands, Heinz Drache.

*The Deadly Bees*
1966 80m col; *pc* Amicus; *d* Freddie Francis; *prod* Max J. Rosenberg, Milton Subotsky; *sc* Robert Bloch, Anthony Marriott; *novel* H.F. Heard; *cast* Suzanna Leigh, Guy Doleman, Frank Finlay, Michael Ripper.

*Dracula Prince of Darkness*
1966 90m col; *pc* Hammer; *d* Terence Fisher; *prod* Anthony Nelson Keys; *sc* John Samson, John Elder; *cast* Christopher Lee, Barbara Shelley, Andrew Keir, Francis Matthews.

*The Frozen Dead*
1966 96m col; *pc* Gold Star; *d* Herbert J. Leder; *prod* Herbert J. Leder; *sc* Herbert J. Leder; *cast* Dana Andrews, Philip Gilbert, Anna Palk, Alan Tilvern.

*The Hand of Night*
1966 88m col; *pc* Associated British, Pathé; *d* Frederic Goode; *prod* Harry Field; *sc* Bruce Stewart; *cast* William Sylvester, Diane Clare, Aliza Gur, Edward Underdown.

*Island of Terror*
1966 89m col; *pc* Planet Film; *d* Terence Fisher; *prod* Tom Blakeley; *sc* Edward Andrew Mann, Alan Ramsen; *cast* Peter Cushing, Edward Judd, Carole Gray, Eddie Byrne.

*It!*
1966 95m col; *pc* Gold Star; *d* Herbert J. Leder; *prod* Herbert J. Leder; *sc* Herbert J. Leder; *cast* Roddy McDowall, Jill Haworth, Paul Maxwell, Noel Trevarthen.

*Let's Kill Uncle*
1966 92m col; *pc* Universal; *d* William Castle; *prod* William Castle; *sc* Mark Rodgers; *novel* Rohan O'Grady; *cast* Nigel Green, Mary Badham, Pat Cardi, Robert Pickering.

*Naked Evil (US: Exorcism at Midnight)*
1966 80m col; *pc* Gibraltar; *d* Stanley Goulder; *prod* Richard Fernback, Steven Pallos; *sc* Stanley Goulder; *play* Jon Manchip White; *cast* Anthony Ainley, Richard Coleman, Basil Dignam, Dan Jackson.

*Plague of the Zombies*
1966 91m col; *pc* Hammer; *d* John Gilling; *prod* Anthony Nelson Keys; *sc* Peter Bryan; *cast* André Morell, Diane Clare, Brook Williams, Jacqueline Pearce.

*The Psychopath*
1966 83m col; *pc* Amicus; *d* Freddie Francis; *prod* Max J. Rosenberg, Milton Subotsky; *sc* Robert Bloch; *cast* Patrick Wymark, Margaret Johnston, John Standing, Alexander Knox.

*Rasputin: The Mad Monk*
1966 91m col; *pc* Hammer, Seven Arts; *d* Don Sharp; *prod* Anthony Nelson Keys; *sc* John Elder; *cast* Christopher Lee, Barbara Shelley, Richard Pasco, Francis Matthews.

*The Reptile*
1966 91m col; *pc* Hammer; *d* John Gilling; *prod* Anthony Nelson Keys; *sc* John Elder; *cast* Noel Williams, Jennifer Daniel, Ray Barrett, Jacqueline Pearce.

*The Vulture*
1966 91m col; *pc* Homeric, Illiad, Film Financial; *d* Lawrence Huntington; *prod* Lawrence Huntington; *sc* Lawrence Huntington; *cast* Robert Hutton, Akim Tamiroff, Broderick Crawford, Diane Clare.

*The Witches (US: The Devil's Own)*
1966 90m col; *pc* Hammer; *d* Cyril Frankel; *prod* Anthony Nelson Keys; *sc* Nigel Kneale; *novel* Peter Curtis; *cast* Joan Fontaine, Kay Walsh, Alec McCowen, Ann Bell.

*The Blood Beast Terror (US" The Vampire Beast Craves Blood)*
1967 88m col; *pc* Tigon British; *d* Vernon Sewell; *prod* Tony Tenser; *sc* Peter Bryan; *cast* Peter Cushing, Robert Flemyng, Wanda Ventham, Vanessa Howard.

*Catacombs (US: The Woman Who Wouldn't Die)*
1967 90m bw; *pc* Parroch, McCallum; *d* Gordon Hessler; *prod* Jack Parsons; *sc* Dan Mainwaring; *novel* Jay Bennett; *cast* Gary Merrill, Jane Merrow, Georgina Cookson, Neil McCallum.

*The Day the Fish Came Out*
1967 109m col; *pc* Michael Cacoyannis; *d* Michael Cacoyannis; *prod* Michael Cacoyannis; *sc* Michael Cacoyannis; *cast* Tom Courtenay, Sam Wanamaker, Colin Blakely, Candice Bergen.

*Eye of the Devil*
1967 92m (US 90m) bw; *pc* Filmway Pictures, MGM; *d* J. Lee Thompson; *prod* John Calley, Martin Ransohoff; *sc* Robin Estridge, Dennis Murphy; *novel* Philip Loraine; *cast* Deborah Kerr, David Niven, Donald Pleasence, Edward Mulhare.

*Frankenstein Created Woman*
1967 86m col; *pc* Hammer; *d* Terence Fisher; *prod* Anthony Nelson Keys; *sc* John Elder; *cast* Peter Cushing, Susan Denberg, Thorley Walters, Robert Morris.

*The Mummy's Shroud*
1967 90m col; *pc* Hammer; *d* John Gilling; *prod* Anthony Nelson Keys; *sc* John Elder, John Gilling; *cast* André Morell, John Phillips, David Buck, Elizabeth Sellars.

*Quatermass and the Pit (US: Five Million Years to Earth)*
1967 97m col; *pc* Hammer; *d* Roy Ward Baker; *prod* Anthony Nelson Keys; *sc* Nigel Kneale; *cast* James Donald, Andrew Keir, Barbara Shelley, Julian Glover.

*The Shuttered Room*
1967 99m col; *pc* Seven Arts, Troy-Schenk, Warner Brothers; *d* David Greene; *prod*

Philip Hazelton; *sc* D.B. Ledrov, Nathaniel Tanchuck; *story* August Derleth, H.P. Lovecraft; *cast* Gig Young, Carol Lynley, Oliver Reed, Flora Robson.

*The Sorcerers*
1967 86m col; *pc* Tigon, Curtwel, Global; *d* Michael Reeves; *prod* Patrick Curtis, Tony Tenser; *sc* Michael Reeves, Tom Baker; *cast* Boris Karloff, Catherine Lacey, Ian Ogilvy, Elizabeth Ercy.

*Theatre of Death (aka Blood Fiend)*
1967 91m col; *pc* Pennea; *d* Samuel Gallu; *prod* M. Smedley-Aston; *sc* Ellis Kadison, Roger Marshall; *cast* Christopher Lee, Julian Glover, Lelia Goldoni, Jenny Till.

*Torture Garden*
1967 93m col; *pc* Amicus; *d* Freddie Francis; *prod* Max J. Rosenberg, Milton Subotsky; *sc* Robert Bloch; *cast* Burges Meredith, Beverly Adams, Barbara Ewing, Jack Palance.

*The Anniversary*
1968 95m col; *pc* 20th Century Fox, Hammer, Seven Arts Production; *d* Roy Ward Baker; *prod* Jimmy Sangster; *sc* Jimmy Sangster; *play* Bill MacIlwraith; *cast* Bette Davis, Sheila Hancock, Jack Hedley, James Cossins.

*Beserk*
1968 96m col; *pc* Columbia; *d* Jim O'Connolly; *prod* Herman Cohen; *sc* Herman Cohen, Aben Kandel; *cast* Joan Crawford, Ty Hardin, Diana Dors, Michael Gough.

*Corruption*
1968 91m col; *pc* Titan; *d* Robert Hartford-Davis; *prod* Peter Newbrook; *sc* Donald and Derek Ford; *cast* Peter Cushing, Sue Lloyd, Noel Trevarthan, Kate O'Mara.

*Curse of the Crimson Altar (US: The Crimson Cult)*
1968 89m col; *pc* Tigon British, American International; *d* Vernon Sewell; *prod* Louis M. Heyward; *sc* Mervyn Haisman, Henry Lincoln, Gerry Levy; *cast* Boris Karloff, Christopher Lee, Mark Eden, Barbara Steele.

*The Devil Rides Out (US: The Devil's Bride)*
1968 92m col; *d* Terence Fisher; *prod* Anthony Nelson Keys; *sc* Richard Matheson; *novel* Dennis Wheatley; *cast* Christopher Lee, Charles Gray, Nike Arrighi, Leon Greene.

*Dracula Has Risen from the Grave*
1968 92m col; *pc* Hammer; *d* Freddie Francis; *prod* Aida Young; *sc* John Elder; *cast* Christopher Lee, Rupert Davies, Veronica Carlson, Barbara Ewing.

*Journey into Darkness*
1968 107m col; *pc* Hammer; *d* James Hill, Peter Sasdy; *prod* Joan Harrison; *sc* John Gould, Oscar Millard; *cast* Robert Reed, Michael Tolan, Jennifer Hilary, Nanette Newman.

*Journey into Midnight*
1968 100m col; *pc* Hammer; *d* Roy Ward Baker, Alan Gibson; *prod* Joan Harrison; *sc* Robert Bloch, Jeremy Paul; *cast* Tom Adams, Chad Everett, Edward Fox, Julie Harris.

*Twisted Nerve*
1968 118m col; *pc* British Lion, Charter Films; *d* Roy Boulting; *prod* George W. George; *sc* Roy Boulting, Leo Marks; *cast* Hayley Mills, Hywel Bennett, Billie Whitelaw, Phyllis Calvert.

*Witchfinder General (US: The Conqueror Worm)*
1968 83m col; *d* Michael Reeves; *prod* Louis M. Heyward, Philip Waddilove; *sc* Tom Baker, Michael Reeves; *novel* Ronald Bassett; *cast* Vincent Price, Ian Ogilvy, Rupert Davies, Hilary Dwyer.

*Frankenstein Must Be Destroyed*
1969 99m col; *pc* Hammer; *d* Terence Fisher; *prod* Anthony Nelson Keys; *sc* Bert Batt; *cast* Peter Cushing, Veronica Carlson, Freddie Jones, Simon Ward.

*The Haunted House of Horror (US: Horror House)*
1969 79m col; *pc* Tigon; *d* Michael Armstrong; *prod* Louis M. Heyward, Tony Tenser; *sc* Michael Armstrong, Peter Marcus; *cast* Frankie Avalon, Jill Haworth, Dennis Price, Mark Wynter.

*Night, After Night, After Night*
1969 87m col; *pc* Dudley Birch Films; *d* Lewis J. Force (Lindsay Shonteff); *prod* James Mellor; *sc* Dail Ambler; *cast* Jack May, Justine Lord, Gilbert Wynne, Linda Marlowe.

*The Oblong Box*
1969 91m col; *pc* American International; *d* Gordon Hessler; *prod* Gordon Hessler; *sc* Lawrence Huntington, Christopher Wicking; *cast* Vincent Price, Christopher Lee, Rupert Davies, Uta Levka.

*Scream and Scream Again*
1969 95m col; *pc* AIP, Amicus; *d* Gordon Hessler; *prod* Max J. Rosenberg, Milton Subotsky; *sc* Christopher Wicking; *novel* Peter Saxon; *cast* Vincent Price, Christopher Lee, Peter Cushing, Judy Huxtable.

*And Soon the Darkness*
1970 100m col; *pc* Associated British; *d* Robert Fuest; *prod* Albert Fennell, Brian Clemens; *sc* Brian Clemens, Terry Nation; *cast* Pamela Franklin, Michele Dotrice, Sandor Eles, John Nettleton.

*The Beast in the Cellar*
1970 101m (89m) col; *pc* Cannon, Leander, Tigon; *d* James Kelley; *prod* Graham Harris; *sc* James Kelley; *cast* Beryl Reid, Flora Robson, John Hamill, Tessa Wyatt.

*Blood on Satan's Claw*
1970 100m col; *pc* Tigon British, Chilton Films; *d* Piers Haggard; *prod* Peter L. Andrews, Malcolm B. Heyworth; *sc* Piers Haggard, Robert Wynne-Simmons; *cast* Patrick Wymark, Linda Hayden, Barry Andrews, Michele Dotrice.

*The Corpse (US: Crucible of Horror)*
1970 (released 1972) 90m col; *pc* London Cannon, Abacus; *d* Viktors Ritelis; *prod* Gabrielle Beaumont; *sc* Olaf Pooley; *cast* Michael Gough, Yvonne Mitchell, Sharon Gurney, Simon Gough.

*Countess Dracula*
1970 93m col; *pc* Hammer; *d* Peter Sasdy; *prod* Alexander Paal; *sc* Alexander Paal, Jeremy Paul, Peter Sasdy; *novel* Valentine Penrose; *cast* Ingrid Pitt, Nigel Green, Sandor Eles, Maurice Denham.

*Crescendo*
1970 95m col; *pc* Hammer; *d* Alan Gibson; *prod* Michael Carreras; *sc* Jimmy Sangster, Alfred Shaughnessy; *cast* Stefanie Powers, James Olson, Margaretta Scott, Jane Lapotaire.

*Cry of the Banshee*
1970 87m col; *pc* AIP; *d* Gordon Hessler; *prod* Louis M. Heyward; *sc* Tim Kelly, Christopher Wicking; *cast* Vincent Price, Essy Persson, Hugh Griffith, Patrick Mower.

*Dorian Gray*
1970 93m col; *pc* Towers of London, Regal Film, Terra Film; *d* Massimo Dallamano; *prod* Harry Alan Towers; *sc* Massimo Dallamano; *cast* Helmut Berger, Richard Todd, Herbert Lom, Marie Liljedahl.

*Fragment of Fear*
1970 95m col; *pc* Columbia; *d* Richard C. Serafian; *prod* John R. Sloan; *sc* Paul Dehn; *cast* David Hemmings, Gayle Hunnicutt, Flora Robson, Wilfrid Hyde White.

*The Horror of Frankenstein*
1970 95m col; *pc* Hammer; *d* Jimmy Sangster; *prod* Jimmy Sangster; *sc* Jeremy Burnham, Jimmy Sangster; *cast* Ralph Bates, Kate O'Mara, Veronica Carlson, Dennis Price.

*The House that Dripped Blood*
1970 102m col; *pc* Amicus; *d* Peter Duffell; *prod* Max J. Rosenberg, Milton Subotsky; *sc* Robert Bloch; *cast* John Bennett, Denholm Elliott, Peter Cushing, Christopher Lee.

*Incense for the Damned (US: Bloodsuckers)*
1970 87m col; *pc* Lucinda Films, Titan; *d* Robert Hartford-Davis; *prod* Graham Harris; *sc* Julian More; *novel* Simon Raven; *cast* Patrick MacNee, Johnny Sekka, Alexander Davison, Peter Cushing.

*The Man Who Haunted Himself*
1970 94m col; *pc* Excalibur, ABP; *d* Basil Dearden; *prod* Michael Relph; *sc* Basil Dearden, Michael Relph; *story* Anthony Armstrong; *cast* Roger Moore, Hildegard Neil, Olga Georges-Picot, Anton Rogers.

*The Mind of Mr Soames*
1970 95m col; *pc* Amicus; *d* Alan Cooke; *prod* Max J. Rosenberg, Milton Subotsky; *sc* John Hale, Edward Simpson; *cast* Terence Stamp, Robert Vaughn, Nigel Davenport, Christian Roberts.

*Mumsy, Nanny, Sonny and Girly (US: Girly)*
1970 101m col; *pc* Fitzroy-Francis Films; *d* Freddie Francis; *prod* Ronald J. Kahn; *sc* Brian Comport; *play* Maisie Mosco; *cast* Michael Bryant, Ursula Howells, Pat Heywood, Howard Trevor.

*The Scars of Dracula*
1970 96m col; *pc* Hammer; *d* Roy Ward Baker; *prod* Aida Young; *sc* John Elder; *cast* Christopher Lee, Dennis Waterman, Jenny Hanley, Christopher Matthews.

*Taste the Blood of Dracula*
1970 95m col; *pc* Hammer; *d* Peter Sasdy; *prod* Aida Young; *sc* John Elder; *cast* Christopher Lee, Geoffrey Keen, Gwen Watford, Linda Hayden.

*Ten Rillington Place*
1970 111m col; *pc* Genesis; *d* Richard Fleischer; *prod* Martin Ransohoff, Leslie Linder; *sc* Clive Exton; *cast* Richard Attenborough, Judy Geeson, John Hurt, Pat Heyward.

*Trog*
1970 93m col; *pc* Herman Cohen Productions; *d* Freddie Francis; *prod* Herman Cohen; *sc* Peter Bryan, John Gilling, Aben Kandel; *cast* Joan Crawford, Michael Gough, Bernard Kay, Kim Braden.

*The Vampire Lovers*
1970 91m col; Hammer, AIP; *d* Roy Ward Baker; *prod* Harry Fine, Michael Style; *sc* Tudor Gates; *story* Sheridan Le Fanu; *cast* Ingrid Pitt, Pippa Steel, Madeline Smith, Peter Cushing.

*The Abominable Dr Phibes*
1971 93m col; *pc* AIP; *d* Robert Fuest; *prod* Louis M. Heyward, Ronald S. Dunas; *sc* James Whiton, William Goldstein; *cast* Vincent Price, Joseph Cotten, Virginia North, Hugh Griffith.

*Assault (US: Tower of Terror)*
1971 88m col; *pc* Peter Rogers Productions; *d* Sidney Hayers; *prod* George H. Brown; *sc* John Kruse; *novel* Kendal Young; *cast* Suzy Kendall, Frank Finlay, James Laurenson, Lesley Anne Down.

*Blind Terror (US: See No Evil)*
1971 89m col; *pc* Genesis; *d* Richard Fleischer; *prod* Leslie Linder, Martin Ransohoff; *sc* Brian Clemens; *cast* Mia Farrow, Dorothy Alison, Robin Bailey, Diane Grayson.

*Blood From the Mummy's Tomb*
1971 94m col; *pc* Hammer; *d* Seth Holt, Michael Carreras (uncredited); *prod* Howard Brandy; *sc* Christopher Wicking; *novel* Bram Stoker; *cast* Andrew Keir, Valerie Leon, James Villiers, Hugh Burden.

*Burke and Hare*
1971 98m col; *pc* Armitage, Kenneth Shipman; *d* Vernon Sewell; *prod* Guido Coen; *sc* Ernie Bradford; *cast* Harry Andrews, Glynn Edwards, Derren Nesbitt, Dee Shenderey.

*A Clockwork Orange*
1971 137m col; *pc* Stanley Kubrick, Polaris; *d* Stanley Kubrick; *prod* Stanley Kubrick; *sc* Stanley Kubrick; *novel* Anthony Burgess; *cast* Malcolm McDowell, Patrick Magee, Michael Bates, Adrienne Corri.

*Crucible of Terror*
1971 91m col; *pc* Glendale; *d* Ted Hooker; *prod* Tom Parkinson; *sc* Ted Hooker, Tom Parkinson; *cast* Mike Raven, John Arnatt, James Bolam, Mary Maude.

*Demons of the Mind*
1971 89m col; *pc* Hammer; *d* Peter Sykes; *prod* Frank Godwin; *sc* Christopher Wicking; *cast* Robert Hardy, Shane Briant, Gillian Hills, Yvonne Mitchell.

*The Devils*
1971 111m col; *pc* Russo, Warner Brothers; *d* Ken Russell; *prod* Ken Russell, Robert H. Solo; *sc* Ken Russell; *play* John Whiting; *novel* Aldous Huxley; *cast* Oliver Reed, Vanessa Redgrave, Dudley Sutton, Max Adrian.

*The Devil's Widow (Tam Lin)*
1971 (UK release 1977) 106m col; *pc* Commonwealth United Entertainment, Wincast; *d* Roddy McDowall; *prod* Elliott Kastner, Alan Ladd Jnr, Stanley Mann; *sc* William Spier; *cast* Ava Gardner, Ian McShane, Stephanie Beacham, Cyril Cusack.

*Dr Jekyll and Sister Hyde*
1971 97m col; *pc* Hammer, EMI; *d* Roy Ward Baker; *prod* Albert Fennell, Brian Clemens; *sc* Brian Clemens; *cast* Ralph Bates, Martine Beswick, Gerald Sim, Lewis Fiander.

*The Fiend (US: Beware the Brethren)*
1971 92m col; *pc* World Arts Media; *d* Robert Hartford-Davis; *prod* Robert Hartford-Davis; *sc* Brian Comport; *cast* Ann Todd, Patrick Magee, Tony Beckley, Madeleine Hinde.

*Fright*
1971 87m col; *pc* Fantale; *d* Peter Collinson; *prod* Harry Fine, Michael Style; *sc* Tudor Gates; *cast* Honor Blackman, Susan George, Ian Bannen, John Gregson.

*Hands of the Ripper*
1971 85m col; *pc* Hammer; *d* Peter Sasdy; *prod* Aida Young; *sc* L.W. Davidson; *story* Edward Spencer Shew; *cast* Eric Porter, Angharad Rees, Jane Merrow, Derek Godfrey.

*I, Monster*
1971 75m col; *pc* Amicus, British Lion; *d* Stephen Weeks; *prod* Max J. Rosenberg, Milton Subotsky; *sc* Milton Subotsky; *story* Robert Louis Stevenson; *cast* Christopher Lee, Peter Cushing, Mike Raven, Richard Hurndall.

*Lust for a Vampire*
1971 95m col; *pc* Hammer; *d* Jimmy Sangster; *prod* Harry Fine, Michael Style; *sc* Tudor Gates; *story* Sheridan Le Fanu; *cast* Ralph Bates, Barbara Jefford, Suzanna Leigh, Michael Johnson.

*The Nightfcomers*
1971 96m col; *pc* Kastner-Kanter-Ladd, Scimitar; *d* Michael Winner; *prod* Elliott Kastner, Michael Winner; *sc* Michael Hastings; *story* Henry James; *cast* Harry Andrews, Stephanie Beacham, Marlon Brando, Christopher Ellis.

*The Night Digger*
1971 100m col; *pc* Leander, Tacitus, Youngstreet; *d* Alastair Reed; *prod* Alan D. Courtney, Norman S. Powell; *sc* Roald Dahl; *novel* Joy Cowley; *cast* Patricia Neal, Pamela Brown, Nicholas Clay, Jean Anderson.

*Revenge*
1971 89m col; *pc* Peter Rogers; *d* Sidney Hayers; *prod* George H. Brown; *sc* John Kruse; *cast* Joan Collins, James Booth, Ray Barrett, Sinead Cusack.

*Twins of Evil*
1971 87m col; *pc* Hammer; *d* John Hough; *prod* Harry Fine; *sc* Tudor Gates; *cast* Peter Cushing, Dennis Price, Mary Collinson, Madelaine Collinson.

*Vampire Circus*
1971 87m col; *pc* Hammer; *d* Robert Young; *prod* Wilbur Stark; *sc* Judson Kinberg; *story* George Baxt; *cast* Adrienne Corri, Thorley Walters, Anthony Corlan, John Moulder-Brown.

*Venom (US: The Legend of Spider Forest)*
1971 91, 79m col; *pc* Action Plus, Cupid; *d* Peter Sykes; *prod* Michael Pearson, Kenneth F. Rowles; *sc* Derek Ford, Donald Ford; *cast* Simon Brent, Sheila Allen, Neda Arneric, Ray Barron.

*Virgin Witch*
1971 88m col; *pc* Tigon, Univista; *d* Ray Austin; *prod* Ralph Solomons; *sc* Klaus Vogel; *cast* Ann Michelle, Vicki Michelle, Keith Buckley, Patricia Haines.

*What Became of Jack and Jill?*
1971 93m col; *pc* Amicus; *d* Bill Bain; *prod* Max J. Rosenberg, Milton Subotsky; *sc* Roger Marshall; *novel* Laurence Moody; *cast* Vanessa Howard, Paul Nicholas, Mona Washbourne.

*Whoever Slew Auntie Roo? (US: Who Slew Auntie Roo?)*
1971 91m col; *pc* AIP, Hemdale Film; *d* Curtis Harrington; *prod* Samuel Z. Arkoff, James H. Nicholson, Jimmy Sangster; *sc* Robert Blees, Gavin Lambert, Jimmy Sangster; *story* David D. Osborn; *cast* Shelley Winters, Mark Lester, Chloe Franks, Ralph Richardson.

*The Asphyx*
1972 99m col; *pc* Glendale; *d* Peter Newbrook; *prod* John Brittany; *sc* Brian Comport; *cast* Robert Stephens, Robert Powell, Jane Lapotaire, Alex Scott.

*Asylum*
1972 88m col; *pc* Amicus, Harbour; *d* Roy Ward Baker; *prod* Max J. Rosenberg, Milton Subotsky; *sc* Robert Bloch; *cast* Peter Cushing, Britt Ekland, Herbert Lom, Patrick Magee.

*The Creeping Flesh*
1972 91m col; *pc* Tigon, World Film Services; *d* Freddie Francis; *prod* Michael Redbourn; *sc* Peter Spenceley, Jonathan Rumbold; *cast* Christopher Lee, Peter Cushing, Lorna Heilbron, George Benson.

*Death Line (US: Raw Meat)*
1972 87m col; *pc* K-L Productions; *d* Gary Sherman; *prod* Paul Maslansky; *sc* Ceri Jones; *story* Gary Sherman; *cast* Donald Pleasence, Norman Rossington, David Ladd, Sharon Gurney.

*Disciple of Death*
1972 84m col; *pc* Chromage; *d* Tom Parkinson; *prod* Tom Parkinson, Churton Fairman; *sc* Tom Parkinson, Churton Fairman; *cast* Mike Raven, Magarite Hardiman, Ronald Lacey, Virginia Wetherell.

*Dr Phibes Rises Again*
1972 88m col; *pc* AIP; *d* Robert Fuest; *prod* Samuel Z. Arkoff, Louis M. Heyward; *sc* Robert Blees, Robert Fuest; *cast* Vincent Price, Robert Quarry, Valli Kemp, Hugh Griffith.

*Doomwatch*
1972 92m col; *pc* Tigon; *d* Peter Sasdy; *prod* Tony Tenser; *sc* Clive Exton; television

serial Kit Pedler, Gerry Davis; *cast* Ian Bannen, Judy Geeson, George Sanders, John Paul.

*Dracula AD 1972*
1972 95m col; *pc* Hammer; *d* Alan Gibson; *prod* Josephine Douglas; *sc* Don Houghton; *cast* Christopher Lee, Peter Cushing, Stephanie Beacham, Christopher Neame.

*Endless Night*
1972 95m col; *pc* Frank Launder and Sidney Gilliat Production; *d* Sidney Gilliat; *prod* Leslie Gilliat; *sc* Sidney Gilliat; *cast* Hywel Bennett, Hayley Mills, Britt Ekland, George Sanders.

*Fear in the Night*
1972 85m col; *pc* Hammer; *d* Jimmy Sangster; *prod* Jimmy Sangster; *sc* Jimmy Sangster, Michael Syson; *cast* Judy Geeson, Joan Collins, Ralph Bates, Peter Cushing.

*The Flesh and Blood Show*
1972 93m col; *pc* Peter Walker (Heritage); *d* Pete Walker; *prod* Pete Walker; *sc* Alfred Shaughnessy; *cast* Ray Brooks, Robin Askwith, Patrick Barr, Jenny Hanley.

*Frenzy*
1972 111m col; *pc* Universal; *d* Alfred Hitchcock; *prod* Alfred Hitchcock; *sc* Anthony Shaffer; *cast* Jon Finch, Barry Foster, Barbara Leigh-Hunt, Anna Massey.

*Horror Express*
1972 90m col; *pc* Benmar, Granada; *d* Eugenio Martin; *prod* Bernard Gordon; *sc* Arnaud d'Usseau, Julian Zimet; *cast* Christopher Lee, Peter Cushing, Alberto de Mendoza, Telly Savalas.

*Neither the Sea Nor the Sand*
1972 94m col; *pc* Tigon; *d* Fred Burnley; *prod* Jack Smith, Peter Fetterman; *sc* Gordon Honeycombe; *novel* Gorden Honeycombe; *cast* Susan Hampshire, Frank Finlay, Michael Petrovitch, Jack Lambert.

*Night Hair Child (US: What the Peeper Saw)*
972 89m col; *pc* Leander; *d* James Kelly; *prod* Graham Harris; *sc* Trevor Preston; *cast* Mark Lester, Britt Ekland, Hardy Kruger, Lilli Palmer.

*Nothing But the Night*
1972 90m col; *pc* Charlemagne, Rank; *d* Peter Sasdy; *prod* Anthony Nelson Keys; *sc* Brian Hayles; *novel* John Blackburn; *cast* Christopher Lee, Peter Cushing, Diana Dors, Georgia Brown.

*Psychomania (US: The Death Wheelers)*
1972 95m col; *pc* Benmar; *d* Don Sharp; *prod* Andrew Donally; *sc* Julian Halevy, Arnaud d'Usseau; *cast* Nicky Henson, Mary Larkin, Ann Michelle, Roy Holder.

*Straight on Till Morning*
1972 96m col; *pc* Hammer; *d* Peter Collinson; *prod* Michael Carreras; *sc* Michael Peacock; *cast* Rita Tushingham, Shane Briant, Tom Bell, Annie Ross.

*Tales from the Crypt*
1972 92m col; *pc* Amicus, Metromedia Producers; *d* Freddie Francis; *prod* Max J. Rosenberg, Milton Subotsky; *sc* Milton Subotsky; *stories* Al Feldstein, Johnny Craig, William Gaines; *cast* Ralph Richardson, Joan Collins, Ian Hendry, Peter Cushing.

*Tower of Evil (US: Horror of Snape Island)*
1972 89m col; *pc* Grenadier Films, Fanfare; *d* Jim O'Connolly; *prod* Richard Gordon; *sc* Jim O'Connolly; *story* George Baxt; *cast* Bryan Haliday, Jill Haworth, Mark Edwards, Jack Watson.

*And Now the Screaming Starts!*
1973 91m col; *pc* Amicus, Harbor; *d* Roy Ward Baker; *prod* Max J. Rosenberg, Milton Subotsky; *sc* Roger Marshall; *novel* David Case; *cast* Peter Cushing, Herbert Lom, Patrick Magee, Stephanie Beacham.

*Blue Blood*
1973 86m col; *pc* Mallard; *d* Andrew Sinclair; *prod* John Trent, Kent Walwin; *sc* Andrew Sinclair; *novel* Alexander Thynne; *cast* Oliver Reed, Fiona Lewis, Anna Gael, Derek Jacobi.

*Dark Places*
1973 91m col; *pc* Sedgley, Glenbeigh; *d* Don Sharp; *prod* James Hannah Jr; *sc* Ed Brennan, Joseph van Winkle; *cast* Christopher Lee, Robert Hardy, Joan Collins, Herbert Lom.

*Don't Look Now*
1973 110m col; *pc* British Lion; *d* Nicholas Roeg; *prod* Peter Katz, Frederick Muller, Steve Previn; *sc* Chris Bryant, Allan Scott; *story* Daphne du Maurier; *cast* Julie Christie, Donald Sutherland, Hilary Mason, Clelia Matania.

*Frankenstein and the Monster From Hell*
1973 93m col; *pc* Hammer; *d* Terence Fisher; *prod* Roy Skeggs; *sc* John Elder; *cast* Peter Cushing, Shane Briant, Madeline Smith, Dave Prowse.

*From Beyond the Grave*
1973 98m col; *pc* Amicus; *d* Kevin Connor; *prod* Max J. Rosenberg, Milton Subotsky; *sc* Robin Clarke, Raymond Christodoulou; *stories* R. Chetwynd-Hayes; *cast* Peter Cushing, David Warner, Ian Bannen, Ian Ogilvy.

*Horror Hospital*
1973 91m col; *pc* Noteworthy Films; *d* Anthony Balch; *prod* Richard Gordon; *sc* Anthony Balch, Alan Watson; *cast* Michael Gough, Robin Askwith, Vanessa Shaw, Ellen Pollock.

*The Legend of Hell House*
1973 94m col; *pc* Academy Pictures; *d* John Hough; *prod* Albert Fennell, Norman T. Herman; *sc* Richard Matheson; *novel* Richard Matheson; *cast* Pamela Franklin, Roddy McDowell, Clive Revill, Gayle Hunnicutt.

*The Mutations*
1973 92m col; *pc* Cyclone, Getty Pictures; *d* Jack Cardiff; *prod* Robert D. Weinbach; *sc* Edward Mann, Robert D. Weinbach; *cast* Donald Pleasence, Tom Baker, Brad Harris, Julie Ege.

*Scream and Die*
1973 99m col; *pc* Blackwater Film; *d* Joseph Larraz; *prod* Diana Daubeney; *sc* Derek Ford; *cast* Andrea Allan, Karl Lanchbury, Maggie Walker, Peter Forbes-Robertson.

*Tales that Witness Madness*
1973 90m col; *pc* World Film Services; *d* Freddie Francis; *prod* Norman Priggen; *sc* Jay Fairbank; *cast* Donald Pleasence, Jack Hawkins, Russell Lewis, Georgia Brown.

*Theatre of Blood*
1973 103m col; *pc* Cineman, Harbor; *d* Douglas Hickox; *prod* John Kohn, Stanley Mann; *sc* Anthony Greville-Bell; *cast* Vincent Price, Diana Rigg, Ian Hendry, Harry Andrews.

*Vault of Horror*
1973 86m col; *pc* Amicus, Metromedia Producers; *d* Roy Ward Baker; *prod* Max J. Rosenberg, Milton Subotsky; *sc* Milton Subotsky; *stories* Al Feldstein, William Gains; *cast* Daniel Massey, Anna Massey, Michael Pratt, Terry Thomas.

*Voices*
1973 91m col; *pc* Morden; *d* Kevin Billington; *prod* Robert Enders; *sc* Robert Enders, George Kirgo; *cast* Gayle Hunnicutt, David Hemmings, Lynn Farleigh, Russell Lewis.

*The Wicker Man*
1973 102m (87m) col; *pc* British Lion; *d* Robin Hardy; *prod* Peter Snell; *sc* Anthony Shaffer; *cast* Edward Woodward, Christopher Lee, Diane Cilento, Britt Ekland.

*The Beast Must Die*
1974 93m col; *pc* Amicus; *d* Paul Annett; *prod* Max J. Rosenberg, Milton Subotsky; *sc* Michael Winder; *cast* Calvin Lockhart, Peter Cushing, Charles Gray, Anton Diffring.

*Captain Kronos: Vampire Hunter*
1974 91m col; *pc* Hammer; *d* Brian Clemens; *prod* Brian Clemens, Albert Fennell; *sc* Brian Clemens; *cast* Horst Janson, John Carson, Caroline Munro, Shane Briant.

*Craze*
1974 96m col; *pc* Harbor, Herman Cohen; *d* Freddie Francis; *prod* Herman Cohen; *sc* Herman Cohen, Aben Kandel; *novel* Henry Seymour; *cast* Jack Palance, Diana Dors, Julie Ege, Edith Evans.

*Frightmare*
1974 86m col; *pc* Peter Walker (Heritage); *d* Pete Walker; *prod* Pete Walker; *sc* David McGillivray; *cast* Rupert Davies, Sheila Keith, Deborah Fairfax, Paul Greenwood.

*Ghost Story*
1974 89m col; *pc* Stephen Weeks Company; *d* Stephen Weeks; *prod* Stephen Weeks; *sc* Rosemary Sutcliffe, Stephen Weeks; *cast* Larry Dann, Murray Melvin, Vivian Mackerall, Marianne Faithfull.

*The Ghoul*
1975 88m col; *pc* Tyburn; *d* Freddie Francis; *prod* Kevin Francis; *sc* John Elder; *cast* Peter Cushing, John Hurt, Gwen Watford, Alexandra Bastedo.

*House of Whipcord*
1974 102m col; *pc* Peter Walker (Heritage); *d* Pete Walker; *prod* Pete Walker; *sc* David McGillivray; *cast* Barbara Markham, Patrick Barr, Ray Brooks, Ann Michelle.

*The Legend of the Seven Golden Vampires*
1974 89m 110m col; *pc* Hammer, Shaw Brothers; *d* Roy Ward Baker; *prod* Don Houghton, Vee King Shaw; *sc* Don Houghton; *cast* Peter Cushing, David Chiang, Julie Ege, Shih Szu.

*Legend of the Werewolf*
1974 90m col; *pc* Tyburn; *d* Freddie Francis; *prod* Kevin Francis; *sc* John Elder; *cast* Peter Cushing, Ron Moody, Hugh Griffith, Lynn Dalby.

*Madhouse*
1974 92m col; *pc* Amicus, AIP; *d* Jim Clark; *prod* Max J. Rosenberg, Milton Subotsky; *sc* Greg Morrison, Ken Levison; *novel* Angus Hall; *cast* Vincent Price, Peter Cushing, Robert Quarry, Adrienne Corri.

*Persecution (US: The Terror of Shoba)*
1974 96m col; *pc* Tyburn; *d* Don Chaffey; *prod* Kevin Francis; *sc* Robert B. Hutton, Frederick Warner, Rosemary Wooten; *cast* Lana Turner, Ralph Bates, Olga Georges-Picot, Trevor Howard.

*The Satanic Rites of Dracula (US: Count Dracula and His Satanic Bride)*
1974 87m col; *pc* Hammer; *d* Alan Gibson; *prod* Roy Skeggs; *sc* Don Houghton; *cast* Christopher Lee, Peter Cushing, Michael Coles, William Franklyn.

*Symptoms*
1974 91m (US 81) col; *pc* Finition; *d* Joseph Larraz; *prod* Jean Dupuis; *sc* Joseph Larraz, Stanley Miller; *cast* Angela Pleasence, Lorna Heilbron, Peter Vaughan, Ronald O'Neil.

*Vampyres*
1974 87m col; *pc* Essay Films; *d* Joseph Larraz; *prod* Brian Smedley-Aston; *sc* Diana Daubeney; *cast* Marianne Morris, Anulka, Murray Brown, Brian Deacon.

*Whispers of Fear*
1974 73m col; *pc* Sideline; *d* Harry Bromley Davenport; *prod* Ian Merrick; *sc* Harry Bromley Davenport; *cast* Ika Hindley, Charles Seeley, William Jones, Johnny Johnson.

*Exposé (US: The House on Straw Hill; aka Trauma)*
1975 82m col; *pc* Norfolk International; *d* James Kenelm Clarke; *prod* Brian Smedley-Aston; *sc* James Kenelm Clarke; *cast* Udo Kier, Linda Hayden, Fiona Richmond, Patsy Smart.

*House of Mortal Sin (US: The Confessional)*
1975 104m col; *pc* Peter Walker (Heritage) Ltd; *d* Pete Walker; *prod* Pete Walker; *sc* David McGillivray; *cast* Anthony Sharp, Susan Penhaligon, Stephanie Beacham, Norman Eshley.

*I Don't Want to be Born (US: The Devil Within Her)*
1975 94m col; *pc* Unicapital; *d* Peter Sasdy; *prod* Norma Corley; *sc* Stanley Price; *cast* Joan Collins, Eileen Atkins, Donald Pleasence, Ralph Bates.

*The Lifetaker*
1975 103m col; *pc* Onyx; *d* Michael Papas; *prod* Michael Papas; *sc* Michael Papas; *cast* Terence Morgan, Peter Ducan, Lea Dregorn, Dimitris Andreas.

*The Spiral Staircase*
1975 89m col; *pc* Raven; *d* Peter Collinson; *prod* Peter Shaw; *sc* Chris Bryant, Mel Dinelli, Allan Scott; *cast* Jacqueline Bisset, Christopher Plummer, Sam Wanamaker, Sheila Brennan.

*The Devil's Men*
1976 94m col; *pc* Getty Pictures, Poseidon; *d* Costas Carayiannis; *prod* Frixos Constantine; *sc* Arthur Rowe; *cast* Donald Pleasence, Peter Cushing, Luan Peters, Nikos Verlakis.

*Full Circle (US: The Haunting of Julia)*
1976 97m col; *pc* Fetter, Classic Film Industries; *d* Richard Loncraine; *prod* Peter Fetterman, Alfred Pariser; *sc* Dave Humphries; *novel* Peter Straub; *cast* Keir Dullea, Mia Farrow, Tom Conti, Jill Bennett.

*Satan's Slave*
1976 86m (89m) col; *pc* Monumental Pictures; *d* Norman J. Warren; *prod* Richard Crafter, Les Young; *sc* David McGillivray; *cast* Candace Glendenning, Michael Gough, Martin Potter, Barbara Kellerman.

*Schizo*
1976 109m col; *pc* Peter Walker (Heritage) Ltd; *d* Pete Walker; *prod* Pete Walker; *sc* David McGillivray; *cast* Lynne Frederick, John Leyton, Stephanie Beacham, John Fraser.

*To the Devil a Daughter*
1976 92m col; *pc* Hammer, Terra Filmkunst; *d* Peter Sykes; *prod* Roy Skeggs; *sc* Christopher Wicking; *novel* Dennis Wheatley; *cast* Richard Widmark, Christopher Lee, Natassja Kinski, Honor Blackman.

*The Black Panther*
1977 98m col; *pc* Impics; *d* Ian Merrick; *prod* Ian Merrick; *sc* Michael Armstrong; *cast* Donald Sumpter, Debbie Farrington, Marjorie Yates, Sylvia O'Donnell.

*The Cat and the Canary*
1977 98m col; *pc* Grenadier; *d* Radley Metzger; *prod* Richard Gordon; *sc* Radley Metzger; *play* John Willard; *cast* Honor Blackman, Carol Lynley, Michael Callan, Edward Fox.

*Holocaust 2000*
1977 102m col; *pc* Embassy Pictures; *d* Alberto de Martino; *prod* Edmondo Amanti; *sc* Alberto de Martino, Aldo de Martino, Sergio Donati, Michael Robson; *story* Sergio Donati; *cast* Kirk Douglas, Simon Ward, Agostina Belli, Anthony Quayle.

*Prey*
1977 85m col; *pc* Tymar Film; *d* Norman J. Warren; *prod* Terence Marcel, David Wimbury; *sc* Max Cuff; *story* Quinn Donohue; *cast* Glory Annen, Sally Faulkner, Barry Stokes, Sandy Chimney.

*The Uncanny*
1977 85m col; *pc* Cinevideo, Tor; *d* Denis Heroux; *prod* Claude Heroux, Rene Dupont; *sc* Michael Parry; *cast* Peter Cushing, Ray Milland, Susan Penhaligon, Simon Williams.

*The Comeback*
1978 100m col; *pc* Peter Walker (Heritage) Ltd; *d* Pete Walker; *prod* Pete Walker; *sc* Michael Sloan, Murray Smith; *cast* Jack Jones, Pamela Stephenson, David Doyle, Sheila Keith.

*Dominique*
1978 100m col; *pc* Grand Prize, Sword and Sorcery; *d* Michael Anderson;

*prod* Andrew Donally, Milton Subotsky; *sc* Edward Abraham, Valerie Abraham; *story* Harold Lawlor; *cast* Jean Simmons, Cliff Robertson, Jenny Agutter, Simon Ward.

### Killer's Moon
1978 90m col; *pc* Rothernorth; *d* Alan Birkinshaw; *prod* Alan Birkinshaw, Gordon Keymer; *sc* Alan Birkinshaw; *cast* Anthony Forrest, Tom Marshall, Georgina Kean, Nigel Gregory.

### The Legacy
1978 102m col; *pc* Pethurst, Turman-Foster; *d* Richard Marquand; *prod* David Foster; *sc* Jimmy Sangster, Patrick Tilley, Paul Wheeler; *cast* Katherine Ross, Sam Elliott, John Standing, Ian Hogg.

### The Medusa Touch
1978 109m col; *pc* Bulldog, Citeca, Coatesgold; *d* Jack Gold; *prod* Anne V. Coates, Jack Gold; *sc* John Briley; *novel* Peter van Greenaway; *cast* Richard Burton, Lee Remick, Lino Ventura, Alan Badel.

### The Playbirds
1978 94m col; *pc* Roldvale; *d* Willy Roe; *prod* Willy Roe; *sc* Robin O'Conner, Bud Tobin; *cast* Mary Millington, Glynn Edwards, Gavin Campbell, Alan Lake.

### The Shout
1978 86m col; *pc* NFFC, Rank, Recorded Pictures; *d* Jerzy Skolimowksi; *prod* Jeremy Thomas; *sc* Michael Austin, Jerzy Skolimowksi; *story* Robert Graves; *cast* Alan Bates, Susannah York, John Hurt, Robert Stephens.

### Terror
1978 84m col; *pc* Crystal Films; *d* Norman J. Warren; *prod* Richard Crafter, Les Young; *sc* David McGillivray; *story* Les Young, Moira Young; *cast* Carolyn Courage, John Nolan, James Aubrey, Sarah Keller.

### Alien
1979 117m col; *pc* Brandywine-Ronald Shusett; *d* Ridley Scott; *prod* Gordon Carroll, David Giler, Walter Hill; *sc* Dan O'Bannon; *story* Dan O'Bannon, Ronald Shusett; *cast* Tom Skerritt, Sigourney Weaver, Veronica Cartwright, Harry Dean Stanton.

### Dracula
1979 112m col; *pc* Mirisch, Universal; *d* John Badham; *prod* Walter Mirisch; *sc* W.D. Richter; *novel* Bram Stoker; *cast* Frank Langella; Laurence Olivier, Donald Pleasence, Kate Nelligan.

*The Godsend*
1979 93m col; *pc* Cannon; *d* Gabrielle Beaumont; *prod* Gabrielle Beaumont; *sc* Olaf Pooley; *novel* Bernard Taylor; *cast* Cyd Hayman, Malcolm Stoddard, Patrick Barr, Joanne Boorman.

*Murder by Decree*
1979 120m col; *pc* Saucy Jack, Decree; *d* Bob Clark; *prod* Bob Clark, Rene Dupont; *sc* John Hopkins; *cast* Christopher Plummer, James Mason, David Hemmings, Suzan Clark.

*The Awakening*
1980 105m col; *pc* British Lion, EMI, Orion; *d* Mike Newell; *prod* Robert H. Solo; *sc* Chris Bryant, Clive Exton, Allan Scott; *novel* Bram Stoker; *cast* Charlton Heston, Susannah York, Jill Townsend, Stephanie Zimbalist.

*Blood Tide*
1980 83m col; *pc* Athon, Connaught International; *d* Richard Jeffries; *prod* Luigi Cingolani, Donald Langdon, Nico Mastorakis, Brian Trenchard-Smith; *sc* Richard Jeffries, Donald Langdon, Nico Mastorakis; *cast* James Earl Jones, José Ferrer, Lila Kedrova, Mary Louise Weller.

*Death Ship*
1980 91m col; *pc* Bloodstar; *d* Alvin Rakoff; *prod* Derek Gibson, Harold Greenberg; *sc* John Robins; *cast* George Kennedy, Richard Crenna, Nick Mancuso, Sally Anne Howes.

*Inseminoid (US: Horror Planet)*
1980 93m col; *pc* Jupiter Film, Shaw Brothers; *d* Norman J. Warren; *prod* Richard Gordon, David Speechley; *sc* Gloria Maley, Nick Maley; *cast* Robin Clarke, Jennifer Ashley, Stephanie Beacham, Steven Grives.

*The Monster Club*
1980 97m col; *pc* Chips, Sword and Sorcery; *d* Roy Ward Baker; *prod* Milton Subotsky; *sc* Edward Abraham, Valerie Abraham; *stories* R. Chetwynd-Hayes; *cast* Vincent Price, John Carradine, Anthony Steel, Roger Sloman.

*The Shining*
1980 146m (143m, 119m) col; *pc* Hawk Films, Peregrine, Producer Circle; *d* Stanley Kubrick; *prod* Robert Fryer, Stanley Kubrick; *sc* Diane Johnson, Stanley Kubrick; *novel* Stephen King; *cast* Jack Nicholson, Shelley Duvall, Danny Lloyd, Scatman Crothers.

*An American Werewolf in London*
1981 97m col; *pc* American Werewolf Inc, Lycanthrope Films, Polygram; *d* John Landis; *prod* George Folsey Jr; *sc* John Landis; *cast* David Naughton, Griffin Dunne, Jenny Agutter, John Woodvine.

*Venom*
1982 92m col; *pc* Morison, Venom; *d* Piers Haggard; *prod* Martin Bregman; *sc* Robert Carrington; *novel* Alan Scholefield; *cast* Klaus Kinski, Oliver Reed, Nicol Williamson, Sarah Miles.

*Xtro*
1982 86m col; *pc* Ashley, Amalgamated Film Enterprises; *d* Harry Bromley Davenport; *prod* Mark Forstater; *sc* Iain Cassie, Robert Smith; *story* Harry Bromley Davenport, Michael Parry; *cast* Philip Sayer, Bernice Stegers, Danny Brainin, Maryam d'Abo.

*House of the Long Shadows*
1983 101m col; *pc* Cannon; *d* Pete Walker; *prod* Yoram Globus, Menahem Golan; *sc* Michael Armstrong; *novel* Earl Derr Biggers; *cast* Desi Arnaz Jr, Julie Peasgood, Christopher Lee, Peter Cushing.

*Screamtime*
1983 88m col; *pc* Salon; *d* Al Beresford; *prod* Al Beresford; *sc* Michael Armstrong; *cast* Vincent Russo, Michael Gordon, Marie Scinto, Kevin Smith.

*The Company of Wolves*
1984 95m col; *pc* Palace Pictures; *d* Neil Jordan; *prod* Chris Brown; *sc* Neil Jordan; *story* Angela Carter; *cast* Sarah Patterson, Angela Lansbury, David Warner, Graham Crowden.

*The Bride*
1985 119m col; *pc* Colgems, Columbia, Delphi III; *d* Franc Roddam; *prod* Victor Drai, Chris Kenny; *sc* Lloyd Fonvielle; *novel* Mary Shelley; *cast* Sting, Jennifer Beals, Anthony Higgins, Clancy Brown.

*The Doctor and the Devils*
1985 92m col; *pc* 20th Century Fox, Brooksfilm; *d* Freddie Francis; *prod* Jonathan Sanger; *sc* Ronald Harwood; *story* Dylan Thomas; *cast* Timothy Dalton, Jonathan Pryce, Twiggy Lawson, Julian Sands.

*Don't Open Till Christmas*
1985 86m col; *pc* Spectacular Trading International; *d* Edmond Purdom; *prod* Steve Minasian, Dick Randall; *sc* Derek Ford; *cast* Edmond Purdom, Alan Lake, Belinda Mayne, Gerry Sundquist.

*The Hills Have Eyes II*
1985 88m col; *pc* New Realm, VTC; *d* Wes Craven; *prod* Barry Cahn, Peter Locke; *sc* Wes Craven; *cast* Michael Berryman, John Laughlin, Tamara Stafford, Kevin Blair.

*Link*
1985 116m col; *pc* Thorn EMI; *d* Richard Franklin; *prod* Richard Franklin; *sc* Everett De Roche; *cast* Elizabeth Shue, Terence Stamp, Steven Pinner, Richard Garnett.

*Daemon*
1986 71m col; *pc* Children's Film Unit; *d* Colin Finbow; *prod* Colin Finbow; *sc* Colin Finbow; *cast* Arnuad Morell, Susannah York, Bert Parnaby, Sadie Herlighy.

*Gothic*
1986 87m col; *pc* Virgin; *d* Ken Russell; *prod* Penny Corke; *sc* Stephen Volk; *cast* Gabriel Byrne, Julian Sands, Natasha Richardson, Miriam Cyr.

*Rawhead Rex*
1986 89m col; *pc* Green Man; *d* George Pavlou; *prod* Kevin Attew, Don Hawkins; *sc* Clive Barker; *story* Clive Barker; *cast* David Dukes, Kelly Piper, Ronan Wilmot, Niall Toibin.

*White of the Eye*
1986 111m col; *pc* Mrs White's Productions; *d* Donald Cammell; *prod* Sue Baden-Powell; *sc* China Cammell, Donald Cammell; *cast* David Keith, Cathy Moriarty, Alan Rosenberg, Art Evans.

*Hellraiser*
1987 93m col; *pc* New World, Film Futures; *d* Clive Barker; *prod* Christopher Figg; *sc* Clive Barker; *story* Clive Barker; *cast* Andrew Robinson, Clare Higgins, Ashley Laurence.

*Slaughter High*
1987 88m col; *pc* Vestron; *d* George Dugdale, Mark Ezra, Peter Litten; *prod* Steve Minasian, Dick Randall; *sc* George Dugdale, Mark Ezra, Peter Litten; *cast* Caroline Munro, Simon Scuddamore, Carmine Iannaccone, Donna Yeager.

*Dream Demon*
1988 89m col; *pc* Spectrafilm, Palace; *d* Harley Cokliss; *prod* Paul Webster; *sc* Harley Cokliss, Chris Wicking; *cast* Jemma Redgrave, Kathleen Wilhoite, Timothy Spall, Jimmy Nail.

*Edge of Sanity*
1988 90m col; *pc* Allied Vision; *d* Gerard Kikoine; *prod* Edward Simmons, Harry Allan Towers; *sc* J.P. Felix, Ron Raley; *cast* Anthony Perkins, Glynis Barber, Sarah Maur-Thorp, David Lodge.

*Hellbound: Hellraiser II*
1988 99m col; *pc* New World; *d* Tony Randel; *prod* Christopher Figg; *sc* Peter Atkins; *story* Clive Barker; *cast* Ashley Laurence, Clare Higgins, Kenneth Cranham, Imogen Boorman.

*The Lair of the White Worm*
1988 93m col; *pc* Vestron; *d* Ken Russell; *prod* Ken Russell; *sc* Ken Russell; *story* Bram Stoker; *cast* Amanda Donohoe, Sammi Davis, Catherine Oxenburg, Hugh Grant.

*Cold Light of Day*
1989 75m col; *d* Fhiona Louise; *prod* Richard Driscoll; *sc* Fhiona Louise; *cast* Bob Flag, Martin Byrne-Quinn, Geoffrey Greenhill, Mark Hawkins.

*The Hand of Death*
1989 84m col; *d* Anders Palm; *prod* Mark Cutforth; *sc* Mark Cutforth; *cast* Gregory Cox, Fiona Evans, Edward Brayshaw.

*Living Doll*
1989 92m col; *pc* Living Doll Productions; *d* George Dugdale, Peter Litten; *prod* Dick Randall; *sc* George Dugdale, Peter Litten; *cast* Mark Jax, Katie Orgill, Eartha Kitt, Sean Aita.

*Paperhouse*
1989 92m col; *pc* Vestron; *d* Bernard Rose; *prod* Tim Bevan, Sarah Radcliffe; *sc* Matthew Jacobs; *cast* Charlotte Burke, Ben Cross, Glenne Headly, Elliott Speirs.

*Hardware*
1990 93m col; *pc* Palace; *d* Richard Stanley; *prod* Jo-Anne Sellar, Paul Trijbits; *sc* Mike Fallon, Richard Stanley; *story* Steve MacManus, Kevin O'Neill; *cast* Dylan McDermott, Stacey Travis, John Lynch, William Hootkins.

*Mr Frost*
1990 103m col; *pc* AAA, Hugo Films; *d* Philip Setbon; *prod* Xavier Gelin; *sc* Brad Lynch, Philip Setbon; *cast* Jeff Goldblum, Alan Bates, Kathy Baker, Jean-Pierre Cassel.

*Afraid of the Dark*
1991 91m col; *pc* Sovereign, Telescope, Les Films Ariane, Cine Cinq; *d* Mark Peploe; *prod* Simon Bosanquet; *sc* Mark Peploe; *cast* Ben Keyworth, James Fox, Fanny Ardant, Paul McGann.

*Dawn*
1991 78m col; *pc* Shooting Gallery; *d* Niall Johnson; *prod* Niall Johnson; *sc* Niall Johnson; *cast* Elizabeth Rees, Geoff Sloan, Craig Johnson, Kate Jones Davies.

*The Monk*
1991 106m col; *pc* Celtic Films, Mediterraneo; *d* Paco Lara; *prod* Paco Lara, Muir Sutherland; *sc* Paco Lara; *cast* Paul McGann, Sophie Ward, Isla Blair, Freda Dowie.

*The Lawnmower Man*
1992 108m col; *pc* Allied Vision, Lane Pringle; *d* Brett Leonard; *prod* Gimel Everett;

*sc* Gimel Everett, Brett Leonard; *story* Stephen King; *cast* Pierce Brosnan, Jef Fahey, Jenny Wright, Mark Bringleson.

*Naked Lunch*
1992 115m col; *pc* Fox; *d* David Cronenberg; *prod* Jeremy Thomas; *sc* David Cronenberg; *novel* William S. Burroughs; *cast* Peter Weller, Judy Davis, Ian Holm, Roy Scheider.

*Tale of a Vampire*
1992 100m col; *pc* State Screen; *d* Shimako Sato; *prod* Simon Johnson; *sc* Jane Corbett, Shimako Sato; *cast* Julian Sands, Suzanna Hamilton, Kenneth Cranham, Marian Diamond.

*Turn of the Screw*
1992 95m col; *pc* Electric Pictures; *d* Rusty Lemorande; *prod* Steffan Ahrenberg; *sc* Rusty Lemorande; *cast* Patsy Kensit, Stephane Audran, Marianne Faithfull, Claire Szekeres.

*Beyond Bedlam*
1993 89m col; *pc* Metrodome Films; *d* Vadim Jean; *prod* Paul Brooks; *sc* Vadim Jean, Rob Walker; *novel* Harry Adam Knight; *cast* Craig Fairbrass, Elizabeth Hurley, Keith Allen, Anita Dobson.

*Dark Waters*
1993 85m col; *d* Mariano Baino; *prod* Victor Zuev; *sc* Mariano Baino, Andy Bark; *cast* Louise Salter, Vencra Simmons, Maria Kapnist, Valeri Bassel.

*Dust Devil*
1993 107m col; *pc* Palace; *d* Richard Stanley; *prod* Jo-Anne Sellar; *sc* Richard Stanley; *cast* Robert Burke, Chelsea Field, Zakes Mokae, Marianne Sagebrecht.

*White Angel*
1993 96m col; *pc* Living Spirit Pictures; *d* Chris Jones; *prod* Genevieve Jolliffe; *sc* Genevieve Jolliffe, Chris Jones; *cast* Harriet Robinson, Peter Firth, Don Henderson, Anne-Catherine Arton.

*Boy Meets Girl*
1994 89m col; *pc* Kino-eye Ltd; *d* Ray Brady; *prod* Ray Brady, Chris Read; *sc* Ray Brady, Jim Crosbie; *cast* Tim Poole, Daniele Sanderson, Margot Steinberg, Susan Warren.

*Demonsoul*
1994 81m col; *pc* Gothic Films, Vista Street Entertainment; *d* Elisar Cabrera; *prod* Elisar Cabrera, Matt Devlen, Gerard Feifer, Daniel Figuero; *sc* Elisar Cabrera; *cast* Kerry Norton, Eileen Daly, Daniel Jordan, Janine Ulfane.

*Funny Man*
1994 90m col; *pc* Victor; *d* Simon Sprackling; *prod* Nigel Odell, David Redman; *sc* Simon Sprackling; *cast* Tim James, Christopher Lee, Benny Young, Matthew Devitt.

*Mary Shelley's Frankenstein*
1994 123m col; *pc* American Zoetrope, Indieprod, Tristar; *d* Kenneth Branagh; *prod* Francis Ford Coppola, James V. Hart, John Veitch; *sc* Frank Darabont, Steph Lady; *novel* Mary Shelley; *cast* Kenneth Branagh, Robert De Niro, Tom Hulce, Helena Bonham-Carter.

*Death Machine*
1995 99m col; *pc* Fugitive Features; *d* Stephen Norrington; *prod* Dominic Anciano; *sc* Stephen Norrington; *cast* Brad Dourif, Ely Pouget, William Hootkins, John Sharian.

*Haunted*
1995 108m col; *pc* Lumière Pictures; *d* Lewis Gilbert; *prod* Anthony Andrews, Lewis Gilbert; *sc* Lewis Gilbert, Bob Kellett, Tony Prager; *novel* James Herbert; *cast* Aidan Quinn, Kate Beckinsale, Anthony Andrews, John Gielgud.

*Proteus*
1995 97m col; *pc* Metrodome Films; *d* Bob Keen; *prod* Paul Brooks; *sc* John Brosnan; *novel* John Brosnan (as Harry Adam Knight); *cast* Craig Fairbrass, Toni Barry, William Marsh, Jennifer Calvert.

*Darklands*
1997 90m col; *pc* Arts Council of Wales, Lluniau Lliw, Metrodome, Prolific Films; *d* Julian Richards; *prod* Paul Brooks; *sc* Julian Richards; *cast* Craig Fairbrass, Jon Finch, Rowena King, Roger Nott.

*Breeders*
1998 92m col; *pc* Peak Viewing Atlantic; *d* Paul Matthews; *prod* Elizabeth Matthews; *sc* Paul Matthews; *cast* Samantha Janus, Clifton Lloyd Brian, Wendy Cooper, Todd Jensen.

*Razor Blade Smile*
1998 98m (US 101m) col; *pc* Eye Deal Image, Beatnik Films; *d* Jake West; *prod* Robert Mercer, Jake West; *sc* Jake West; *cast* Eileen Daly, Grahame Wood, Christopher Adamson, Isabel Brook.

*Urban Ghost Story*
1998 82m col; *pc* Living Spirit Pictures; *d* Geneviève Jolliffe; *prod* Chris Jones; *sc* Genenviève Jolliffe, Chris Jones; *cast* Stephanie Buttle, Heather Ann Foster, Jason Connery, Alan Owen.

*The Wisdom of Crocodiles*
1998 98m col; *pc* Arts Council, Film Foundry Partners, Goldwyn Films, Zenith Productions; *d* Po-Chih Leong; *prod* Carolyn Choa, David Lascelles; *sc* Paul Hoffman; *cast* Jude Law, Timothy Spall, Elina Lowensohn, Kerry Fox.

*Witchcraft X: Mistress of the Craft*
1998 90m col; *pc* Armadillo Films; *d* Elisar Cabrera; *prod* Jon Blay, Elisar Cabrera; *sc* Elisar Cabrera; *cast* Wendy Cooper, Eileen Daly, Stephanie Beaton, Kerry Knowlton.

*Lighthouse (US: Dead of Night)*
1999 95m col; *pc* Arts Council, British Screen, Tungsten Pictures, Winchester Films; *d* Simon Hunter; *prod* Tim Dennison, Mark Leake; *sc* Simon Hunter; *cast* James Purefoy, Rachel Shelley, Don Warrington, Christopher Adamson.

*Ravenous*
1999 100m col; *pc* 20th Century Fox, ETIC, Engulf and Devour Productions, Heyday Films; *d* Antonia Bird; *prod* Adam Fields, David Heyman; *sc* Ted Griffin; *cast* Guy Pearce, Robert Carlyle, David Arquette, Jeremy Davies.

*The Asylum*
2000 99m col; *pc* Nunhead Films; *d* John Stewart; *prod* Carol Lemon; *sc* John Stewart; *cast* Steffanie Pitt, Nick Waring, Ingrid Pitt, Patrick Mower.

*Blood*
2000 90m col; *pc* Omni International, Yorkshire Media Production; *d* Charly Cantor; *prod* Simon Markham; *sc* Charly Cantor; *cast* Adrian Rawlins, Lee Blakemore, Phil Cornwell, Elizabeth Marmor.

*Nine Tenths*
2000 80m col; *pc* Big Picture Productions; *d* Jon Gritton; *prod* Simon Vause; *sc* Simon Vause; *cast* Sarah Cartwright, Phil Craven, Luke Goss, Elisabeth Heaney.

*Shadow of the Vampire*
2000 91m col; *pc* BBC, Delux Productions, Long Shot Pictures, Luxembourg Film Fund, Metrodome Films, Satrun Films; *d* E. Elias Merhige; *prod* Nicolas Cage, Jeff Levine; *sc* Steven Katz; *cast* John Malkovich, Willem Dafoe, Udo Kier, Cary Elwes.

*The 13th Sign*
2000 85m col; *pc* Paranoid Celluloid; *d* Jonty Acton, Adam Mason; *prod* Adam Mason, Nadya Mason; *sc* Jonty Acton; *cast* Nadja Brand, Eric Colvin, Jonathan Coote, Justin Ellis.

*The Hole*
2001 102m col; *pc* Cowboy Films, Film Council, Granada Film Productions, Impact Pictures, Le Studio Canal+, Pathe Pictures; *d* Nick Hamm; *prod* Jeremy Bolt, Lisa Bryer, Pippa Cross; *sc* Ben Cort, Caroline Ip; *novel* Guy Burt; *cast* Thora Birch, Desmond Harrington, Daniel Brocklebank, Laurence Fox.

# Index